# WEB DESIGN INDEX
# 5

Compiled by Günter Beer

**THE PEPIN PRESS / AGILE RABBIT EDITIONS**
AMSTERDAM AND SINGAPORE

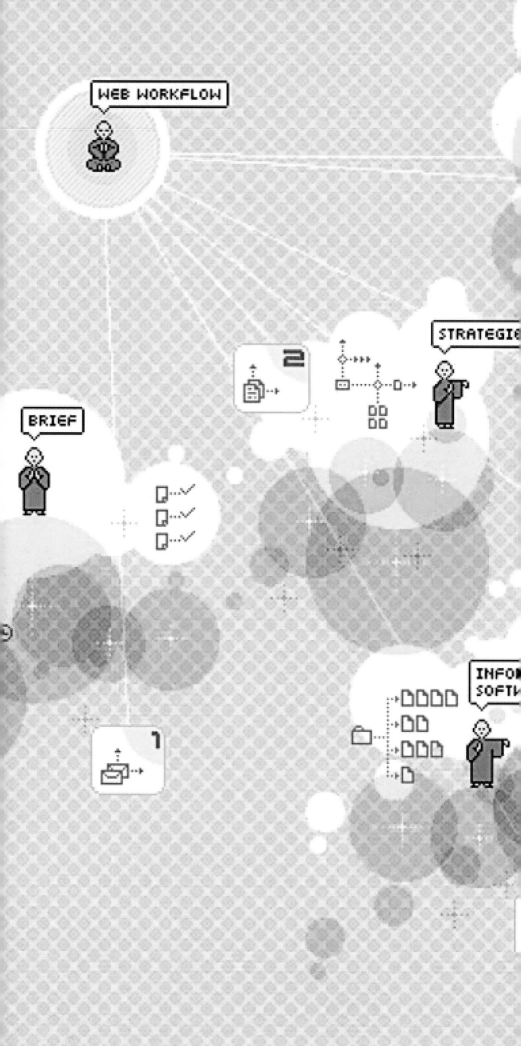

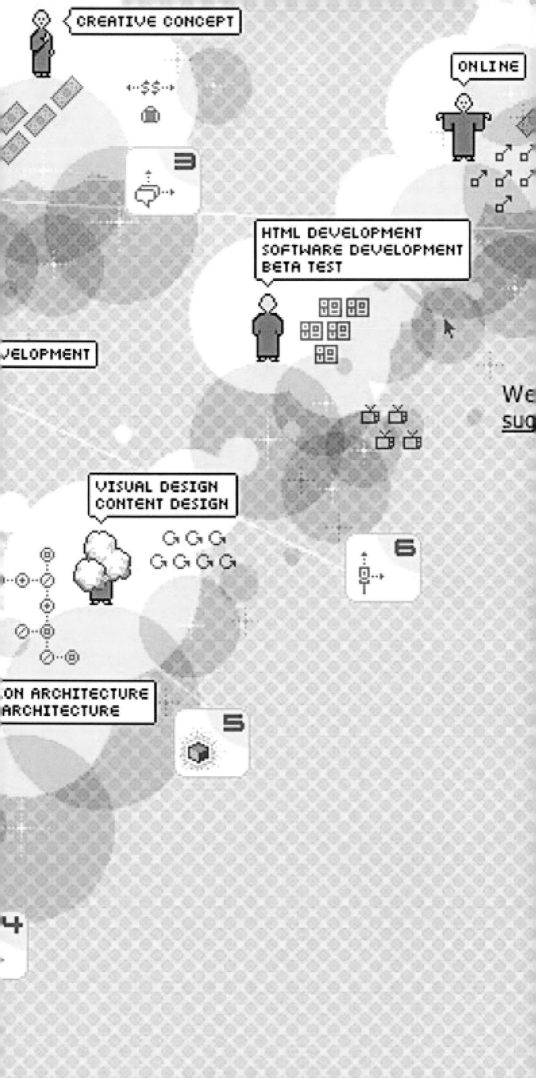

With special thanks to Magda Garcia Masana
of LocTeam S.L., Barcelona

Compiled and edited by Günter Beer
(www.webdesignindex.org)
Compilation and CD-ROM content
copyright © 2004 Günter Beer

Cover, CD label and book design by Pepin van Roojen
Layout by Sabine Reibeholz
CD master by Günter Beer and Sabine Reibeholz

Introduction by Pepin van Roojen
Translations by LocTeam, Barcelona (German, Spanish,
French, Italian and Portuguese), and The Big Word,
Leeds (Japanese, Chinese, Korean, Russian and Arabic).

ISBN 90 5768 068 8
The Pepin Press — Agile Rabbit Editions


The Pepin Press BV
P.O. Box 10349
1001 EH Amsterdam
The Netherlands


Tel +31 20 4202021
Fax +31 20 4201152
mail@pepinpress.com
www.pepinpress.com


10  9  8  7  6  5  4  3  2
2008  07  06  05


Manufactured in Singapore

Free CD-Rom in the inside back cover

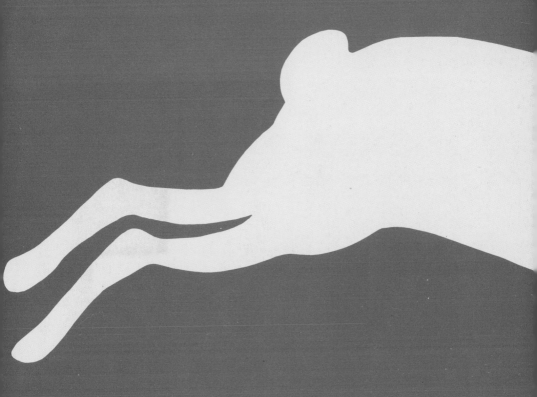

# CONTENTS

Since its first edition in the year 2000, the annual Web Design Index has developed into one of the most important publications in its field. Year after year, it gives an accurate overview of the state of the art in web design.

Websites can range from simple, single-page layouts to sophisticated constructions featuring the latest digital capabilities. Selection for the Web Design Index is based on design quality, innovation, and effectiveness — regardless of complexity. So, in this book you will find examples of all conceivable forms and styles.

Every Web Design Index contains 1002 outstanding web pages. With each page, the URL is indicated. The names of those involved in the design and programming of the sites are stated as follows:

**D**     design
**C**     coding
**P**     production
**A**     agency
**M**     designer's email address

In the inside back cover you will find a CD-ROM containing all the pages, arranged according to their location in the book. You can view them on your computer with a minimum of loading time, and access the Internet to explore the selected site in full.

**Submissions**
Each year, a brand new edition of the Web Design Index is published. Should you wish to submit or recommend a design for consideration for the next edition, please access the submission form at www.webdesignindex.org.

**Web Design by Content**
In addition to the Web Design Indexes, The Pepin Press/ Agile Rabbit Editions publishes the annual Web Design by Content. Volumes in this series feature some 600 sites, arranged by content (qualified by trade, profession, vocation, etc.), covering all conceivable uses of the Web. Web Design by Content offers a quick overview of the standard of web design in any particular field.

**The Pepin Press/Agile Rabbit Editions**
The Pepin Press/Agile Rabbit Editions publishes a wide range of books and CD-ROMs with visual reference material and ready-to-use images for designers, for Internet applications as well as high-resolution printed media.

For more information, please visit www.pepinpress.com.

Seit der Erstausgabe im Jahr 2000 hat sich der jährliche Web Design Index zu einer der wichtigsten Veröffentlichungen in diesem Bereich entwickelt. Jahr für Jahr bietet dieses Werk einen genauen Überblick über die neuesten Entwicklungen im Webdesign.

Webdesign reicht von Sites mit nur einer Seite und sehr einfachem Layout bis hin zu komplexen Strukturen mit den neuesten Funktionen. Die Auswahl für den Web Design Index basiert auf der Qualität des Designs, dem Innovationsgrad und der Wirkung und ist von der Komplexität unabhängig. Daher enthält das vorliegende Buch Beispiele aller nur erdenklichen Arten und Stile von Webdesigns.

Jeder Web Design Index stellt 1002 erstklassige Webseiten vor.Für jede Webseite ist auch die entsprechende URL angegeben. Die Namen der für Design und Programmierung der Sites verantwortlichen Personen sind mit folgenden Codes verzeichnet:

**D**        Design
**C**        Code
**P**        Produktion
**A**        Agentur
**M**        E—Mail—Adresse des Designers

In der hinteren Umschlagseite finden Sie eine CD—ROM mit allen Seiten, geordnet nach deren Platzierung im vorliegenden Buch. Sie können diese mit äußerst kurzen Ladezeiten auf dem Bildschirm anzeigen oder diese im Internet aufrufen, um die gesamte Site zu erkunden.

### Einreichungen
Jedes Jahr wird eine komplett neue Ausgabe des Web Design Index herausgegeben.Wenn Sie ein Design für die nächste Ausgabe einreichen oder empfehlen möchten, verwenden Sie bitte das Teilnahmeformular auf www.webdesignindex.org.

### Web Design by Content
Zusätzlich zum Web Design Index veröffentlicht Pepin Press/Agile Rabbit Editions alljährlich Web Design by Content. Die Bände dieser Serie beleuchten 600 Webseiten, nach Inhalt geordnet (unterteilt nach Gewerbe, Beruf, Talent, etc.), die alle nur erdenklichen Anwendungen des Internets abdecken. Web Design by Content bietet einen schnellen Überblick über Webdesign Standards in den verschiedensten Gebieten.

### The Pepin Press/Agile Rabbit Editions
The Pepin Press/Agile Rabbit Editions veröffentlicht eine breite Palette an Büchern und CD—ROMs mit visuellem Referenzmaterial und sofort verwendbaren Bildern für Designer, Internet—Applikationen sowie hoch auflösende Print—Medien.

Weitere Informationen entnehmen Sie bitte der Website www.pepinpress.com.

Depuis ses débuts en 2000, l'édition annuelle de
l'Index de modèles de sites Web est devenue l'une
des publications les plus importantes de son secteur
et propose chaque année un aperçu exhaustif des
toutes dernières tendances dans la conception de
sites Web.

Le design Web reprend des ouvrages très divers, des
sites à page unique à la mise en page simple aux
systèmes plus sophistiqués exploitant les toutes
dernières fonctionnalités. La sélection des sites
pour l'Index de modèles de sites Web se base sur la
qualité de leur design, leur caractère novateur et
leur efficacité — quelle que soit leur complexité.
Vous trouverez donc dans cet ouvrage des exemples de
tous les styles et formes imaginables de sites Web.

Chaque Index de modèles de sites Web présente une
sélection de 1002 sites Web exceptionnels. L'URL
de ces sites est à chaque fois mentionnée. Les noms
des responsables du design et de la programmation
des sites sont mentionnés selon le code suivant :

**D**    design
**C**    codage
**P**    production
**A**    agence
**M**    adresse e-mail du designer

Un CD-ROM inclus à l'intérieur de la quatrième de
couverture contient toutes les pages Web dans l'ordre
de leur apparition dans le livre. Il vous permettra
de les visualiser sur votre ordinateur avec un temps
de chargement minimum et d'accéder à Internet pour
explorer en détail le site choisi.

**Candidatures**
Une édition toute nouvelle de l'Index de modèles
de sites Web paraît chaque année. Si vous souhaitez
soumettre ou recommander un site Web pour notre
prochaine édition, vous pouvez remplir le formulaire
de candidature que vous trouverez à l'adresse
www.webdesignindex.org.

**Web Design by Content**
En plus des Index de modèles de sites Web, The Pepin
Press/Agile Rabbit Editions publie chaque année
Web Design by Content. Les volumes de cette série
incluent quelque 600 sites, répertoriés par contenu
(classés par activité commerciale, profession,
vocation, etc.) couvrant toutes les utilisations
concevables du Web. Web Design by Content vous
offre une vue d'ensemble rapide des standards en
termes de conception de sites Web dans chaque
domaine spécifique.

**The Pepin Press/Agile Rabbit Editions**
Les éditions Pepin Press/Agile Rabbit publient un
vaste choix de livres et de CD-ROM reprenant des
documents visuels de référence et des images prêtes
à l'emploi pour l'usage des designers, pour les
applications destinées à l'Internet ainsi que tout
support imprimé haute définition.

Pour en savoir plus rendez-vous sur
www.pepinpress.com.

A partire dal 2000, anno della sua prima uscita, l'Indice del Disegno Web con pubblicazione annuale è diventata un punto di riferimento nel settore, offrendo ogni anno una rassegna accurata sullo stato dell'arte del web design.

Il web design può variare da semplici siti con una sola pagina a strutture sofisticate elaborate secondo le ultime tecniche. Il criterio di selezione utilizzato per l'Indice del Disegno Web si basa sulla qualità del design, sull'innovazione e sull'efficacia, indipendentemente dalla complessità. Così, in questo libro, troverete degli esempi di ogni forma e stile possibile.

Ogni libro presenta una selezione di 1002 pagine web straordinarie. Per ogni pagina web viene indicata la direzione URL. I nomi delle persone che hanno partecipato alla concezione e alla programmazione dei siti sono preceduti dalle seguenti abbreviazioni:

**D**   design
**C**   codifica
**P**   produzione
**A**   agenzia
**M**   indirizzo e-mail dei disegnatori

All'interno della copertina posteriore troverete un CD-ROM che contiene tutte le pagine web sistemate secondo l'ordine di apparizione nel libro. Appaiono sul monitor in pochissimo tempo e permettono di accedere alla pagina selezionata per navigare nel sito desiderato.

### Candidature
Ogni anno viene pubblicata una nuova edizione di Indice del Disegno Web. Se volete presentare o raccomandare una creazione perché venga inclusa nella prossima edizione, potete accedere al modulo di candidatura nel sito www.webdesignindex.org.

### Web Design by Content
Oltre ai libri della collezione Indice del Disegno Web, The Pepin Press/ Agile Rabbit Editions pubblica anche l'edizione annuale Web Design by Content. I volumi di questa serie presentano circa 600 siti, elencati per contenuto (secondo l'attività commerciale, la professione, l'occupazione, ecc.), che trattano dei possibili usi del Web. Web Design by Content offre una rapida panoramica sullo standard del web design in ogni campo specifico.

### The Pepin Press/Agile Rabbit Editions
The Pepin Press/Agile Rabbit Editions pubblica una vasta gamma di libri e CD-ROM con materiale informativo ed immagini per designer, per applicazioni Internet, e anche per mezzi stampa ad alta risoluzione.

Per ulteriori informazioni potete visitare il sito www.pepinpress.com.

Desde su primera edición en el año 2000, el Índice
de diseño de páginas web se ha convertido en una de
las publicaciones más importantes de su sector, y
año tras año muestra una visión detallada del estado
del diseño de páginas web.

El diseño de páginas web abarca desde sitios forma-
dos por una sola página de composición sencilla
hasta complicadas estructuras con las más novedosas
técnicas. Los criterios de selección de este índice
se basan en la calidad, la innovación y la eficacia
del diseño, sin tener en cuenta su complejidad; por
lo tanto, en este libro encontrará ejemplos de todas
las formas y estilos que pueda imaginar.

Cada Índice de diseño de páginas web presenta una
selección de 1.002 magníficas páginas web (junto
a cada una de ellas se indica la dirección URL
correspondiente). Los nombres de quienes han par-
ticipado en el diseño y la programación de cada
sitio se citan de la siguiente manera:

D       diseño
C       codificación
P       producción
A       agencia
M       correo electrónico del diseñador

En el interior de la contracubierta encontrará un
CD-ROM que contiene todas las páginas web, ordenadas
según aparecen en este libro. Si lo desea, puede
verlas en su ordenador (el tiempo de descarga es
mínimo) y acceder a Internet para explorar en su
totalidad el sitio web seleccionado.

### Sugerencias
Todos los años se publica una nueva edición del
Índice de diseño de páginas web. Si desea sugerir
o recomendar un diseño para que se tenga en cuenta
para la próxima edición, rellene el formulario de
sugerencias que aparece en la dirección
www.webdesignindex.org.

### Web Design by Content
Además de los Índices de diseño de páginas web, The
Pepin Press/Agile Rabbit Editions publica anualmente
Web Design by Content. Los volúmenes de esta serie
presentan alrededor de 600 sitios web ordenados
según su contenido (clasificados por ramo, profesión,
ocupación, etc.) y que abarcan todos los usos imaginables de la red. Web Design by Content ofrece una
pasada rápida por los estándares del diseño web en
todos los campos.

### The Pepin Press/Agile Rabbit Editions
La editorial The Pepin Press/Agile Rabbit Editions
publica una gran variedad de libros y CD-ROM con
material de referencia visual e imágenes destinados
a diseñadores, aplicaciones de Internet y medios
impresos de alta resolución.

Si desea obtener más información visite
www.pepinpress.com.

Desde a sua primeira edição, no ano 2000, o Catálogo de Web Design anual tornou-se uma das publicações mais importantes nesta área, proporcionando, ano após ano, uma descrição geral exacta do estado da arte em web design.

Os sites podem variar entre uma página com formatos simples e estruturas sofisticadas que apresentam as capacidades digitais mais avançadas. A selecção para o Catálogo de Web Design é feita com base na qualidade de design, inovação e eficácia, independentemente da complexidade. Por isso, poderá encontrar neste livro exemplos de todas as formas e estilos concebíveis.

Todos os Catálogos de Web Design apresentam uma selecção de 1002 páginas web notáveis. Com cada página inclui-se a indicação do respectivo URL. Os nomes das pessoas envolvidas no design e na programação dos sites são indicados do seguinte modo:

**D**      design
**C**      codificação
**P**      produção
**A**      agência
**M**      endereço de e-mail do designer

No interior da contracapa, encontrará um CD-ROM com todas as páginas, organizadas de acordo com a sua localização neste livro. Poderá visualizá-las no seu computador com um tempo de carregamento mínimo e aceder à Internet para explorar na totalidade o site seleccionado.

**Envios**
Todos os anos é publicada uma edição completamente nova do Catálogo de Web Design. Caso pretenda enviar ou recomendar um design para ser considerado para a próxima edição, aceda ao formulário para esse efeito em www.webdesignindex.org.

**Web Design by Content**
Para além dos Catálogos de Web Design Indexes, a The Pepin Press/ Agile Rabbit Editions publica anualmente o Web Design by Content. Os volumes desta série apresentam cerca de 600 sites, organizados pelos respectivos conteúdos (qualificados por ocupação, profissão, carreira, etc.), abrangendo todas as utilizações imagináveis da Web. O Web Design by Content oferece uma descrição geral rápida do web design padrão em qualquer área específica.

**The Pepin Press/Agile Rabbit Editions**
A The Pepin Press/Agile Rabbit Editions publica um vasto leque de livros e CD-ROM com material de consulta visual e imagens prontas a utilizar para designers, para aplicações de Internet, e suporte impresso de alta resolução.

Para mais informações, visite www.pepinpress.com.

С момента выхода первого издания в 2000 г., ежегодный «Индекс веб-дизайна» вырос в одну из самых важных публикаций в своей области, из года в года представляя точный обзор положения дел в современном веб-дизайне.

Веб-сайты могут быть самыми разными – от простой постраничной компоновки до сложнейших конструкций, в которых реализованы новейшие цифровые возможности. Выбор для «Индекса веб-дизайна» основывается на качестве, новаторстве и эффективности дизайна – независимо от сложности. Так что в этой книге вы найдете примеры всех мыслимых форм и стилей.

В каждом «Индексе веб-дизайна» представлены 1002 выдающиеся веб-страницы. Указан адрес URL каждой страницы. Имена принимавших участие в дизайне и программировании сайтов указаны следующим образом:

**D**    дизайн
**C**    кодирование
**P**    производство
**A**    агентство
**M**    адрес электронной почты дизайнера

На внутренней стороне задней обложки вы найдете компакт-диск со всеми страницами, расположенными согласно их положению в этой книге. Страницы можно просматривать на компьютере с минимальной длительностью загрузки, также можно войти в Интернет и изучить выбранный сайт целиком.

**Представление заявок**
Каждый год публикуется совершенно новое издание «Индекса веб-дизайна». Если вы пожелаете представить или порекомендовать какой-либо дизайн к рассмотрению для следующего издания, пожалуйста, сделайте это с помощью формы представления на сайте www.webdesignindex.org.

**Веб-дизайн по контенту**
Помимо «Индексов веб-дизайна», издательство The Pepin Press/ Agile Rabbit Editions публикует ежегодный «Веб-дизайн по контенту». В номерах этой серии представлено порядка 600 сайтов – они расположены по контенту (классифицированы по отрасли, профессии, роду занятий и т.п.) и охватывают все мыслимые формы использования Интернета. «Веб-дизайн по контенту» предлагает краткий обзор стандартов веб-дизайна по каждой отдельной области.

**Издательство The Pepin Press/Agile Rabbit Editions**
Издательство The Pepin Press/Agile Rabbit Editions публикует широкий спектр книг и компакт-дисков с визуальными справочными материалами и готовыми к использованию изображениями для дизайнеров, для Интернет-приложений, а также для печатных средств массовой информации с высоким разрешением.

Чтобы получить более подробную информацию, посетите сайт www.pepinpress.com.

2000年に企画開始となった《ウェブデザイン年鑑》も、おかげさまで版を重ね、今ではこの分野の最も重要なレビュー誌となり、年々ウェブデザインの現状を伝える正確な概覧として好評を頂いております。

ここに含まれるウェブサイトのデザインは、レイアウトの単純な1ページのサイトから、最新技術を駆使し洗練された構造を持つサイトまで、実に様々です。《ウェブデザイン年鑑》では、そのサイトがどのくらい複雑かではなく、デザインの質、画期性、効果に注目して掲載サイトの選考を行っています。従ってこの年鑑では、あらゆる形態やスタイルのサイトをご覧になることでしょう。

例年どおり、今回も1002の優れたウェブサイトを選んでお届けします。各ページにサイトのURLも合わせて掲載いたしました。サイトのデザイン及びプログラミングに関わった人名は、以下の記号で示しています:

| | |
|---|---|
| **D** | デザイン |
| **C** | コード化 |
| **P** | 制作 |
| **A** | 代理店 |
| **M** | デザイナーのE-メール |

裏表紙の内側にはCD-ROMが入っており、この本での収録順に従って全掲載ウェブサイトに関する情報が含まれてます。短時間でロードした後、ご自身のPCをインターネットに接続すれば、ご希望の掲載ウェブサイト全てにアクセスできます。

**応募について**
《ウェブデザイン年鑑》は年次刊行されています。次回の年鑑にご自身のウェブデザインを応募なさりたい方、ウェブデザインの推薦をなさりたい方は、www.webdesignindex.org からダウンロードできる応募用紙でお申し込み下さい。

**コンテンツ別ウェブデザイン目録について**
ペピン・プレス/アジール・ラビット・エディションは、ウェブデザイン年鑑の他にもコンテンツ別《ウェブデザイン目録》を年次刊行しています。このシリーズでは、約600のウェブサイトを、考えられる全ての用途のコンテンツごとに(商業用、専門職用、職務用等)紹介いたします。コンテンツ別《ウェブデザイン目録》は、どの分野に関しても標準的なウェブデザインがすぐに参照できる便利な概覧です。

**ペピン・プレス/アジール・ラビット・エディションについて**
ペピン・プレス/アジール・ラビット・エディションは、インターネットのアプリケーションや高解像度印刷媒体で使用できる、デザイナー向けのビジュアル資料やレディーメード素材付きの書籍やCD-ROMを幅広く手がけています。

詳細については www.pepinpress.com でご覧下さい。

《網頁設計索引》年刊自 2000 年誕生起現已發展成?同行業最重要的出版物之一，每年都會對網頁設計的最新趨勢給予準確概述。

網站可簡單到只有一頁，也可以設計為具有最新數位性能的複雜結構。《網頁設計索引》的篩選標準是根據設計品質、創意及效率 － 而不管複雜程度如何。因此在本書中，你可以找到所有可能的樣式和風格的實例。

每輯《網頁設計索引》都展示了 1002 個精彩的網頁。同時提供了每個網頁的 URL。網站設計和編程所用的代碼約定如下：

D　　　設計
C　　　編碼
P　　　製作
A　　　代理商
M　　　設計者的電郵地址

在本書的封底內頁，你會發現一張光碟，它包含了全書內容，其編排順序與本書一致。你可以在最短的時間內將其載入電腦進行瀏覽，也可以連線網際網路，瀏覽所選網站全文。

### 提 交
《網頁設計索引》每年出版一次。如果你希望在下一輯中提交或推薦網頁設計，請訪問 www.webdesignindex.org 填寫提交表。

### 網頁設計分類
除《網頁設計索引》外，The Pepin Press/Agile Rabbit Editions 還每年出版一輯《網頁設計分類》。每期推出約 600 個網站，依照行業、專業、職業等等分類編排，涵蓋各種可能的網頁設計方法。《網頁設計分類》可讓您快速查閱某特定領域的網頁設計標準。

### The Pepin Press/Agile Rabbit Editions 出版社
The Pepin Press/Agile Rabbit Editions 出版了大量的書籍和光碟，為設計者、網際網路應用以及高清晰度的印刷媒體提供直觀的參考材料和圖片素材。

更多資訊請訪問 www.pepinpress.com。

網頁設計索引 中文版

2000년의 초판 발행 이후 매년 발행하는 *웹 디자인 인덱스*는 업계의 가장 중요한 출판물 중 하나로 발전하여 첨단 웹 디자인의 정확한 개요를 제공하고 있습니다.

웹사이트는 단순한 한 페이지짜리 레이아웃을 비롯하여 최신 디지털 기능을 갖춘 정교한 구조까지 갖추고 있습니다. *웹 디자인 인덱스*의 선택은 복잡성과는 상관 없이 디자인 품질, 혁신 및 효율성을 기초로 합니다.

따라서 이 책자에서는 생각할 수 있는 모든 형태와 스타일의 예를 볼 수 있습니다.
모든 *웹 디자인 인덱스*는 1002개의 뛰어난 웹 페이지를 제공합니다. 각 페이지에는 URL이 표시되어 있습니다. 웹사이트의 디자인 및 프로그램에 관련된 이름은 다음과 같이 표시합니다.

**D**     디자인
**C**     코딩
**P**     생산
**A**     에이전시
**M**     디자이너의 이메일 주소

뒷 표지의 안쪽에는 책 속의 위치에 따라 모든 페이지가 나열된 CD-ROM이 있습니다. 여러분은 모니터상에서 최소의 로딩 시간으로 내용을 볼 수 있으며, 인터넷에 액세스하여 선별된 전체 사이트를 검색할 수 있습니다.

## 제출
매년 완전한 *웹 디자인 인덱스*의 신판이 출판됩니다. 다음 판에 고려할 디자인을 제출 또는 추천하려면 www.webdesignindex.org 에서 제출 양식에 액세스하십시오.

## 내용별 웹 디자인
웹 디자인 인덱스와 더불어 페핀 출판사/ 기민한 토끼그림 판은 *내용별 웹 디자인*을 매년 출판합니다. 이 시리즈의 책은 내용별(거래처, 직업, 적성별로 인정)로 나열하고 웹상에서 생각할 수 있는 모든 용도가 포함된 600개의 사이트가 있습니다. *내용별 웹 디자인*은 모든 분야에서 웹 디자인의 기준에 대한 개요를 제공합니다.

## 페핀 출판사/기민한 토끼그림 판
페핀 출판사/기민한 토끼그림 판은 인터넷 응용 프로그램과 고해상도 인쇄 매체를 위한 광범위한 분야의 서적과 가시적 참고 자료 및 디자인에 즉시 사용할 수 있는 이미지가 포함된 CD-ROM을 출판합니다.

자세한 내용은 www.pepinpress.com 을 방문하십시오.

منذ طبعته الأولى في عام 2000، تطور "دليلٍ تصميمٍ الشبكة" إلى واحد من أهم المطبوعات في مجاله، معطياً ـ عاماً بعد عامٍ ـ نظرة شاملة على أحدث ما وصلت إليه التقنية الحديثة في تصميمٍ شبكة الإنترنيت.

وقد تتراوح مواقع الشبكة ما بين تصميمات مبسطة على صفحة واحدة، وبنيات متطورة تضم أحدث القدرات الرقمية. ويستند الانتقاء من "دليل تصميم الشبكة" إلى نوعية التصميم والابتكار والفاعلية بصرف النظر عن التشابك والتعقيد. لذلك ستجد في هذا الكتاب نماذج لكل ما يمكن تصوره من أشكال وأساليب.

ويقدم كل دليل لتصميم الشبكة 1002 صفحة إلكترونية على قدر من الروعة والجمال، مع الإشارة إلى URL في كل صفحة. وقد تم بيان أسماء من اشتركوا في تصميم وبرمجة المواقع كما يلي:

| | |
|---|---|
| D | تصميم |
| C | تكويد |
| P | إنتاج |
| A | وكالة |
| M | عنوان البريد الإلكتروني للمصمم |

وستجد في الغلاف الداخلي الخلفي "سي دي روم" يحتوى على جميع الصفحات مرتبة حسب مواقعها في هذا الكتاب. وبإمكانك الاطلاع عليها في جهاز الكمبيوتر الخاص بك بأقل فترة تحميل ممكنة، وتدخل إلى الإنترنيت كي تسبر أغوار الموقع المنتقى على الوجه الأكمل.

### تقديم التصميمات أوالتوصيات

يجري كل عام نشر طبعة جديدة تماماً من "دليل تصميم الشبكة". فإذا رغبت في تقديم تصميم أو التوصية به لتضمينه في الطبعة التالية، الرجا الدخول إلى استمارة التقديم على الموقع الإلكتروني التالي:
www.webdesignindex.org.

### تصميم الشبكة عن طريق المحتوى

بالإضافة إلى "دليل تصميم الشبكة" تقوم دار The Pepin Press/Agile Rabbit Editions بنشر الكتاب السنوي "تصميم الشبكة عن طريق المحتوى". وتضم مجلدات هذه السلسلة حوالي 600 موقع إلكتروني مرتبة حسب المحتوى (مؤهل حسب الحرفة، المهنة، الوظيفة .. إلخ). وتغطي جميع استعمالات الشبكة التي يمكن تصورها. ويوفر " تصميم الشبكة عن طريق المحتوى" نظرة سريعة وشاملة على مستوى تصميم الشبكة في أي حقل بعينه.

### دار The Pepin Press/Agile Rabbit Editions

تتولى هذه الدار نشر مجموعة متنوعة من الكتب وأقراص "سي دي روم" مع مراجع مرئية وصور جاهزة للاستعمال للمصممين وتطبيقات الإنترنيت، هذا بالإضافة إلى وسائط مطبوعة كاملة الوضوح.

لمزيد من المعلومات الرجا زيارة: www.pepinpress.com.

**WWW.BENES.CZ**
**D:** PAVEL BENES
**A:** PAVEL BENES, **M:** PAVEL@BENES.CZ

**WWW.GRAFIXLIFE.COM**
**D:** SERGIO BROTONS, **C:** JUAN PIERA BELTRAN, **P:** SERGIO BROTONS
**A:** GRAFIXLIFE, **M:** INFO@GRAFIXLIFE.COM

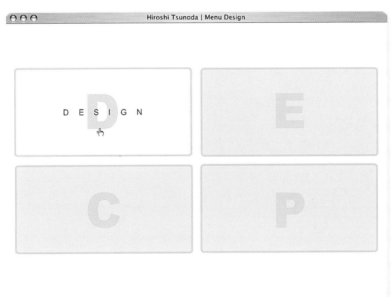

**WWW.HIROSHITSUNODA.COM**
**D:** HIROSHI TSUNODA, **C:** MIKEL SEIJAS
**A:** LA BELLA LOLA, **M:** DE_MIKEL@LABELLALOLA.COM

**WWW.ARNOCHE.COM**
**D:** ARNAUD LACOCHE,
**M:** ARNOCHE@ARNOCHE.COM

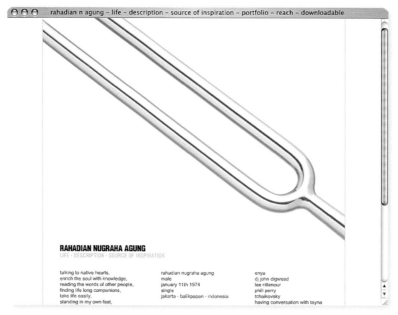

**WWW.SPACECONTROLLER.DK/**
**D:** JAKOB BRANDT-PEDERSEN,
**A:** SPACECONTROLLER, **M:** JBRANDTP@GET2NET.DK

**WWW.RAHADIAN.COM**
**D:** RAHADIAN N AGUNG,
**A:** RAHADIAN EMPEROR, **M:** CONTACT@RAHADIAN.COM

**WWW.GRINTSCH.DE**
**D:** CHUN-HEE HER, **C:** SLAWOMIR CHODNICKI, **P:** ACHIM GRINTSCH
**A:** FRAMEWORK, **M:** MAIL@FRAMEWORK-D.COM

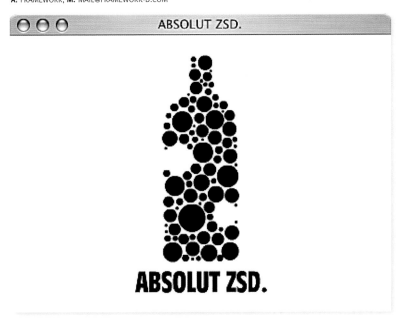

**ZSD.NEASE.NET/**
**D:** ZSD,
**A:** ZSD, **M:** ZS_INFO@YAHOO.COM.CN

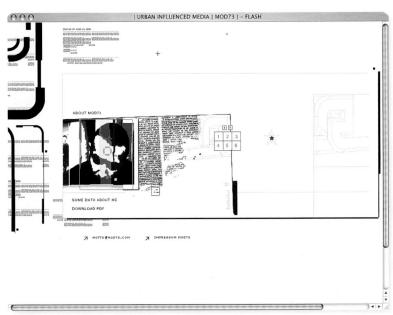

**WWW.MOD73.COM**
**D:** MIKE JOHN OTTO,
**M:** MOTTO@MOD73.COM

La nostra struttura rappresenta una novità nel panorama delle agenzie di pubblicità e marketing operanti tuttora:
è infatti composta esclusivamente da giovani under 30 che dopo diversi anni di esperienza con clienti nazionali ed internazionali, hanno deciso di creare Winkler & Noah, una realtà che in poco tempo di vita è riuscita ad affermarsi ed ottenere diversi

about

W:N

**WWW.WINKLER-NOAH.IT**
**D:** ROMINA RAFFAELLI, STEFANO MARINI, **C:** STEFANO MARINI, **P:** WINKLER NOAH
**A:** WINKLER NOAH, **M:** INFO@WINKLER-NOAH.IT

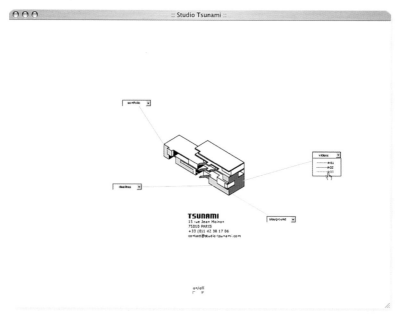

TSUNAMI
15 rue Jean Moinon
75010 PARIS
+33 (0)1 42 38 17 06
contact@studio-tsunami.com

**WWW.STUDIO-TSUNAMI.COM**
**D:** STUDIO-TSUNAMI,
**A:** STUDIO-TSUNAMI, **M:** ANTHONY@STUDIO-TSUNAMI.COM

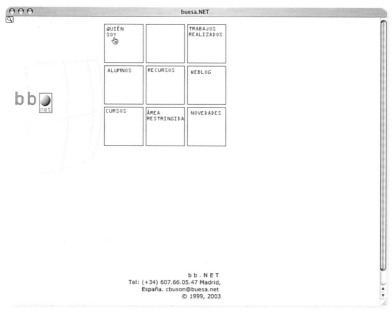

QUIÉN SOY

TRABAJOS REALIZADOS

ALUMNOS

RECURSOS

WEBLOG

CURSOS

ÁREA RESTRINGIDA

NOVEDADES

bb net

b b . N E T
Tel: (+34) 607.66.05.47 Madrid,
España. cbuson@buesa.net
© 1999, 2003

**WWW.BUESA.NET**
**D:** CARLOS BUSÓN BUESA,
**A:** BUESA.NET, **M:** CBUSON@BUESA.NET

○ berlin

○ niederrhein ○ bochum
⦿ wuppertal **process yellow**

○ wiesbaden
○ mainz

⦿ mannheim

○ ○ münchen
○ taufkirchen

○ basel
○ olten

**WWW.PROCESSYELLOW.DE**
**D:** CHRISTOPH PACKHIESER, CLAUDIA SIEPER
**A:** KALT8 KONZEPT BERLIN, **M:** WIR@KALT8.DE

Davide Bressan – pinguini

Davide
bressan

Pubblicità
Editoria
Inediti

Pinguini

L'autore
Contatto

L'incantatore di matite
◀ ▶
Gli amici del Pinguino >>

**WWW.DAVIDEBRESSAN.IT**
**D:** CRISTIANA GIURIATO, **P:** DAVIDE_BRESSAN
**A:** GIURIATO / BRESSAN, **M:** INFO@DAVIDEBRESSAN.IT

Stefano Rosolin Web/Graphic Designer Visualizer

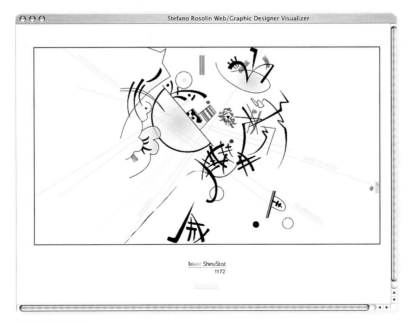

ShinyStat
1172

**STEFANORO.TOO.IT**
**D:** STEFANO ROSOLIN,
**M:** STEFANORO@EMAIL.IT

23

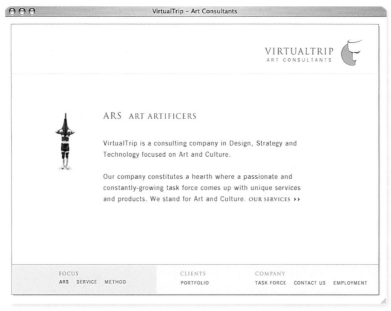

**WWW.SHISSO.ORG**
**D:** BILLY LAW
**A:** QIQ, **M:** CLAW8223@BIGPOND.NET.AU

**WWW.VIRTUALTRIP.COM**
**D:** JULIAN BEDEL, **C:** VIRTUALTRIP, **P:** JULIAN BEDEL
**A:** VIRTUALTRIP, **M:** JULIAN@VIRTUALTRIP.COM

**WWW.PUSULA.COM/JSP/**
**D:** NUMAN PEKGÖZ
**M:** NUMANPEK@HOTMAIL.COM

24

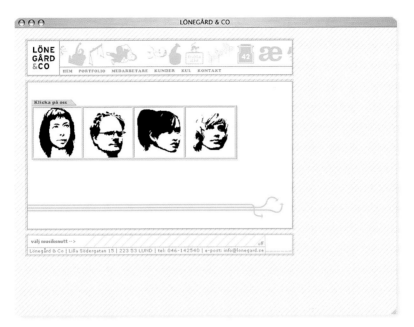

**WWW.LONEGARD.SE**
**C:** SAM SOHLBERG,
**A:** LÖNEGÅRD CO, **M:** SAM@LONEGARD.SE

**WWW.DESIGNUEBERFALL.DE**
**D:** TOBIAS IMMEL, OLIVER LEHMANN, TOM LEMMER, **C:** TOBIAS IMMEL,
**P:** DESIGNUEBERFALL

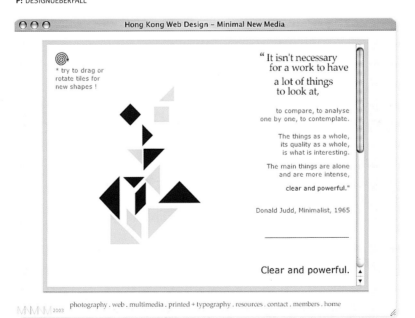

**MNMNM.COM**
**D:** ANTHONY HO,
**A:** MINIMAL NEW MEDIA, **M:** A@MNMNM.COM

## SantiagoOrtiz

INTRODUCCIÓN

TRABAJOS INTERACTIVOS

1. ESPACIOS

2. CINEMÁTICA

3. SONIDO

4. MODELOS BIOLÓGICOS

5. MODELOS NARRATIVOS

6. MÓDULOS PEDAGÓGICOS INTERACTIVOS

ARTÍCULOS

BLANK (revista de cultura digital)

INFINITOARTE (cursos de creación digital)

CURRICULUM

REFERENCIAS

CONTACTO: santiago@moebio.com

Este sitio está optimizado para Safari en Mac OS X y Explorer en Windows
XP. Se recomienda tener instalado el último player de Flash

**WWW.MOEBIO.COM/SANTIAGO**
**D:** SANTIAGO ORTIZ,
**A:** MOEBIO, **M:** SANTIAGO@MOEBIO.COM

## FotoForma

PROFILO     PORTFOLIO     MANIFESTO     CRITICA          CONTATTO

Enrico Sarsini e' nato a Roma nel 1938.

Studia scienze politiche lavorando nello stesso tempo
come fotoreporter per l'Espresso. nel 1960 lascia il
fotogiornalismo per passare alla cinepresa per il
cine-giornale "ieri,oggi,domani". Nel 1962 parte per
gli USA, e riprende la fotografia.

Prima esposizione nel 1964 a Chicago. Entra come
fotogiornalista al settimanale "LIFE". Lavora a LIFE
per 10 anni. Nel 1965 in Vietnam, nel 1968 a Parigi,
Nel 1970 lascia LIFE e lavora per un decennio come
indipendente in Europa per la stampa americana,
francese ed italiana. Negli anni '80 filma e dirige
diversi documentari per la TV francese, in Israele,
Marocco, Finlandia, Turchia...

Nel 1991 fotografo a Mosca per il giornale EQUIPE ed
il settimanale d'economia CAPITAL. Vivendo in
Russia tiene una mostra fotografica al "Museo degli
Artisti" a Mosca dove elabora le sue prime forme

**PROFILO**

*FotoForma*

**WWW.FOTOFORMA.NET**
**D:** APOSTROPHE, **C:** ROBERTO BEFANI, **P:** APOSTROPHE
**A:** APOSTROPHE, **M:** N.CAPPELLETTI@APOSTROPHE.IT

## Salotto

**WWW.VINAVILL.NET**
**D:** GIAMPIERO GIÀ
**A:** VINAVILL, **M:** VINAVILL_WEB@HOTMAIL.COM

## ulrike krappen
### design

| kontakt | intro | referenzen |

WWW.MAD-KLOSE.DE/UKRAPPEN/HOME.HTML
**D:** ULRIKE KRAPPEN,
**A:** ECHTERNACHT NEW MEDIA, **M:** UKRAPPEN22@COMPUSERVE.DE

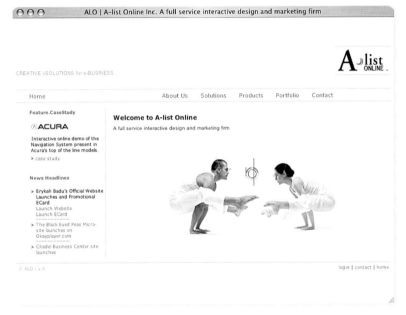

WWW.A-LISTONLINE.COM
**D:** AFRA AMIRSANJARI, **P:** A-LIST ONLINE
**M:** AMIRSANJARI@A-LISTONLINE.COM

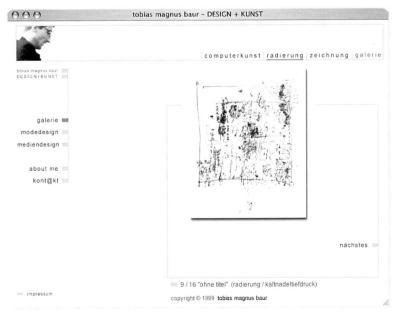

WWW.TOBIASBAUR.DE
**D:** TOBIAS MAGNUS BAUR,
**A:** BAUR, **M:** TMB@TOBIASBAUR.DE

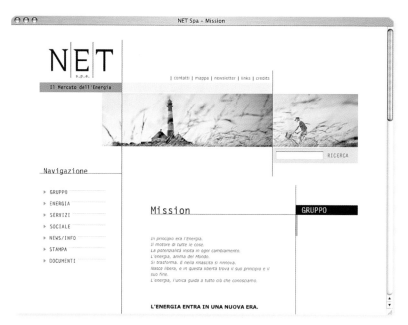

**WWW.NET-ITALY.IT**
**D:** CRISTIANO RASTELLI, **P:** AREA WEB
**A:** AREA WEB, **M:** PUBLIC@DIDOO.NET

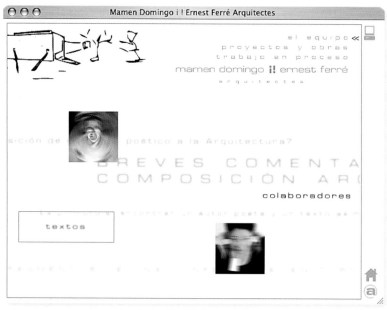

**WWW.DOMINGOFERRE.COM**
**D:** QUICO DOMINGO, SARA ROMERO, **C:** QUICO DOMINGO,
**P:** MAMEN DOMINGO I ! ERNEST FERRÉ ARQUITECTES

Hello, interested in learning or sharing photography?

information     enroll online     enter classroom     the gallery

a bit late is acceptable...

eggy business

Welcome to this Hongkong-based online art gallery and classroom.
last updated: 17 Oct 2003

**EGGY.BIZ**
**D:** ANTHONY HO, **P:** MNMNM.COM
**M:** A@MNMNM.COM

**WWW.BAASCH.COM**
**D:** ANDREW BAASCH, **P:** PREODE
**M:** ANDREW@BAASCH.COM

**WWW.SKYLON.IT**
**D:** MATTEO SONZOGNI
**M:** SONZOBROS@YAHOO.IT

**WWW.GALERIEJAKUBSKA.CZ**
**D:** MILAN NEDVED, **C:** IRI PETVALDSKY, **P:** ISOLAB
**A:** ISOLAB, **M:** E@ISOLAB.CZ

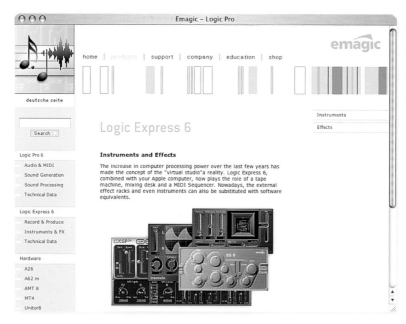

**WWW.EMAGIC.DE**
**D:** PETRA EHLERS, JAN ZIMMERMANN,
**C:** PATRICK BOYER, **P:** EMAGIC

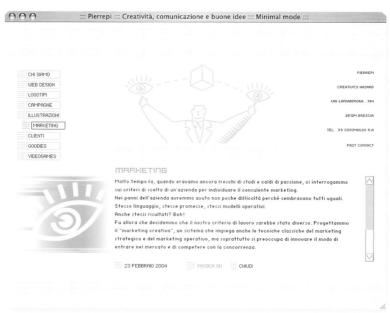

**WWW.PIERREPI.IT**
**D:** MAX SCHIAVETTA, **P:** PIERREPI
**A:** PIERREPI, **M:** MAX.SCHIAVETTA@PIERREPI.IT

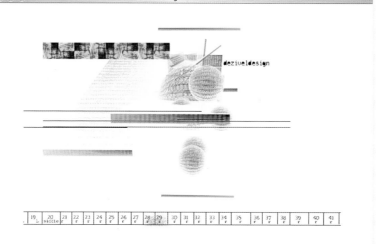

**WWW.DEZIVELDESIGN.5oG.COM/**
**D:** KARIN REYES
**A:** DEZIVE DESIGN, **M:** PINION@OUTGUN.COM

# KWATTA ONTWERPERS

Vernieuwing en originaliteit zijn volgens Kwatta ontwerpers de ingrediënten die ervoor zorgen dat een ontwerp de juiste soort verleiding teweeg brengt. De verleiding om je aandacht erop te vestigen en te blijven houden. Kwatta ontwerpers ontwikkelt concepten, huisstijlen, websites en verschillende soorten drukwerk die van deze ingrediënten voorzien zijn.

De naam Kwatta is vooral gekozen vanwege de nostalgische waarde van de naam (het vroegere chocolade merk) en de speelse klank ervan. Bovendien bestaat natuurlijk de uitdrukking "Aller ogen zijn gericht op Kwatta" welke uitstekend van toepassing is op de ontwerpen van Kwatta.

**WWW.KWATTA.COM/**
**D:** JEROEN HERMES, **P:** KWATTA ONTWERPERS
**A:** KWATTA ONTWERPERS, **M:** JEROEN@KWATTA.COM

[ Gad –Exibition ]

Istanbul Exhibition: Gallerist art gallery, March 6- April 5 2002

Philadelphia Exhibition: Minima Gallery, August 30- September 15 2002

The exhibition explores gad architecture's 10 years work through the lens of three categories: already built buildings; competition and future projects; and renovations restorations and interiors.
The exhibition consists of three dvd films which were about the three different categories and reflected to the walls of the exhibition spaces.

**WWW.GADARCHITECTURE.COM**
**D:** CAN BURAK BIZER
**A:** BIZER WEB SOLUTIONS, **M:** CANBURAK@BIZER.WS

VOODOO192 – Matthew Phillips

VOODOO192  Home   Profile   Portfolio   Sketch Book   Photography   Contact

Photography

#1
#2
#3
#4
#5
#6
#7
#8
#9

night series – Little Lady

Home of Matthew Phillips                Web Design and Creation, Paris France

**WWW.VOODOO192.COM**
**D:** MATTHEW PHILLIPS
**M:** MATTHEW@VOODOO192.COM

| BOUTIQUE
ATTIVITÁ | Metodo   Clienti   Case history
| PORTFOLIO
| NEWS
| GADGETS
| CONTATTI

\\          BOUTIQUE CREATIVA \\ VISUAL DESIGN \\ MILANO–BARCELONA \\

**Ogni progetto di comunicazione è una storia a sé**, tagliato sulle caratteristiche, le esigenze, gli obiettivi del singolo cliente e viene sempre preceduto dall'attenta analisi conoscitiva dell'azienda e del mercato nel quale opera. Un percorso che può coinvolgere la direzione marketing, la ricerca e sviluppo e quant'altri qualificati a fornire un determinante contributo. A questa fase di studio segue l'elaborazione della strategia di comunicazione. La strategia definisce i concetti e le linee guida da seguire nel progetto, identifica ogni elemento di comunicazione, illustra le funzioni e le sinergie tra i vari elementi. Una volta condiviso e approvato il piano di comunicazione, Boutique Creativa si fa carico della sua realizzazione, avvalendosi di tutti i suoi collaboratori e, dove necessario, coordinando altre strutture, per il pieno conseguimento degli obiettivi.

**WWW.BOUTIQUE-CREATIVA.COM**
**D:** PAOLO BOCCARDI, **P:** BOUTIQUE CREATIVA
**A:** BOUTIQUE CREATIVA, **M:** PAOLO@PAOLOBOCCARDI.COM

Oxigenio Design

oxigénio design

| PORTFOLIO | STAFF | CONTACTO | LINKS | CLIENTES

LOGOS
IMPRENSA
CARTAZ
EVENTOS
PUBLICAÇÕES
OUTDOOR
ANUNCIOS TV
SPOTS RÁDIO
MULTIMÉDIA
FONTE

> Light
> Light Italic
> Normal
> Italic
> Medium
> Medium Italic
> Bold
> Bold Italic
> Logotipo

Aa1O

**WWW.OXIGENIODESIGN.COM**
**D:** PEDRO CALHORDAS, **P:** AUGUSTO T. DIAS
**A:** OXIGENIO DESIGN, **M:** PCALHORDASDESIGN@IOL.PT

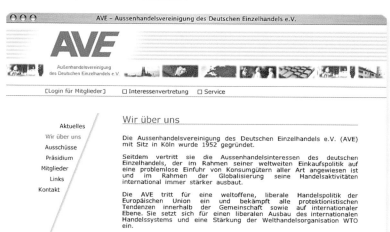

AVE – Aussenhandelsvereinigung des Deutschen Einzelhandels e.V.

AVE
Außenhandelsvereinigung
des Deutschen Einzelhandels e.V.

[Login für Mitglieder]    ☐ Interessenvertretung    ☐ Service

Aktuelles
Wir über uns
Ausschüsse
Präsidium
Mitglieder
Links
Kontakt

## Wir über uns

Die Aussenhandelsvereinigung des Deutschen Einzelhandels e.V. (AVE) mit Sitz in Köln wurde 1952 gegründet.

Seitdem vertritt sie die Aussenhandelsinteressen des deutschen Einzelhandels, der im Rahmen seiner weltweiten Einkaufspolitik auf eine problemlose Einfuhr von Konsumgütern aller Art angewiesen ist und im Rahmen der Globalisierung seine Handelsaktivitäten international immer stärker ausbaut.

Die AVE tritt für eine weltoffene, liberale Handelspolitik der Europäischen Union ein und bekämpft alle protektionistischen Tendenzen innerhalb der Gemeinschaft sowie auf internationaler Ebene. Sie setzt sich für einen liberalen Ausbau des internationalen Handelssystems und eine Stärkung der Welthandelsorganisation WTO ein.

Ihre Mitglieder informiert sie umfassend über handelspolitische und Fragen der Aussenwirtschaftspraxis.

Darüber hinaus können die Mitgliedsunternehmen konkrete Unterstützung bei der Lösung von Zoll- und Verfahrensproblemen, in Anti-Dumping-Verfahren und bei der Überwindung sonstiger Restriktionen des Handels in Anspruch nehmen.

**WWW.AVE-KOELN.DE**
**D:** L.LUDWIG, **C:** M.SEILER, **P:** CHAMEDION
**A:** CHAMEDION, **M:** INFO@CHAMEDION

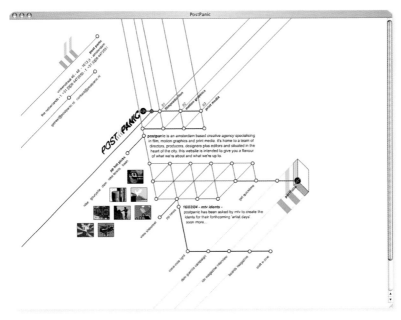

**WWW.POSTPANIC.NL**
**A:** POSTPANIC,
**M:** JULES@POSTPANIC.NL

**WWW.LUFT.COM.MX**
**D:** LUIS FERNANDO CASTRO KARG, **P:** LUIS FERNANDO CASTRO KARG
**A:** LUFT DESIGN, **M:** LIFER@LUFT.COM.MX

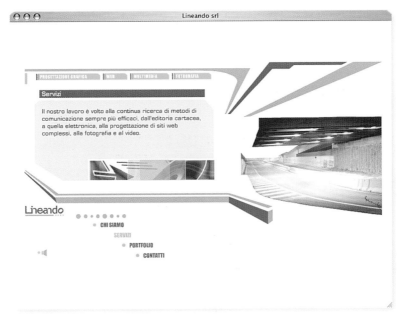

**WWW.LINEANDO.IT**
**D:** GIUSEPPE PRASTI, **C:** LUCA MANCUSI, **P:** GIUSEPPE VOLPI
**A:** LINEANDO SRL, **M:** VOLPI@LINEANDO.IT

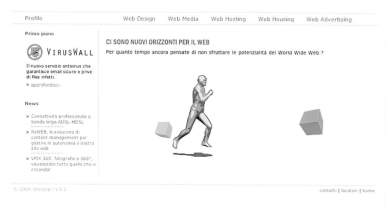

**INTERPOP** DIGITAL MEDIA AGENCY

Profilo    Web Design    Web Media    Web Hosting    Web Housing    Web Advertising

Primo piano

V I R U S W A L L

Il nuovo servizio antivirus che garantisce email sicure e prive di files infetti.
> approfondisci

News

> Connettività professionale a banda larga ADSL-HDSL
> ReWEB, la soluzione di content management per gestire in autonomia il Vostro sito web
> VPIX 360: fotografie a 360°, visualizzate tutto quello che vi circonda!

**CI SONO NUOVI ORIZZONTI PER IL WEB**
Per quanto tempo ancora pensate di non sfruttare le potenzialità del World Wide Web ?

© 2004 interpop | v.6.2    contatti | location | home

**WWW.INTERPOP.IT**
**D:** STEFANO SANVITO, **C:** AVIDE ALDRIGHETTI, **P:** INTERPOP
**A:** INTERPOP S.R.L., **M:** NO.WHERE@KATAMAIL.COM

**WWW.NAUTES-KE.IT**
**P:** NAUTES SRL
**M:** INFO@NAUTES-KE.IT

**WWW.ELASTICBRAND.COM**
**D:** NIK JORDAN, **C:** QASIM BUTT, **P:** ELASTIC BRAND
**M:** NIK@ELASTICBRAND.COM

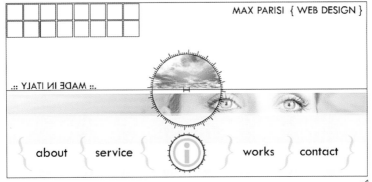

**WWW.MAXPARISI.COM**
**D:** MAXPARISI
**M:** MAXPARISI@MAXPARISI.COM

**WWW.SBT-AG.CH**
**D:** CORNEL BETSCHART, **P:** PETER ULRICH
**A:** NEXUS - CREATIVE COMPANY, **M:** INFO@NCC.CH

**WWW.EVARISTORIERA.COM**
**D:** SANTI SALLÉS ARGILA, **P:** TUNDRABCN
**M:** INFO@TUNDRABCN.COM

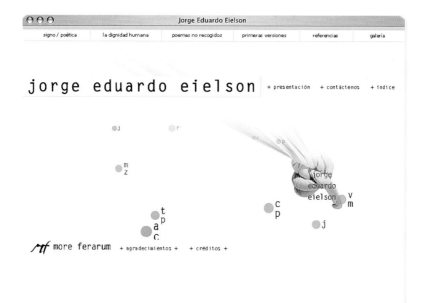

**EIELSON.PERUCULTURAL.ORG.PE**
**D:** CHRISTIAN ARAKAKI, **C:** FAUSTO CÁRDENAS, **P:** FUNDACIÓN TELEFÓNICA
**M:** CHRISTIAN@TSI.COM.PE

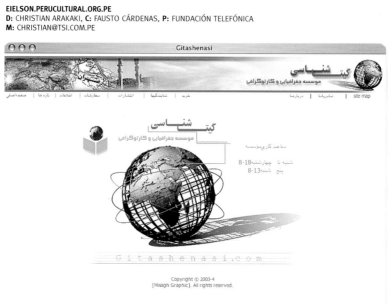

**WWW.GITASHENASI.COM**
**D:** MISAGH GRAPHIC
**A:** MISAGH GRAPHIC, **M:** INFO@SMISAGH.COM

**WWW.CARROGGIO.COM**
**D:** SANTI SALLÉS ARGILA, **P:** TUNDRABCN
**M:** INFO@TUNDRABCN.COM

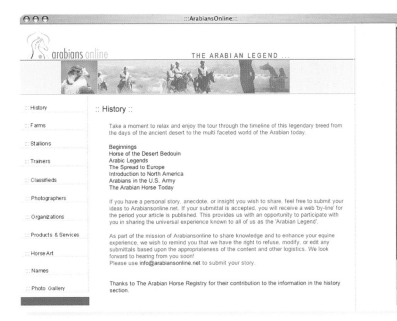

**WWW.ARABIANSONLINE.NET**
**D:** EYAD ABUTAHA, **C:** TIM CHIPMAN, **P:** MUHAMAD ABDELKADER
**A:** WWW.EYAD.COM, **M:** INFO@ARABIANSONLINE.NET

**WWW.MENUURBAIN.COM/ACCUEIL.PHP**
**D:** VALEMBERT XAVIER, **P:** PIX-M
**A:** EXICA, **M:** XAVIER@VALEMBERT.COM

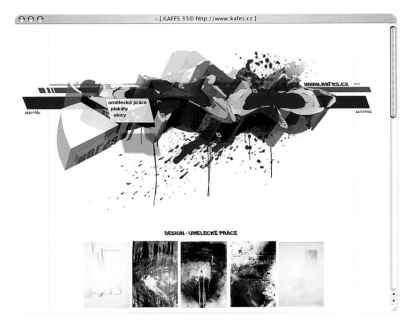

**WWW.KAFES.CZ**
D: KAFES33
**A:** 2IN, **M:** KAFES33@KAFES.CZ

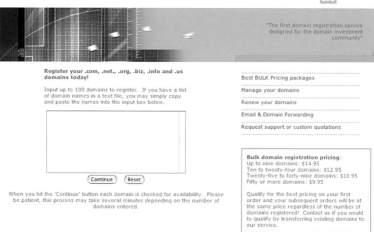

**WWW.BULKNAMES.COM**
**D:** LAWRENCE D'MELLO, **C:** JASON MURRAY, **P:** ELISABETH RIZZI
**M:** LAWRENCE@MELBOURNEIT.COM.AU

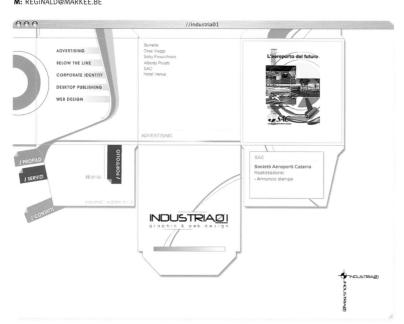

**WWW.MARKEE.BE**
**D:** REGINALD VAN DE VELDE, **C:** BART HEIRWEG, **P:** MARKEE
**M:** REGINALD@MARKEE.BE

**WWW.INDUSTRIA01.IT**
**D:** BAS, **P:** MIASHIGROUP
**A:** INDUSTRIA01, **M:** INFO@INDUSTRIA01.IT

**WWW.BERGENGROUP.COM**
**D:** HELGE WINDISCH, **C:** WOLFGANG LEHMANN, **P:** BERGEN GROUP
**A:** FLANEUR DESIGN

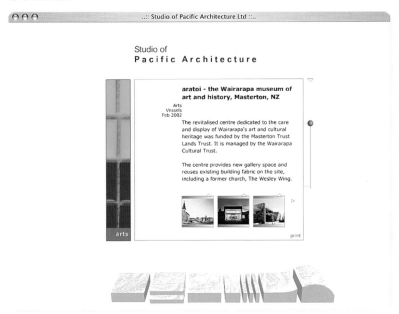

**WWW.STUDIOPACIFIC.CO.NZ**
**D:** ANDREW MAYFIELD, **C:** ANTHONY THORP, **P:** SPIKEFIN MOBILE WEB ARCHITECTURE

**KALIMODJO.NO.SAPO.PT**
**D:** GUSTAVO COUTO
**A:** 2CONTIGO DESIGN

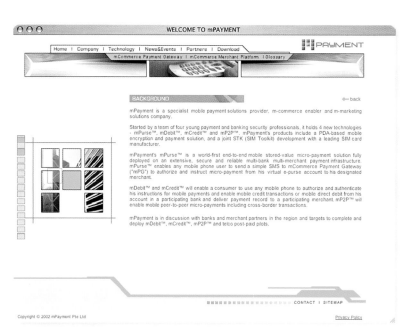

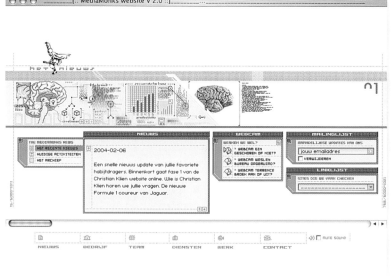

**WWW.MARILULOREN.IT**
**C:** LORENZO MONACO
**M:** INFO@MARILULOREN.IT

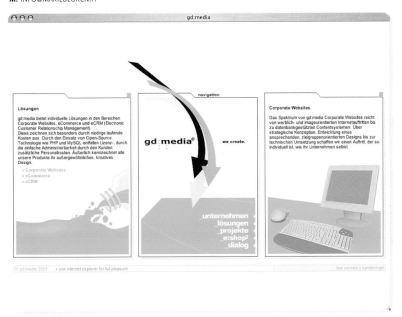

**WWW.GDMEDIA.DE**
**D:** MICHAEL GRAF, ANDREAS DIETERLE
**M:** INFO@GDMEDIA.DE

**WWW.GRAFIKANGELEGENHEITEN.DE**
**D:** JENS MEIER
**A:** MEIER GRAFIKDESIGN, **M:** J.MEIER@GRAFIKANGELEGENHEITEN.DE

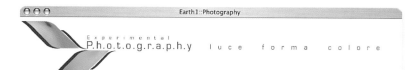

If you want to know when new pictures are published join the newsletter by clicking here

**WWW.MARIOCORALLO.COM**
**D:** MARIO CORALLO
**M:** MARIOCORALLO@HOTMAIL.COM

**WWW.HAACH.COM.SG/**
**D:** LEONG TZI PING / IVAN MP TAN, **P:** ARETAE LTD
**M:** IVAN.TAN@ARETAE.COM

**WWW.PIXELGLOSS.COM**
**D:** JOERN STRATEN
**A:** PIXELGLOSS, **M:** JOERN@PIXELGLOSS.COM

**WWW.ADAGIO.COM.PT**
**D:** DORDIO ESPIGA/PEDRO FERREIRA, **P:** INNOVAGENCY
**M:** RVIANA@INNOVAGENCY.COM

**WWW.BOONDAGO.COM**
**D:** BOONDAGO
**A:** BOONDAGO, **M:** PEPEVERA@BOONDAGO.COM

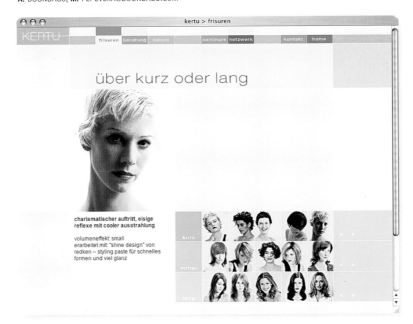

**WWW.KERTU.DE**
**D:** MARION BURBULLA, **C:** STEFAN HAACK
**M:** SCHWARZ.MALER@WEB.DE

**WWW.YO-YOLL.NET**
**D:** FRANCESCO GALLI, **P:** YO-YOLL.NET
**M:** MAIL@YO-YOLL.NET

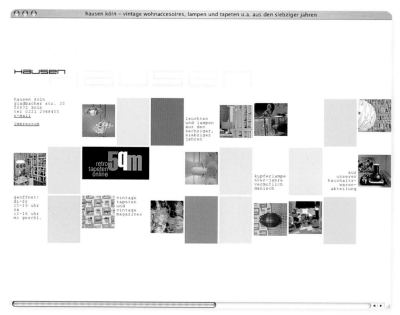

**WWW.WAREN-MIT-CHARME.DE/**
**D:** BERND SASSMANNSHAUSEN, **C:** STEPHAN HERCZEG, **P:** HAUSEN - WAREN MIT CHARME
**A:** NETZRECHERCHE.DE, **M:** HERCZEG@NETZRECHERCHE.DE

**WWW.VIANET.IT**
**D:** SIMONE LEGNO, **C:** FABIO GALLO - EMANUELE PETRUNGARO, **P:** LUCA SIMEONE
**A:** VIANET, **M:** LUCA@VIANET.IT

**WWW.LIFE42.DE**
**P:** LIFE42 - MEDIENDESIGN
**A:** LIFE42 - MEDIENDESIGN, **M:** HL@LIFE42.DE

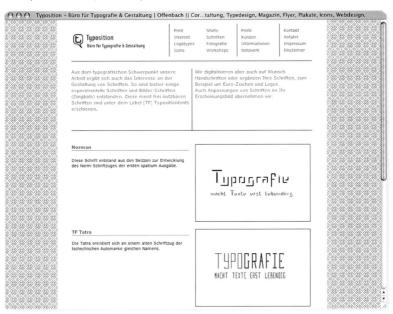

**WWW.TYPOSITION.DE**
**D:** PETER REICHARD/CHRISTOPHER LINDLOHR, **P:** TYPOSITION
**M:** TEAM@TYPOSITION.DE

**WWW.EMPTYDROME.COM**
**D:** J.POU, **C:** MATHIEU, **P:** J.POU
**A:** EMPTYDROME, **M:** ONABRAIN@EMAIL.COM

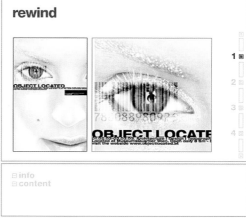

**WWW.KRCHODESIGNS.SK**
**D:** ANDRE KRCHO
**M:** ANDRE@KRCHODESIGNS.SK

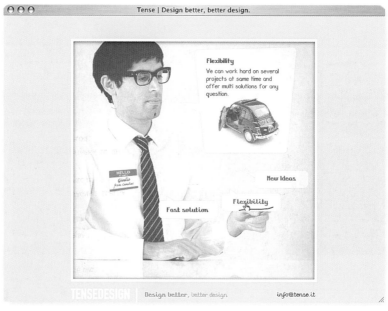

**WWW.TENSE.IT**
**D:** FRANCESCO BERTELLI
**A:** TENSE, **M:** INFO@TENSE.IT

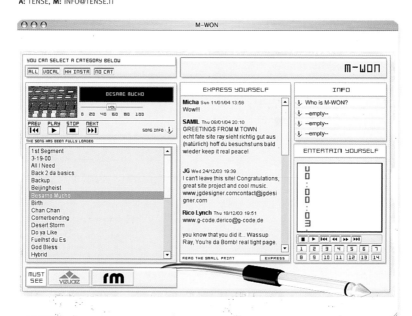

**WWW.MWON.DE**
**D:** RAY MOORE, **P:** CARL WALTER GMBH&CO KG
**A:** STUDIO 39, **M:** ANGELA.WALTER@GMX.DE

OBJE[C]T *

Accessoires_accessories     [Kang] [Xi] [Sampan] [Domido] [Ento] [Bonhomme]
Mobilier_furniture     [Lumiroir] [Bottable] [Plati-plato] [Archiclass] [Zed]
Luminaires_lights     [Apli] [Trio] [Cub]

### Kang
(2002)
Kang est un soliflore prêt à bondir! Il peut
prendre quatre positions différentes.
Tube en verre, polypropylène
L7.5 P16 H13

*Kang is a one-flower vase ready to jump! It can
take four different positions.
Glass, polypropylen
L3 P6.2 H 5*

Suivant
*Next* →

☆ La création d'objets est l'occasion de jouer sur les matériaux comme on joue sur les mots, avec
humour, astuce et poésie... Mes modèles (protégés auprès de l'INPI) sont essentiellement des
objets décoratifs ou du mobilier d'appoint: à cette échelle, je peux réaliser moi-même les
prototypes.

*Creating objects is the occasion for playing with materials as one plays with words, with humor,
artfulness and poetry... My models (all protected by INPI) are decorative objects and extra
furniture: at this scale, I can make prototypes myself.*

[E]SPACE    OBJE[C]T    IMAGE    PROFIL[E]    CONTACT     helene**degroote**.com
                                                   interior design

**HELENEDEGROOTE.COM**
**C:** B. COULMONT / H. DEGROOTE, **P:** HELENEDEGROOTE
**M:** HD@HELENEDEGROOTE

---

Altea Zone – Image

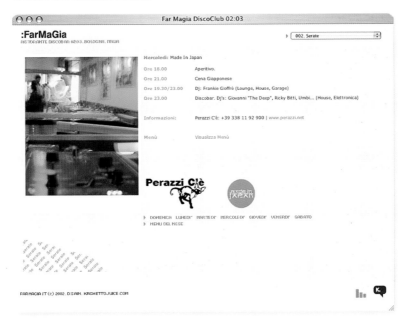

**WWW.PRNETWORK.IT/ALTEAZONE/POSTMSG.HTM**
**D:** RICCARDO IANNARELLI, **P:** FORMAT C
**A:** FORMAT C, **M:** RICCARDO@FORMATC.IT

---

Far Magia DiscoClub 02:03

**WWW.FARMAGIA.IT**
**D:** GIOVANNI PALETTA
**A:** KRGHETTOJUICE, **M:** KRGHETTOJUICE@HOTMAIL.COM

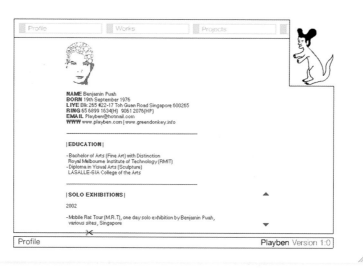

**NAME** Benjamin Puah
**BORN** 19th September 1976
**LIVE** Blk 265 #22-17 Toh Guan Road Singapore 600265
**RING** 65 6899 1634(H)  9061 2076(HP)
**EMAIL** Playben@hotmail.com
**WWW** www.playben.com | www.greendonkey.info

| EDUCATION |

- Bachelor of Arts (Fine Art) with Distinction
  Royal Melbourne Institute of Technology (RMIT)
- Diploma in Visual Arts (Sculpture)
  LASALLE-SIA College of the Arts

| SOLO EXHIBITIONS |

2002

- Mobile Rat Tour (M.R.T), one day solo exhibition by Benjamin Puah,
  various sites, Singapore

Profile                                    Playben Version 1:0

**WWW.PLAYBEN.COM**
**D:** GERARD TAN, **P:** PLAYBEN
**M:** PLAYBEN@HOTMAIL.COM

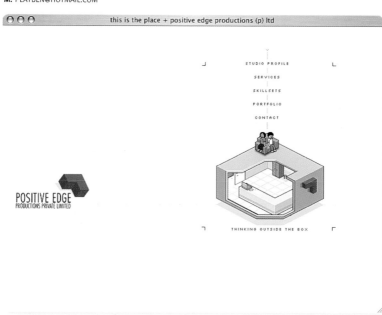

**WWW.POSITIVEEDGE.BIZ**
**D:** MANOJ PAUL, **P:** POSITIVE EDGE PRODUCTIONS PVT LTD
**A:** MANOJ PAUL, **M:** POSITIVEDGE@VSNL.COM

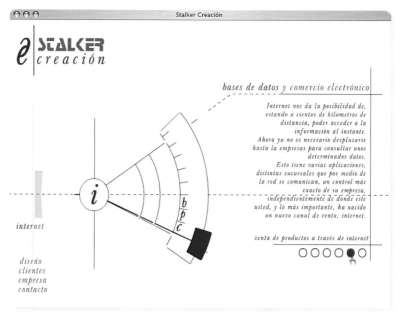

**WWW.STALKERCREACION.COM**
**D:** ELOY MORENO OLARIA, **P:** STALKER CREACIÓN S.L.
**M:** INFO@STALKERCREACION.COM

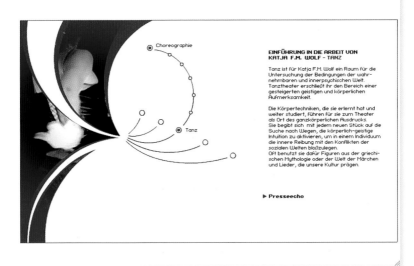

**EINFÜHRUNG IN DIE ARBEIT VON
KATJA F.M. WOLF - TANZ**

Tanz ist für Katja F.M. Wolf ein Raum für die
Untersuchung der Bedingungen der wahr-
nehmbaren und innerpsychischen Welt.
Tanztheater erschließt ihr den Bereich einer
gesteigerten geistigen und körperlichen
Aufmerksamkeit.

Die Körpertechniken, die sie erlernt hat und
weiter studiert, führen für sie zum Theater
als Ort des ganzkörperlichen Ausdrucks.
Sie begibt sich mit jedem neuen Stück auf die
Suche nach Wegen, die körperlich-geistige
Intuition zu aktivieren, um in einem Individuum
die innere Reibung mit den Konflikten der
sozialen Welten bloßzulegen.
Oft benutzt sie dafür Figuren aus der griechi-
schen Mythologie oder der Welt der Märchen
und Lieder, die unsere Kultur prägen.

▶ **Presseecho**

**WWW.KATJA-F-M-WOLF.DE**
**D:** ZELLTEILUNG
**A:** ZELLTEILUNG, **M:** SABINE@ZELLTEILUNG.DE

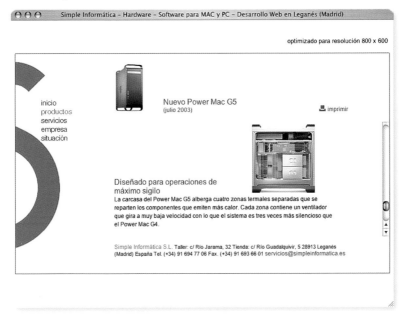

**WWW.SIMPLEINFORMATICA.ES**
**D:** MANUEL ESTRADA   **P:** SIMPLE INFORMATICA
**M:** DIGITAL@MANUELESTRADA.COM

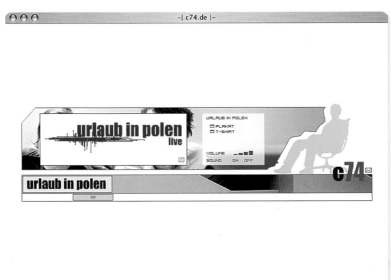

**WWW.C74.DE**
**D:** CHRISTIAN STEIN
**M:** F.KLAUS@GMX.NET

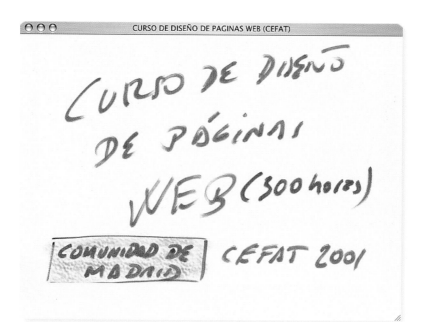

**WWW.BUESA.NET/CURSOS/CEFAT01**
**D:** CARLOS BUSÓN BUESA, **P:** BUESA.NET
**M:** CBUSON@BUESA.NET

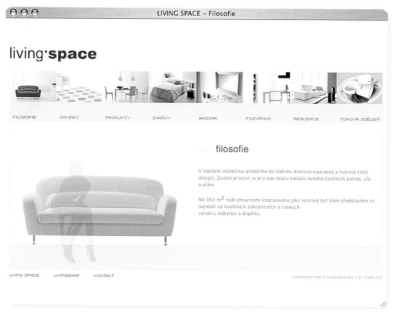

**WWW.LIVINGSPACE.CZ**
**D:** BARBORA KUKLÍKOVÁ, **C:** RADEK BALKOVSK , **P:** BARBORA KUKLÍKOVÁ
**A:** D-SIGN, **M:** KUKLIKOVA@D-SIGN.CZ

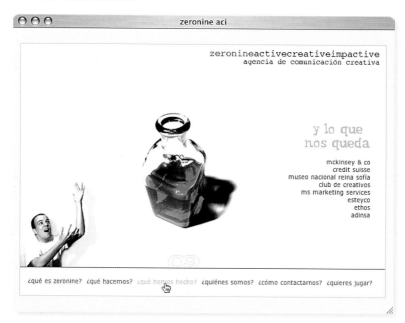

**WWW.ZERO9INE.COM**
**D:** RAFAEL PAVÓN, **C:** MIGUEL COBIÁN, **P:** ZERONINE ACI, SL
**M:** RPAVON@ZERO9INE.COM

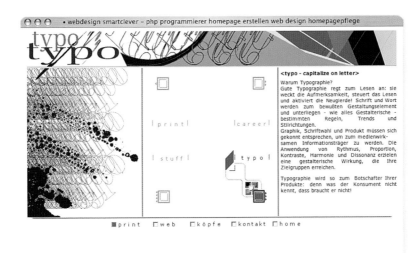

**WWW.SMARTCLEVER.DE**
**D:** ROBERT RAJDA, **C:** BIRGIT HUTMACHER
**A:** DESIGNBÜRO SMARTCLEVER, **M:** KONTAKT@SMARTCLEVER.DE

**WWW.E-BI.IT**
**D:** ROMINA RAFFAELLI, **C:** STEFANO MARINI
**A:** WINKLER NOAH, **M:** INFO@WINKLER-NOAH.IT

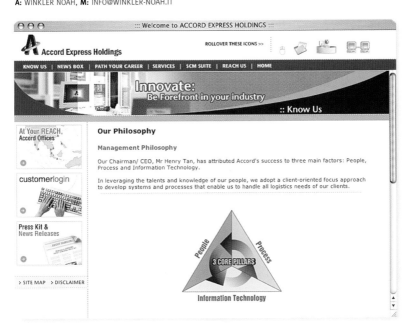

**WWW.ACCORDHOLDINGS.COM.SG**
**D:** HENDRI, **P:** VOXMEDIA
**M:** JOE@VOXMEDIA.COM.SG

WWW.IRENIGRANDI.ORG/A_SITO2003/HOME2003.HTM
**D:** BORMOLINI NICOLA
**M:** NIKKO74@TIN.IT

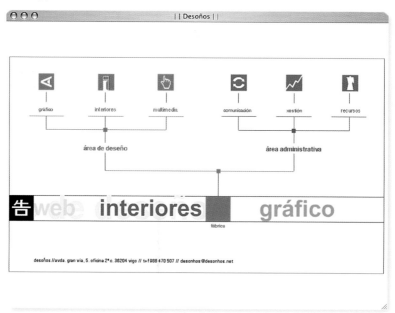

WWW.DESONHOS.NET
**D:** DESOÑOS
**M:** MULTIMEDIA@DESONHOS.NET

WWW.PROFESSIONECASA.IT
**D:** PAOLO CHIESA
**M:** INFO@FACTORYGROUP.IT

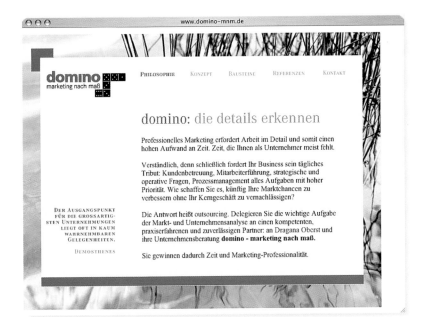

**WWW.DOMINO-MNM.DE**
**D:** STEFAN BEHRINGER, **C:** JUERGEN WUNDERLE, **P:** D:\SIGN CREATIVECONCEPTS
**A:** D:\SIGN CREATIVECONCEPTS, **M:** BEHRINGER@DSIGN.DE

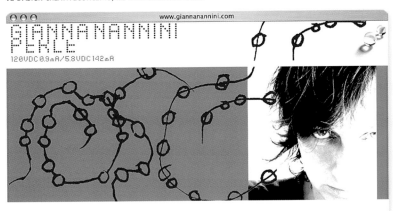

**WWW.GIANNANANNINI.COM**
**D:** LAURA SANTORO
**M:** LAURASANTORO@ROCKETMAIL.COM

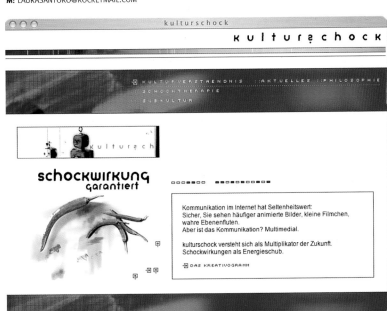

**WWW.KULTUR-SCHOCK.NET**
**D:** BORIS HAHN, **C:** KATJA BÖHM, **P:** BORIS HAHN
**A:** KULTURSCHOCK, **M:** BOEHM@KULTUR-SCHOCK.NET

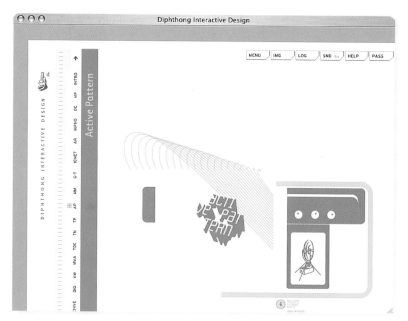

**WWW.DIPHTHONG.COM**
**D:** MAX HANCOCK, **P:** DIPHTHONG INTERACTIVE DESIGN
**A:** DIPHTHONG INTERACTIVE DESIGN, **M:** MAX@DIPHTHONG.COM

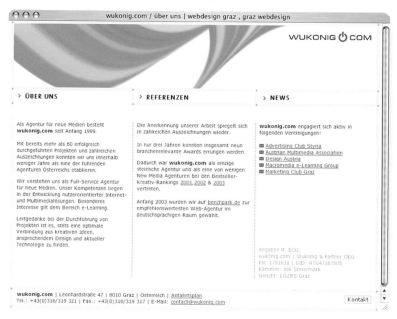

**WWW.WUKONIG.COM**
**D:** WUKONIG JOERG
**A:** WUKONIG, **M:** OFFICE@WUKONIG.COM

**WWW.CREACIONESOLIMPIA.ES**
**D:** CARLES LORIENTE, **P:** LORIENTE INTERACTIVE MEDIA
**M:** CARLES@LORIENTE.TV

**WWW.INNOVATECH-ANSBACH.DE**
**D:** STEPHAN KURZ, **C:** MATTHIAS MESSERER, **P:** QUERFORMAT - DIE WERBEAGENTUR
**A:** QUERFORMAT - DIE WERBEAGENTUR, **M:** MESSERER@QUERFORMAT.INFO

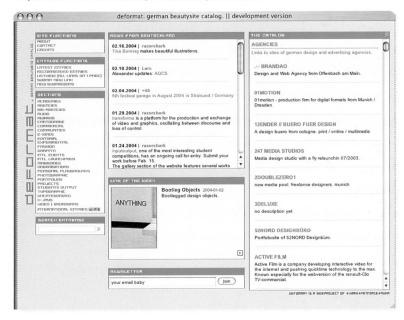

**WWW.DEFORMAT.DE**
**D:** LARS WOEHNING, **P:** V2A**NETFORCE**RUHR
**M:** LW@V2A.NET

**WWW.HKDESIGNCENTRE.ORG**
**D:** YAN PANG, **C:** SAMUEL CHENG, **P:** EUREKA DIGITAL LTD
**A:** EUREKA DIGITAL, **M:** KELLY@EUREKA-DIGITAL.COM

**WWW.COAPI.ORG**
**D:** SANTI SALLÉS, **C:** TUNDRABCN
**A:** TUNDRABCN, **M:** INFO@TUNDRABCN.COM

**WWW.ROCKCENTRO.COM**
**D:** CARLOS MURILLO
**M:** CARLOS@ROCKCENTRO.COM

**WWW.ULF-NOLL.DE**
**D:** PETER HANKEL DESIGN, **C:** CHRISTIAN ITTNER
**A:** PETER HANKEL DESIGN, **M:** INFO@PETER-HANKEL-DESIGN.DE

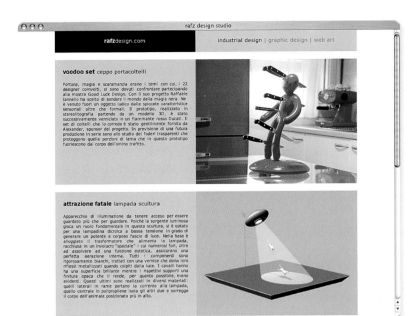

**WWW.RAFZDESIGN.COM**
**D:** RAFFAELE IANNELLO
**M:** RAFZ@RAFZ.IT

**WWW.ITFASHION.COM**
**D:** VILASECA ALVAREZ, **C:** ESTEL VILASECA, **P:** ESTEL MUNNE
**A:** ITEAM, **M:** POSTMASTER@ITFASHION.COM

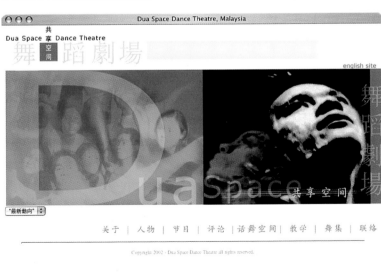

**WWW.DUASPACE.COM.MY**
**D:** HENRY KHOR, **P:** DUA SPACE DANCE THEATRE
**M:** HENRYKHOR@LYCOS.COM

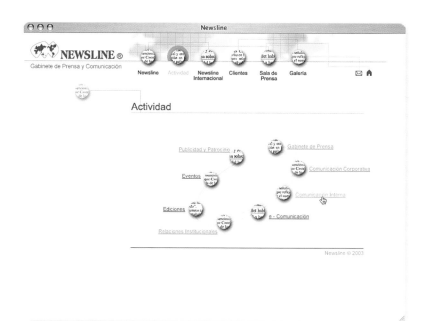

WWW.NEWSLINE-PR.COM/
**D:** SANTI SALLÉS ARGILA
**A:** TUNDRABCN, **M:** INFO@TUNDRABCN.COM

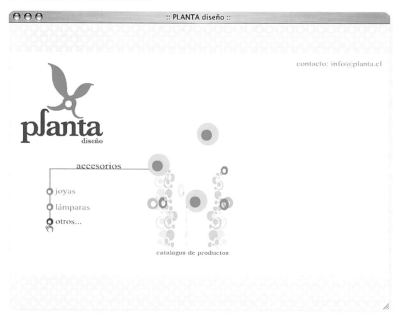

WWW.PLANTA.CL
**D:** MAURICIO OLGUIN, **P:** PISTA2.COM
**A:** PISTA2.COM, **M:** CONTACTO@MAURICIOOLGUIN.COM

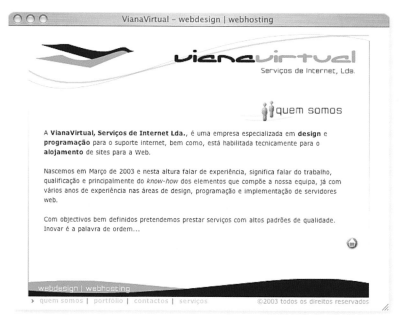

WWW.VIANAVIRTUAL.COM
**D:** JOSÉ VIANA
**A:** VIANAVIRTUAL, **M:** JOSE-VIANA@VIANAVIRTUAL.COM

58

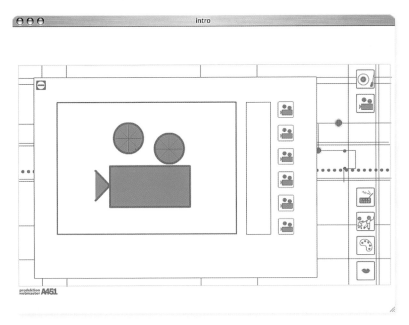

**WWW.EYECANHEARIT.DE/**
**D:** KARIN GEURTZ

**WWW.GEOLOGO.COM**
**D:** JOHNNIE MANEIRO
**A:** GRAFF.NET

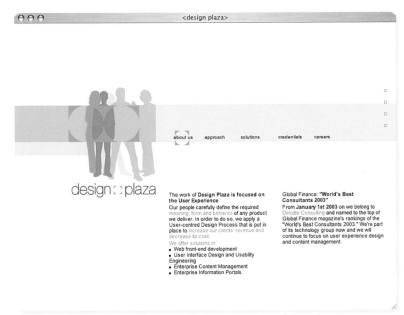

**WWW.DESIGNPLAZA.NET**
**D:** ANICK LE CERF
**A:** ANDERSEN - DESIGN PLAZA

Poligono de Roces 5, Nave 3
Gijón. Asturias. Tf: 985.307.017

QUIENES SOMOS    DONDE ESTAMOS    QUE HACEMOS    SEGURIDAD INDIVIDUAL    SEGURIDAD COLECTIVA    PIDA INFORMACION

Tejanort es una empresa fundada en 1997, joven en su creación, pero con gran experiencia acumulada entre los profesionales que la forman.

Preocupada desde sus inicios por los avances que en su campo se desarrollan, y especialmente aquellos que tienen que ver con la seguridad, Tejanort ha dado un paso adelante, con la introducción en España de nuevos sistemas de protección, individual y colectiva.

Tejanort no solo aporta las ideas y avances que se desarrollan en Europa, sino que además los pone en práctica a través de los múltiples trabajos que realiza: renovación de tejados, impermeabilizaciones…

**WWW.TEJANORT.COM**
**D:** ELIAS MEGIDO, **P:** EMVISUAL
**M:** EMVISUAL@IMEDIA.ES

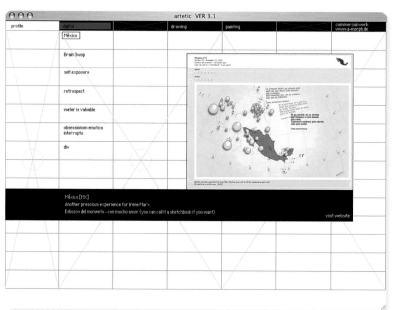

**WWW.ARTETIC.COM**
**D:** IRENE MARX, **P:** ARTETIC
**M:** IRENE@ARTETIC.COM

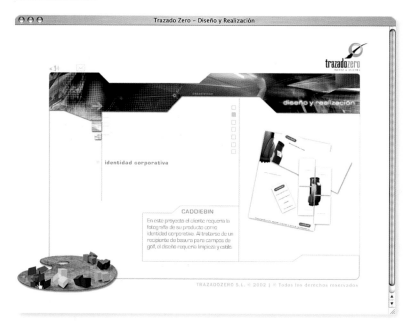

**WWW.TRAZADOZERO.COM**
**D:** IBAÑEZ VILCHES, **P:** TRAZADOZERO S.L
**A:** IBAÑEZ VILCHES, **M:** INFO@TRAZADOZERO.COM

**WWW.ERBORISTERIADEIFRATI.IT**
**D:** ILARIA BOZ, **P:** VILLAGE S.R.L.
**M:** IBOZ@VILLAGE.IT

**WWW.DESCONECTAYDISFRUTA.COM**
**D:** LUIS JUAN, **C:** SALVA ALBORS, **P:** SELERED
**A:** SELERED, **M:** SELERED@SELERED.COM

**WWW.CAPUTA-DESIGN.COM/ENG/**
**D:** GRZEGORZ CAPUTA, **C:** PIOTR KOSTECKI
**A:** CAPUTA-DESIGN, **M:** GRZEGORZ@CAPUTA-DESIGN.COM

**WWW.VALLESDELOSO.ORG**
**D:** ELIAS MEGIDO
**A:** EMVISUAL, **M:** EMVISUAL@IMEDIA.ES

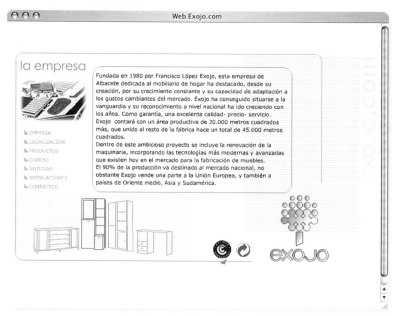

**WWW.EXOJO.COM**
**D:** ELENA JIMENEZ ARBOLEDA, **C:** MANUEL ALTAMIRANO, **P:** LUIS ZORNOZA
**A:** TECON, **M:** EJIMENEZ@TECON.ES

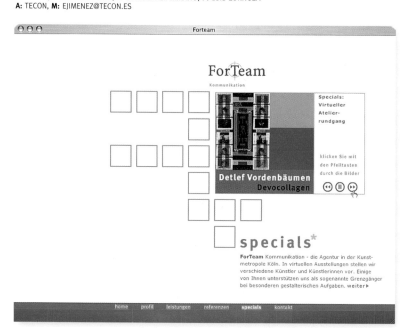

**WWW.FORTEAM.DE**
**D:** TIM FISCHER, **C:** THOMAS SCHÜSSLER, **P:** MEDIENBÜRO UKB
**A:** MEDIENBÜRO UKB, **M:** FISCHER@MEDIENBUERO-UKB.DE

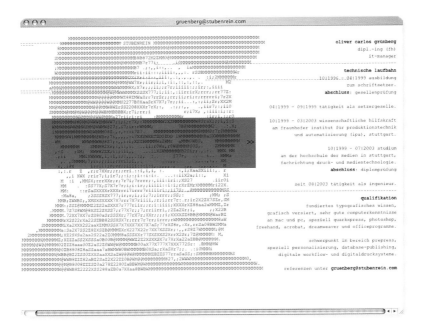

WWW.STUBENREIN.COM
**D:** OLIVER CARLOS GRUENBERG
**M:** OLI@STUBENREIN.COM

WWW.GRAPHISMEDIA.COM/MAG
**D:** ANTHONY THIBAULT, **C:** DELPHINE LECHAT, **P:** GRAPHISMEDIA
**A:** GRAPHISMEDIA, **M:** CONTACT@GRAPHISMEDIA.COM

WWW.ELINCENETWORKS.COM
**D:** MIRIAM CAMPILLO, **C:** DENIS DUREUX, **P:** ELINCE NETWORKS S.L.
**A:** ELINCE NETWORKS S.L., **M:** MCAMPILLO@ELINCENETWORKS.COM

**WWW.RADKE-INTERAKTIV.DE**
**D:** SONJA RADKE, **C:** OLIVER MANZ, **P:** RADKE INTERAKTIV
**M:** INFO@RADKE-INTERAKTIV.DE

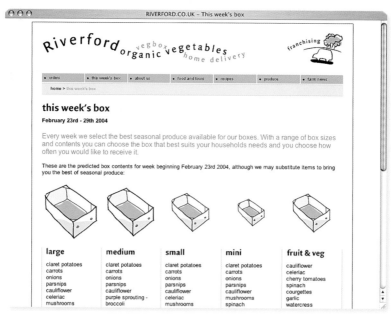

**WWW.RIVERFORD.CO.UK**
**D:** NATHAN KINGSTONE, **C:** DAVID MORLEY, **P:** MARCUS PULLEN
**A:** ASPIN INTERACTIVE, **M:** MARCUSP@ASPIN.CO.UK

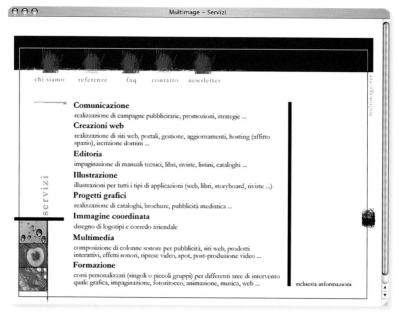

**WWW.MULTIMAGE.NET**
**D:** GIANLUCA RANIERI
**A:** MULTIMAGE, **M:** INFO@MULTIMAGE.NET

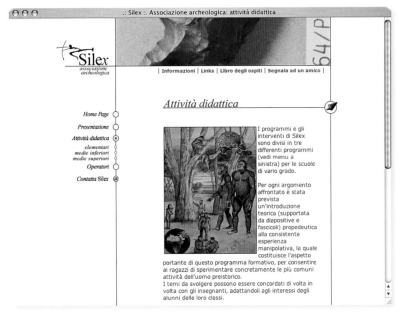

**WWW.ARCHEOSILEX.IT**
**D:** DOMENICO MANES, **P:** SILEX
**M:** MANES@LIBERO.IT

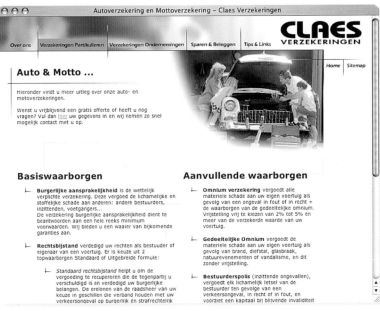

**WWW.CLAESVERZEKERINGEN.BE**
**D:** SVEN GODIJN, **C:** JAN BOLS
**A:** ENCOUNTERS MEDIASCIENCE, **M:** INFO@ENCOUNTERS.BE

**WWW.1210-CLUB.DE**
**D:** HANNES ULBRICH
**A:** JMS MULTIMEDIA, **M:** HANNES.ULBRICH@JMSMULTIMEDIA.DE

**WWW.MAX.HI-HO.NE.JP/ASTRONAUT2001/**
**D:** TADASHI MINEMURA
**M:** ASTRONAUT2001@MAX.HI-HO.NE.JP

**WWW.ZIFRI.DE**
**D:** CHRISTINA KÖNIG, **C:** ANITA HRSAK, **P:** ZIMMER + FRISCHEMEYER
**A:** VS.42, **M:** RECEPTION@VS42.COM

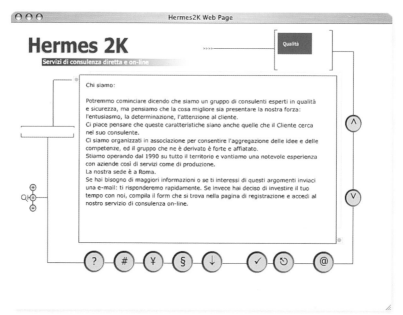

**WWW.HERMES2K.IT**
**D:** MICHELE VOLPE, **P:** HERMES2K
**M:** HERMES@HERMES2K.IT

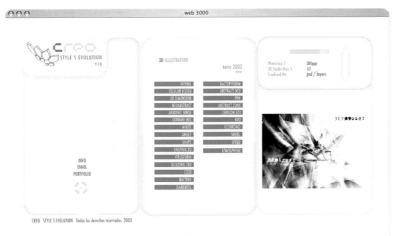

**WWW.C230.NET**
**D:** CREO, **C:** MIGUEL ANGEL, **P:** MIGUEL ANGEL
**A:** CREO STYLE´S EVOLUTION, **M:** CREOART@HOTMAIL.COM

**WWW.SITEUP.COM/FIDO/**
**P:** BOB GIBBONS
**A:** EASTERN | WEBMEDIA, **M:** KALIS@NEXTRA.SK

**WWW.MBB-AIRBAGSYSTEMS.DE**
**D:** STEFAN BEHRINGER, **C:** JUERGEN WUNDERLE
**A:** D:\SIGN CREATIVECONCEPTS, **M:** BEHRINGER@DSIGN.DE

**WWW.RICCARDOTURCATO.COM**
**D:** RICCARDO TURCATO
**M:** INFO@RICCARDOTURCATO.COM

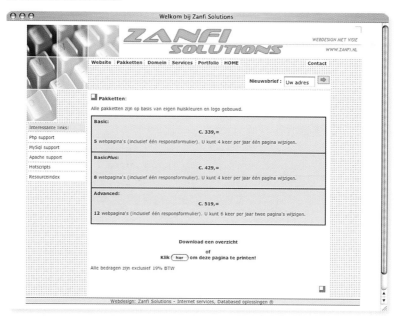

**WWW.ZANFI.NL**
**D:** GIANLUCA ZANFERRARI
**M:** INFO@ZANFI.NL

**WWW.LOB-DIABETES.DE**
**D:** AXEL BERGER, **C:** HOLGER NEUJAHR, **P:** PETER DAHLHAUSEN
**A:** GEE-INTERACTIVE, **M:** AB@GEE-INTERACTIVE.COM

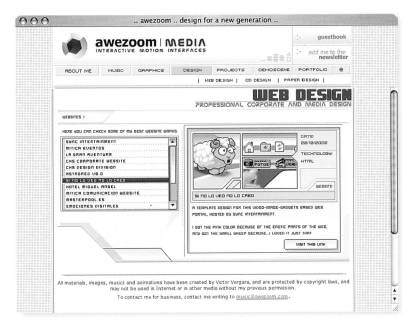

**WWW.AWEZOOM.COM**
**D:** AWEZOOM
**M:** AWEZOOM@AWEZOOM.COM

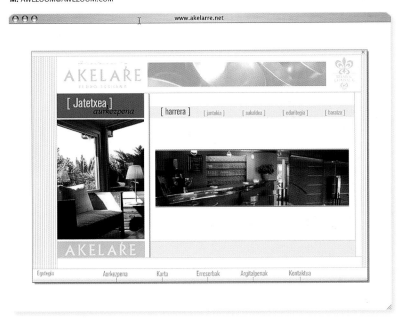

**WWW.AKELARRE.NET**
**D:** ZOÉ , EVA, **C:** JOHN COWEN, AINHOA GARCÍA, PEPE, **P:** GONZALO PEREA
**A:** DEDO MULTIMEDIA

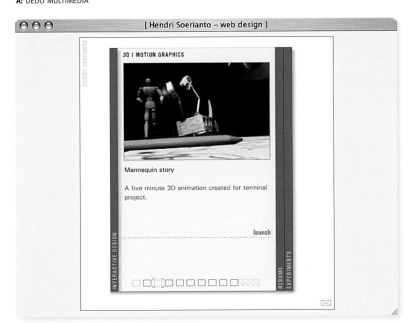

**WWW.SOERIANTO.NET**
**D:** HENDRI SOERIANTO
**M:** HENDRI@SOERIANTO.NET

69

**MANUELONLINE.TK**
**D:** MANUEL GOMEZ
**A:** SCIPIO DESIGN, **M:** MEGDANKA@YAHOO.ES

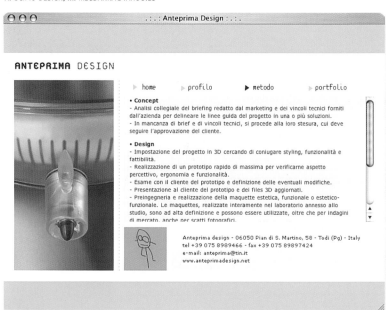

**ANTEPRIMADESIGN.IT**
**D:** NICOLA CAPPELLETTI, **C:** R.BEFANI
**A:** APOSTROPHE, **M:** N.CAPPELLETTI@APOSTROPHE.IT

**WWW.FASHCAT.COM**
**D:** BORILLO CÉSPEDES, **C:** SALVADOR CATALÀ, **P:** BORILLO CÉSPEDES
**A:** FASHCAT, **M:** ESTUDIO@FASHCAT.COM

**WWW.MILDMAC.ES**
**D:** CHRISTIAN RUGE, **C:** LUIS DORADO
**A:** ESPACIO DIGITAL, **M:** CRUGE@EDIGITAL.ES

**WWW.KOLUMBUS.FI/ARKKITEHTIPIENOISMALLI/**
**D:** KARRI LAITALAINEN
**A:** VADELMA, **M:** KARRI_L@POCZTA.ONET.PL

**WWW.HAIKU-MEDIA.COM**
**D:** HAIKU MEDIA
**M:** A@HAIKU-MEDIA.COM

**WWW.SOLUTIONROOM.DE**
**D:** CINDY FISCHER   **C:**   MICHAEL SCHAAB   **P:**   SOLUTIONROOM GBR
**M:** CINDY.FISCHER@SOLUTIONROOM.DE

**WWW.ACADEMIAGLOBAL.COM**
**D:** HUGO SILVA
**A:** FACTOR DIGITAL, **M:** HUGOS@FACTORDIGITAL.COM

**WWW.FBTO.NL**
**D:** HENKJAN BERKHOFF, **P:** CLOCKWORK
**M:** HENKJAN@CLOCKWORK.NL

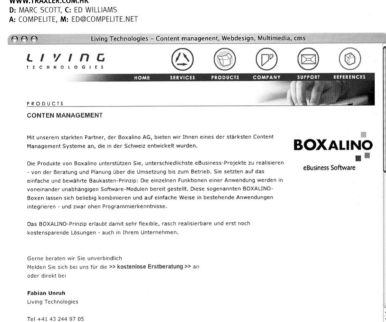

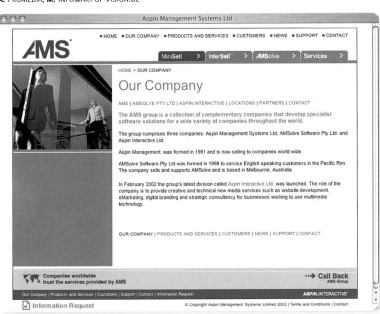

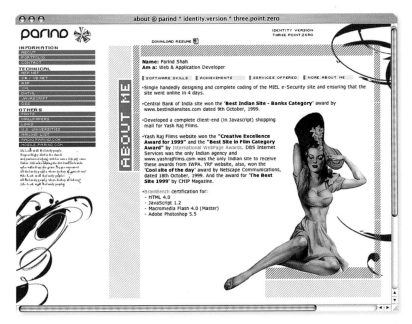

PORTADAS

**HORACIOTORRENT.COM**
**D:** HORACIO TORRENT
**A:** HORACIOTORRENT, **M:** ELGORY@HORACIOTORRENT.COM

Spannbauer, Rolladen, Markisen, Jalousien und Sonnenschutz in Neureichenau

**WWW.SPANNBAUER.DE**
**D:** LUDWIG GUTSMIEDL, **P:** ROLLADEN SPANNBAUER
**A:** G-2000 WERBUNG+DESIGN, **M:** INFO@SPANNBAUER.DE

Artigianfer di Benedetti e Campagnacci Spello, ferro battuto, ferro forgiato a mano.

**WWW.ARTIGIANFERONLINE.IT**
**D:** ROSITA PAPARELLI
**A:** GRAFICHERÒ, **M:** INFO@GRAFICHERO.IT

76

**WWW.NETEFFECTS1.NET**
**D:** KEVIN GENTRY, **C:** MISTY TRANG, **P:** KEVIN GENTRY
**A:** NETEFFECTS 1 DESIGN, **M:** KEVIN@NETEFFECTS1.NET

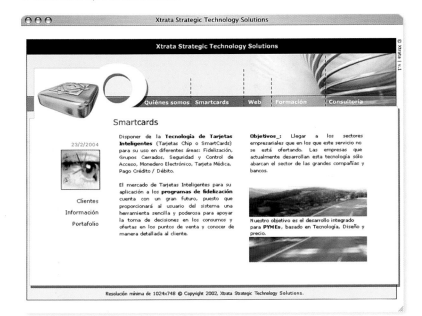

**WWW.MARS.DE**
**D:** MICHAEL SCHLÜTER, **C:** VISTA NOVA GMBH, **P:** MASTERFOODS GMBH
**A:** VISTA NOVA GMBH, **M:** INFO@VISTANOVA.DE

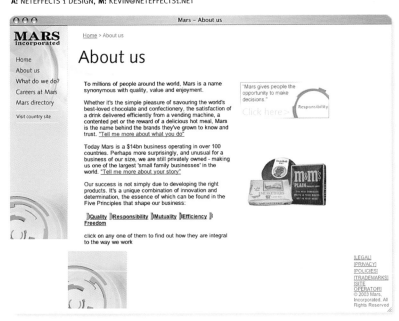

**WWW.XTRATA.COM**
**D:** SILVIA PÉREZ LUIÑA, **C:** MANUEL GARCÍA GARCÍA,
**P:** XTRATA STRATEGIC TECHNOLOGY SOLUTIONS **M:** MGARCIAGA@XTRATA.COM

**SINFONICADETENERIFE.COM**
**D:** JORGE ZUBIRIA TOLOSA, **P:** ORQUESTA SINFÓNICA DE TENERIFE
**M:** JORGE@ZUBIRIA.COM

**WWW.POSTMAN.IT**
**D:** JOHNNIE MANEIRO
**A:** GRAFF.NET, **M:** JOHNNIEMANEIRO@MAC.COM

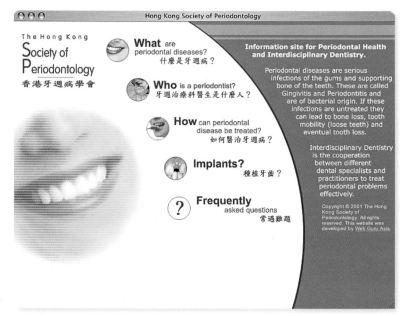

**WWW.HKPERIO.ORG/**
**D:** KATHY LO
**A:** WEB GURU ASIA, **M:** KATHY@WEBGURUASIA.COM

**SINFONICADEGALICIA.COM**
**D:** JORGE ZUBIRIA TOLOSA
**M:** JORGE@ZUBIRIA.COM

**WWW.CREATIVESENSES.DE**
**D:** CHRISTOPHER JONES
**A:** CREATIVESENSES, **M:** CHRIS@CREATIVESENSES.DE

**ANABELEN.IESPANA.ES**
**D:** CARLOS G. PEDREGOSA
**M:** CARLOSPEDREGOSA@ERESMAS.COM

## Objetos Publicitarios

home | quiénes somos | nuestros clientes | productos | promoción especial | presupuesto

¿quienes somos?

OBJETOS PUBLICITARIOS es una empresa especializada en la creación y distribución de Regalos PUBLICITARIOS Y PROMOCIONALES, con una experiencia de más de 20 años en el sector.

Si Usted está buscando una empresa de regalos publicitarios con:
- un catálogo de más de 500 artículos
- personalización de los productos
- presupuesto a medida, descuentos importantes
- imbatible relación calidad-precio
**Somos la empresa a su medida.**

¿Necesita reforzar sus campañas publicitarias haciendo un regalo, poner en marcha una promoción, tener un detalle con sus clientes o empleados, obsequiándoles en alguna feria o en ciertas fechas especialmente indicadas? Nosotros nos encargamos de todo, desde un simple bolígrafo a un viaje, pasando por artículos de escritorio, metal, piel, cristal o cualquier regalo que usted se imagine.

Le ofrecemos el asesoramiento que usted necesita, orientándole en la forma de aprovechar al máximo su presupuesto, presentándole los artículos que mas se ajusten a sus necesidades, personalizándoselo con los mejores medios, láser, tampografía, bordados, etc,... según cual sea más adecuado para cada artículo.

contacte

**WWW.OBJETOSPUBLI.COM**
**D:** DAVID MARTIN, **C:** JAIME SÁNCHEZ, **P:** ANTONIO CARRASCOSA
**A:** CONVIERTA COMERCIALIZACIÓN, **M:** JIMMY20ES@ERESMAS.COM

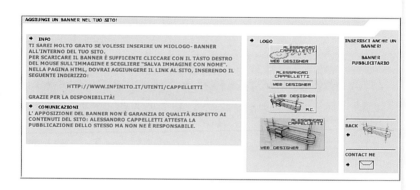

AGGIUNGI UN BANNER NEL TUO SITO!

**+ INFO**
TI SAREI MOLTO GRATO SE VOLESSI INSERIRE UN MIOLOGO- BANNER ALL'INTERNO DEL TUO SITO.
PER SCARICARE IL BANNER È SUFFICENTE CLICCARE CON IL TASTO DESTRO DEL MOUSE SULL'IMMAGINE E SCEGLIERE "SALVA IMMAGINE CON NOME".
NELLA PAGINA HTML, DOVRAI AGGIUNGERE IL LINK AL SITO, INSERENDO IL SEGUENTE INDIRIZZO:

HTTP://WWW.INFINITO.IT/UTENTI/CAPPELLETTI

GRAZIE PER LA DISPONIBILITÀ!

**+ COMUNICAZIONI**
L' APPOSIZIONE DEL BANNER NON È GARANZIA DI QUALITÀ RISPETTO AI CONTENUTI DEL SITO: ALESSANDRO CAPPELLETTI ATTESTA LA PUBBLICAZIONE DELLO STESSO MA NON NE È RESPONSABILE.

+ LOGO

INSERISCI ANCHE UN BANNER!

BANNER PUBBLICITARIO

BACK

CONTACT ME

**WWW.INFINITO.IT/UTENTI/CAPPELLETTI**
**D:** ALESSANDRO CAPPELLETTI
**M:** CAPPELLETTI@INFINITO.IT

VSTUP
BIOGRAFIE
VÝSTAVY
KNIHY
CENY
FOTOGALERIE
SOUČASNÉ PROJEKTY
KONTAKT
ROZHOVORY
ENGLISH

**VÝSTAVY**

Jak jsem potkal kulturu, 1987, Praha
Listopad 1989, 1990, Augsburg
Václav Havel, 1993, Praha
Módní fotografie, 1995, Olomouc
MAFA, 1993, 1994, 1995, 1996, Praha
Deset let fotografie MAFA, 1999, Praha
Olympijské hry, 1999, Varšava
Atletická MS, 1997, Atény
Olympijské hry Sydney, 2000, Praha
Tváře/Faces, 2003, Praha, Moskva

**ZASTOUPENÍ V GALERIÍCH**

Leica Gallery Praha
Komorní galerie Domu fotografie J. Sudka Praha

© 2003 Webmaster+WebdesignerD-sign.cz

**WWW.HERBERTSLAVIK.CZ**
**D:** BARBORA KUKLÍKOVÁ, **C:** RADEK BALKOVSK , **P:** BARBORA KUKLÍKOVÁ
**A:** D-SIGN, **M:** KUKLIKOVA@D-SIGN.CZ

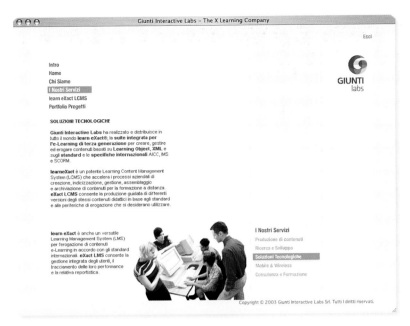

WWW.GIUNTILABS.COM
**D:** LUCAS OBER, **C:** CRISTIANO BOZZO, **P:** GIUNTI INTERACTIVE LABS
**M:** L.OBER@GIUNTILABS.COM

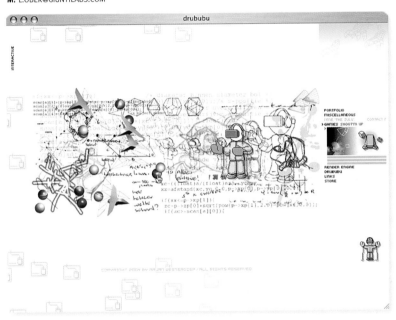

WWW.DRUBUBU.COM
**D:** ARJAN WESTERDIEP
**A:** DRUBUBU, **M:** ARJAN@DRUBUBU.COM

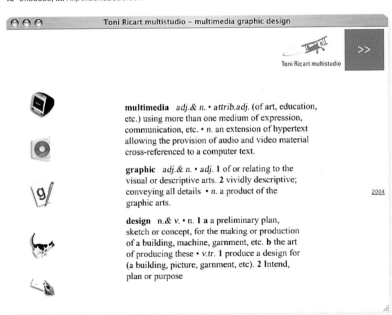

WWW.MULTISTUDIO.COM
**D:** TONI RICART
**A:** TONI RICART MULTISTUDIO SCP, **M:** TRICART@MULTISTUDIO.COM

*l'aperitivo*

*stop music*

### Perché "an Advertising Agency"?

*Tra tanti buoni ristoranti e buonissimi menù
solo uno sarà il piatto che sceglierete.*

*Così come tra tante cose, case, auto, solo una è la vostra:
quella che vorrete che vi accompagni nella vita.
Magari non sarà la più bella, ma per voi è la migliore che ci sia.
Noi non saremo i migliori, i più creativi o i più convenienti,
ma tra tante buone Agenzie e ottimi cibi, uno solo sarà
il vostro piatto pubblicitario preferito.*

Aperitivo
Primo piatto
Il sugo
Il pranzo
Il dolce

ADV web Card   Anti, isto   Contattaci

Maggiolo Adv
*an Advertising Agency*

**MAGGIOLO.COM**
**D:** GIORGIO MAGGIOLO
**A:** MAGGIOLO ADV, **M:** INFO@MAGGIOLO.COM

---

d d s · n l

Internet, maar dan anders.

Nieuws   Basispakket   ADSL   Helpdesk   Webmail   Vdrive   Accountbeheer

algemene voorwaarden, contact, rechten DDS©

**WWW.DDS.NL**
**D:** ANTON BENSDORP, **C:** BAS JANSEN EN BART VAN DER SCHANS,
**A:** ANTON COMMUNICATION DESIGN, **M:** ANTON@BENSDORP.NL

---

**CALCOGRAFIA NACIONAL**
REAL ACADEMIA DE BELLAS ARTES DE SAN FERNANDO

■■ FRANCISCO DE GOYA

HISTORIA   DEPARTAMENTOS   ESTAMPA DIGITAL   BIBLIOGRAFÍA ARTE GRÁFICO   GOYA   EXPOSICIONES Y ACTIVIDADES

01. Caprichos
02. Desastres de la Guerra
03. Tauromaquia
04. Disparates

### PRESENTACIÓN

El principal tesoro conservado en la Calcografía
Nacional son las láminas de cobre grabadas al
aguafuerte por Francisco de Goya, obras cumbres de
la historia universal del grabado.

El estudio, investigación y difusión de la obra de
Goya ocupan un lugar destacado en las actuaciones
de la institución.

La historia de la estampa moderna tiene su
referente inicial en la producción gráfica de Francisco
de Goya. Sus series gráficas -Caprichos, Desastres de
la Guerra, Tauromaquia y Disparates-, constituyen el
punto de inflexión entre la estampa de reproducción
tradicional en talla dulce y el grabado de creación en
sentido moderno.

La evolución de la técnica en el arte gráfico goyesco
fue continua. Alcanzó un extraordinario dominio de
los útiles y una perfecta combinación de los

imágenes

NOTICIAS   DESTACADOS
> HOME

**WWW.CALCOGRAFIANACIONAL.COM**
**D:** SERGIO SEGOVIA · LAURA CASTILLO, **C:** DANIEL SEGOVIA
**A:** SYNAPSIS DIGITAL, **M:** LAURA@SYNAPSISDIGITAL.COM

WWW.AIPPI.ES
**D:** SANTI SALLÉS
**A:** TUNDRABCN, **M:** INFO@TUNDRABCN.COM

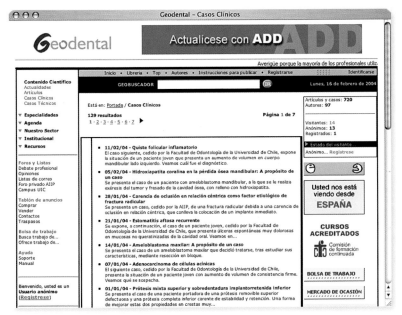

WWW.NEVEBLUES.COM
**D:** DÉSIRÉE TONUS, **C:** LAURA SANTORO
**A:** FLYWDESIGN, **M:** DTONUS@TISCALINET.IT

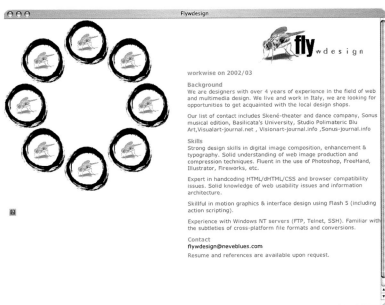

WWW.GEODENTAL.COM
**D:** SANTI SALLÉS, **C:** TUNDRABCN
**A:** TUNDRABCN, **M:** INFO@TUNDRABCN.COM

**WWW.FESTIVALMUSICAEARTESACRA.NET**
**D:** KAI GREIM
**A:** GRAFIKAI, **M:** INFO@GRAFIKAI.DE

**WWW.LIBRERIACARNEVALI.IT**
**D:** ALESSANDRA COMPAROZZI
**A:** GRAFICHERÒ, **M:** INFO@GRAFICHERO.IT

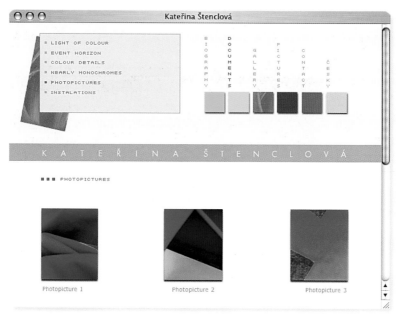

**WWW.STENCLOVA.COM**
**D:** BARBORA KUKLÍKOVÁ, **C:** RADEK BALKOVSK , **P:** BARBORA KUKLÍKOVÁ
**M:** KUKLIKOVA@D-SIGN.CZ

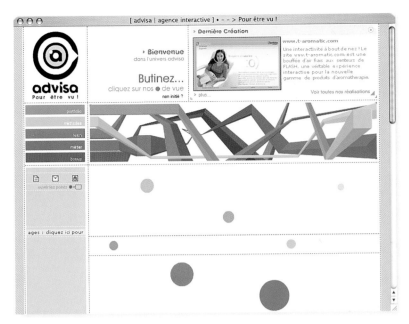

**WWW.ADVISA.FR**
**D:** TINSEL FRÉDÉRIC, **C:** GALLEANO OLIVIER
**A:** ADVISA, **M:** FTINSEL@ADVISA.FR

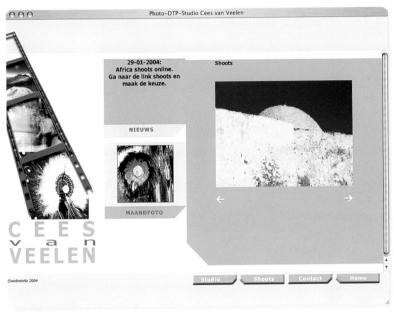

**WWW.CEESVEELEN.COM**
**D:** MARTIJN SCHOUWE
**A:** WEBWORKZ, **M:** INFO@WEBWORKZ.NL

**WWW.E-AGALMA.COM**
**D:** SILVIA PÉREZ, **C:** MANUEL GARCÍA Y RAFAEL TERRERO
**M:** INFO@XTRATA.COM

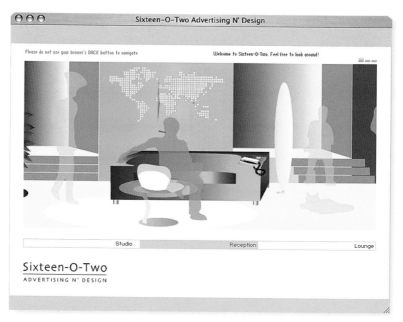

**WWW.16-0-2.COM**
**D:** AGNES TAN, **P:** SIXTEEN O TWO
**A:** JUNKFLEA, **M:** MAIL@16-0-2.COM

**WWW.MILOMEDIA.CO.UK**
**D:** GRANT FORREST, **P:** MILOMEDIA
**M:** GRANT@MILOMEDIA.CO.UK

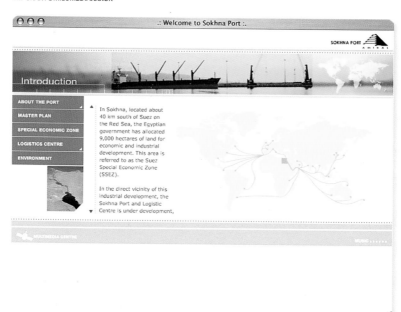

**WWW.SPDC.COM**
**D:** NTNZ
**M:** O.MAERNHOUT@NTNZ.COM

**WWW.JELLYCOM.DE**
**D:** FRANK SCHIER
**A:** JELLYCOM INTERACTIVE, **M:** ASK@JELLYCOM.DE

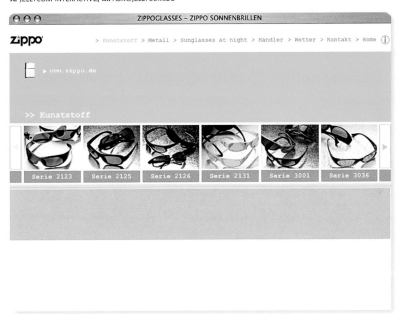

**WWW.ZIPPOGLASSES.DE**
**D:** VERA HEIMANN, **C:** CHRISTOPH FRERICKS, **P:** ISION SALES + SERVICES GMBH CO KG
**M:** VERA.HEIMANN@ENERGIS-ISION.COM

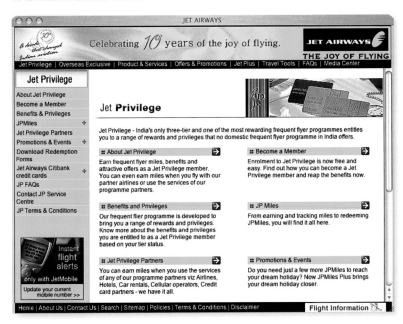

**WWW.JETAIRWAYS.COM**
**D:** KUNAL SHAH, **C:** SUDEEP NAMBIHAR
**A:** OGILVY INTERACTIVE WORLDWIDE, **M:** KUNAL.SHAH@OGILVY.COM

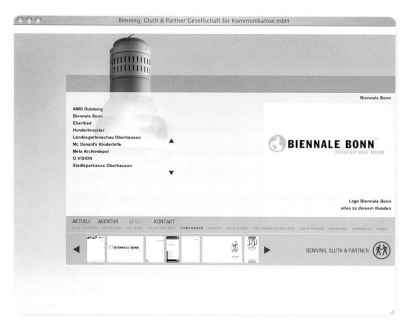

**WW.BGP.DE**
**D:** PAUL BAUMANN **C:** JENS RAUTNER, **P:** GLUTH PARTNER
**A:** BENNING, GLUTH PARTNER, **M:** BENNING@BGP.DE

**WWW.LONGEDESIGN.COM**
**D:** HERIC LONGE ABRAM
**M:** LONGE@LONGEDESIGN.COM

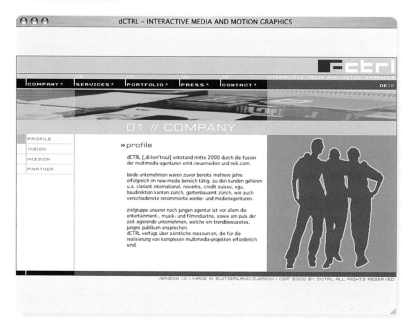

**WWW.DCTRL.COM**
**D:** LORENZ ANDREAS, **C:** ROBERTO EBERHARD,
**A:** NTERACTIVE MEDIA AND MOTION GRAPHICS, **M:** AL@DCTRL.COM

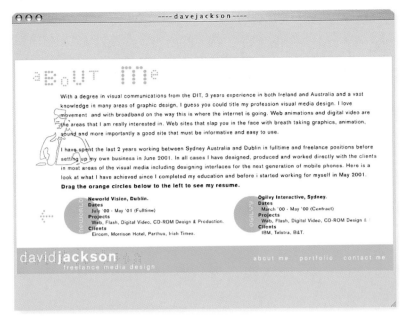

**HOMEPAGE.NTLWORLD.IE/DAVEJACKO**
**D:** DAVID JACKSON
**A:** DAVID JACKSON, **M:** DAVEJACKO@NTLWORLD.IE

**WWW.NICEMOTION.IT**
**D:** NICOLA BOCCHIO
**A:** NICEMOTION, **M:** NICOLA@NICEMOTION.IT

**WWW.NTX.RO**
**D:** ALEXANDRU DUTULESCU
**A:** FLAVORADE, **M:** HI@FLAVORADE.COM

**WWW.FILIPPOROMANO.COM**
**D:** ALESSANDRO AMODIO
**A:** ALCHIMEDIA S.R.L., **M:** AAMODIO@ALCHIMEDIA.COM

**WWW.MINIMALCOMUNICACION.COM**
**D:** MAR SAN ALBERTO
**A:** MINIMAL COMUNICACIÓN, **M:** MAR@MINIMALCOMUNICACION.COM

**WWW.ORANGEBABIES.COM**
**D:** YACCO VIJN, **P:** HANS VAN DIJK, YACCO VIJN
**A:** SKIPINTRO, **M:** YACCO@SKIPINTRO.NL

LAUNDRETTE SOAP

PROGRAMMA
  SPETTACOLI
  INCONTRI
  AZIONI

PROGETTO SPECIALE

FORUM

CONTATTI

Programma | Progetto Speciale | Forum | Contatti | Area riservata

**WWW.LAUNDRETTESOAP.IT**
**D:** DAVID BOARDMAN
**M:** PAOLOGERBO@TISCALI.IT

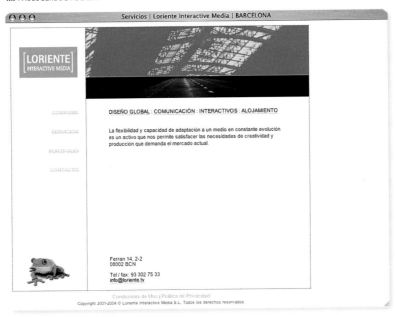

Servicios | Loriente Interactive Media | BARCELONA

[LORIENTE]
INTERACTIVE MEDIA

COMPAÑIA

SERVICIOS

PORTFOLIO

CONTACTO

DISEÑO GLOBAL : COMUNICACIÓN : INTERACTIVOS : ALOJAMIENTO

La flexibilidad y capacidad de adaptación a un medio en constante evolución
es un activo que nos permite satisfacer las necesidades de creatividad y
producción que demanda el mercado actual.

Ferran 14, 2-2
08002 BCN

Tel / fax: 93 302 75 33
info@loriente.tv

Condiciones de Uso | Política de Privacidad
Copyright 2001-2004 © Loriente Interactive Media S.L. Todos los derechos reservados.

**WWW.LORIENTE.TV**
**D:** CARLES LORIENTE
**A:** LORIENTE INTERACTIVE MEDIA, **M:** CARLES@LORIENTE.TV

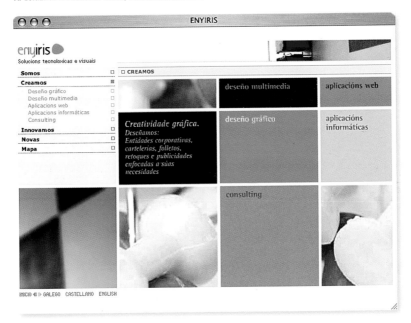

enyiris
Solucións tecnolóxicas e visuais

Somos
**Creamos**
  Deseño gráfico
  Deseño multimedia
  Aplicacións web
  Aplicacións informáticas
  Consulting
**Innovamos**
**Novas**
**Mapa**

☐ CREAMOS

deseño multimedia          aplicacións web

*Creatividade gráfica.*      deseño gráfico        aplicacións
*Deseñamos:*                                       informáticas
*Entidades corporativas,*
*cartelerias, folletos,*
*retoques e publicidades*
*enfocadas a súas*
*necesidades*

                           consulting

INICIO ◀ ▶ GALEGO  CASTELLANO  ENGLISH

**WWW.ENYIRIS.COM**
**D:** ANTONIO FERREIRO RODRIGUEZ, **C:** MIGUEL ANGEL CASTRO FERNÁNDEZ, **P:** ENYIRIS
**M:** MIGUEL@ENYIRIS.COM

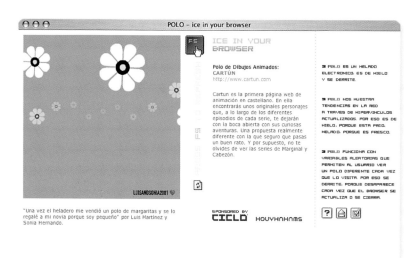

**ELELEC.COM/POLO**
**D:** EDUARDO DE FELIPE, **C:** HECTOR GARZON
**A:** ELEC, **M:** EDUARDO@ELELEC.COM

**WWW.LABELLO.COM**
**P:** BEIERSDORF AG

**WWW.N-IMAGE.DE**
**D:** ANDRE NITZE, **C:** YARO V. FLOCKEN **P:** NEW IMAGE
**A:** NEW IMAGE, **M:** NITZE@N-IMAGE.COM

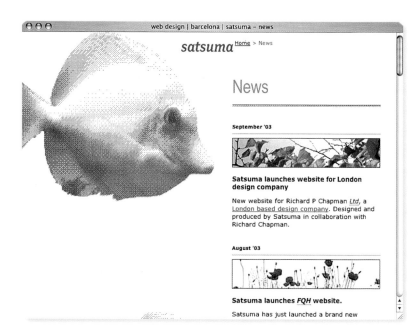

WWW.ERPNCOLLECTIVE.COM
**D:** BEN O'HEAR, STEPHANIE KIEFFER, **C:** BEN O'HEAR
**A:** THE EUROPEAN COLLECTIVE, **M:** STEFFI@ERPNCOLLECTIVE.COM

WWW.ACHELON.IT
**D:** FABRIZIO PASQUERO, **C:** ROBERTO BRONDOLO
**A:** ACHELON WEB DESIGN, **M:** INFO@ACHELON.IT

WWW.SCHOENGEIST.DE/
**D:** JAN RIDDER
**A:** DESIGN KONZEPTION, **M:** INFO@SCHOENGEIST.DE

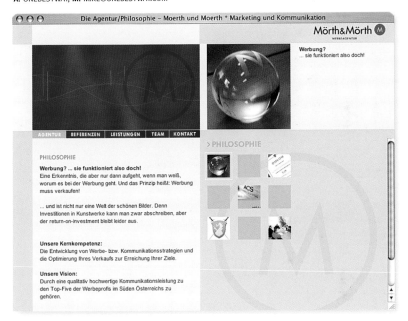

### what we do
introduction

Today we live in an environment in which turbulence seems 'the norm' and change is the only constant. Many factors are forcing organisations to look for new ways to meet market demands quickly, efficiently and effectively. Such factors include the need for speed, to respond to vast technological change, the trend towards globalisation, increased market pressures, and the need to perform more efficiently.

To succeed in this high-pressure, ever-changing environment the knowledge, skills, experience and perspectives of a wide range of **people** must be brought together. Only in this way can organisations solve problems, make effective decisions and deliver optimal solutions to their customers.

◄ 1 of 3 ►

**WWW.QABI.CO.UK**
**D:** JUSTIN COCKBURN, **C:** PHELIM CAVLAN,
**A:** ONEBESTWAY, **M:** MIKE@ONEBESTWAY.COM

**WWW.MOERTH.AT/**
**D:** CHRISTIAN POLTENSTEINER
**A:** WUKONIG, **M:** OFFICE@WUKONIG.COM

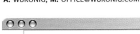

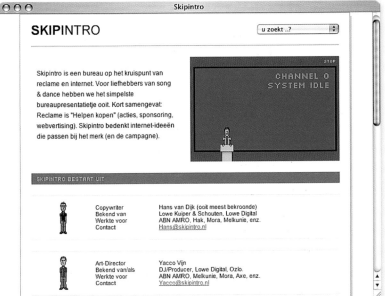

**WWW.SKIPINTRO.NL**
**D:** YACCO VIJN, **P:** HANS VAN DIJK, BJORN BRUINSMA
**A:** SKIPINTRO, **M:** YACCO@SKIPINTRO.NL

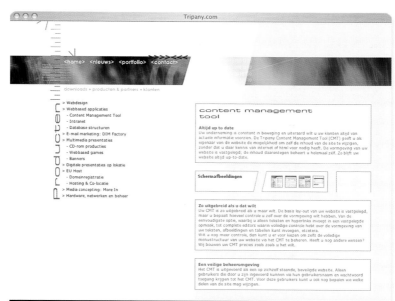

**WWW.TRIPANY.COM**
**D:** TRIPANY TEAM
**A:** TRIPANY INTERNET, **M:** INFO@TRIPANY.COM

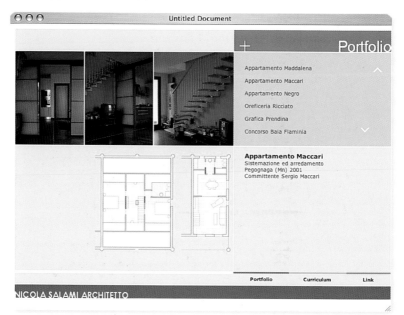

**WWW.ASEPTIC404.NET**
**D:** ALESSANDRO RANDI
**A:** ASEPTIC404, **M:** STERILE@ASEPTIC404.NET

**WWW.NICOLASALAMI.COM**
**D:** MAX BOSCHIN, **P:** NICOLA SALAMI
**A:** GELATINA, **M:** IO@MAXBOSCHINI.COM

COSMOPOLITAN
C O S M E T I C S
D E U T S C H L A N D

□ home    □ rechtliche hinweise    □ kontakt    □ suche    □ impressum

**unternehmen**
unser antrieb
daten & fakten
weltweit präsent
innovation & qualität
kontakt
tradition
anfahrt
□ vertriebsgesellschaften
□ presseinformationen
□ jobs & karriere

[ _____ ]   suche

## Junge Werte und wahre Qualität.

**Cosmopolitan Cosmetics setzt Markenzeichen.**

Empfehlen Sie diese
Seite weiter!

Unsere gesamten Aktivitäten in der internationalen Kosmetik- und Duftbranche haben eines gemeinsam: Wir setzen auf inspirierende Innovationen, lebendigen Lifestyle, zukunftsweisende Trends und qualitativen Vorsprung durch hochwertige Markenprodukte.

Das Portfolio von Cosmopolitan Cosmetics umfasst 30 Markenfamilien – Anna Sui, Gucci, Mexx, Montblanc, Naomi Campbell, Rochas und 4711, um nur einige zu nennen – die weltweit bedeutende Bekanntheit und Präsenz besitzen. Mit unseren Düften sind wir sowohl im Prestige- als auch im Bridge-Segment erfolgreich vertreten.

Kontinuierlich greifen wir in der Entwicklung neuer Duftmarken weitreichende und weltumspannende Trends auf. Multikulturelle Teams in Köln, London, Paris und New York setzen ihre Kreativität, Kompetenz und unkonventionellen *lust for life* immer wieder in faszinierende Ideen um – die schon bald international gefragt sein werden.

**WWW.COSMOPOLITAN-COSMETICS.COM**
**D:** DIETMAR SCHMIDT, **C:** KRUEGER/MÜLLER, **P:** COSMOPOLITAN COSMETICS
**A:** KINGMEDIA, **M:** SCHMIDT@UNIT-MEDIENHAUS.DE

design-stop

□ welcome
□ **philosophy**
□ services
□ portfolio
□ impressum
□ contact

euer erfolg ist unser erfolg

um ihre zielanforderungen zu erreichen, arbeiten wir mit einem pool von freien fachleuten zusammen; strategische planer, designer, texter, system-administratoren - jeder einzelne ein spezialist auf seinem gebiet. so stellen wir je nach anforderung ein spezielles team für sie zusammen. ganz nach ihren wünschen entwickeln wir für sie und ihr unternehmen die massgeschneiderte strategie, klassische werbung, web-design, corporate identity, wir unterstützen sie in ihrem vorhaben.

**WWW.DESIGN-STOP.DE**
**D:** ADAM MAJEWSKI
**A:** DESIGN-STOP, **M:** MAJEWSKI@DESIGN-STOP.DE

KOSMO

**KOSMO**

**Menu**

>> KOSMO home
>> about KOSMO
>> wellness
>> healthy food & beverages
>> merchandise
>> KOSMO card
>> outlets
>> news
>> franchise
>> contact

**KOSMO Food & Beverages**

>> healing juice
>> fruit smoothie
>> power smoothie
>> organic healing tea
>> organic Well-Bean coffee
>> coffee beverages
>> anti-aging food

go organic

KOSMO, a leading
international group of
healthy lifestyle cafés
serving naturally inspired
food & beverages

**NAME**

KOSMO is derived from the word 'cosmopolitan' which is spelled "KOSMOpolitan' in its original Greek form.

It is about a world where healthy living transcends national boundaries, ethnic groups & cultural barriers.

**ORIGIN**

KOSMO is owned by a group of international investors, including a well-known London-based time piece and jewellery maker, a New York-based specialist health food company and a group of surgeons and medical doctors.

**VISION**

To be the world's leading healthy lifestyle café and a leader of the rapidly emerging wellness industry.

**MARKET GAP**

Sitting in a space between fine dining and the traditional cafés, KOSMO has created a new category – a healthy lifestyle café – to fill a market gap, making naturally inspired food and beverages affordable to health conscious consumers.

We acknowledge our responsibility as a global pioneer and a leader of the wellness industry.

**KOSMONAUTS**

Everyone who shares our passion that healthy eating is the foundation of healthy living. Professional, gym-goers, yuppies, the urban chic crowd and health conscious people have all been loyal customers in our quest to promote healthy living.

**Claudia Del Vecchio**

Claudia Del Vecchio is the chief

**WWW.KOSMOLIVING.COM**
**D:** MARC SCOTT, **C:** MATTHEW SILLS
**A:** COMPELITE, **M:** ED@COMPELITE.NET

# molecule

Graphic design for print, web or screen

Mike Vlack is the head designer at Molecule.

He has been freelance graphic designing and photo retouching since 1992.

Despite full time employment in the Film, Television and Music industries; he still had time and creative energy for diverse projects; so he founded Molecule.

Currently, the head designer at *Panavision Australia*. He designs the print and web marketing for the following companies in the group:
*Panavision* (Motion Picture Camera Rentals)
*Panavision Lighting* (Lighting Rental)

who
what
where

**WWW.MOLECULE.COM.AU**
**D:** MIKE VLACK
**A:** MOLECULE, **M:** MIKEV@MOLECULE.COM.AU

---

**Artificio lab**
Artificio è un'associazione per la promozione di lavori interdisciplinari legati alla sfera elettronica e digitale. Dal 1996 al 1998 abbiamo portato avanti un progetto galleristico nel cuore della capitale ticinese, proponendo eventi, workshop, installazioni e concerti di musica elettronica.
Tutte queste attività sono documentate in questa sezione "version 2.0" come documentazione del progetto. Ora la galleria è virtuale e non esiste più fisicamente, e gli sforzi di artificio si sono direzionati verso progetti più piccoli e legati al web.
Non è detto che in futuro ci saranno dei cambiamenti ma per ora la galleria in piazza Magoria rimane uno splendido ricordo ricco di creatività e soddisfazioni.

Demian Conrad

**Grazie**
Ringraziamo tutti gli artisti che hanno contribuito al progetto e a tutte le persone che con il loro sostegno e aiuto han fatto si che questa piccola realtà potesse esprimersi in un territorio non ancora fertile per accogliere le arti eletroniche e informatiche.

**WWW.ARTIFICIO.COM**
**D:** CONRAD DEMIAN, **P:** ARTIFICIO
**A:** POINTPIXEL | COMMUNICATION DESIGN, **M:** INFO@POINTPIXEL.COM

---

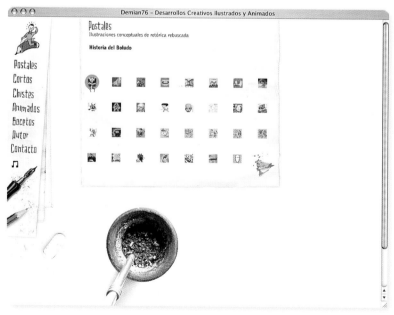

Postales
Cortos
Chistes
Animados
Bocetos
Autor
Contacto

**Postales**
Ilustraciones conceptuales de retórica rebuscada.
**Historia del Boludo**

**WWW.DEMIAN76.COM.AR**
**D:** MATIAS GILLI
**M:** DEMIAN76@CIUDAD.COM.AR

**WWW.FU-HO.COM**
**D:** UHO FUHOLEE
**M:** U_HO_LEE@HOTMAIL.COM

**WWW.VISUALDRUG.COM**
**D:** JOOST KUIJPERS, **C:** FRANK VAN DELFT, **P:** DRUG
**A:** OIN, **M:** FRANK@VISUALDRUG.COM

**WWW.MAUROBARTOCCELLI.COM**
**D:** MAURO BARTOCCELLI
**M:** MAIL@MAUROBARTOCCELLI.COM

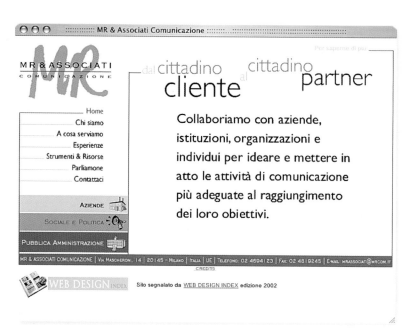

**WWW.MRCOM.IT**
**D:** LOGICAL NET
**M:** GIUSEPPE@LOGICAL.IT

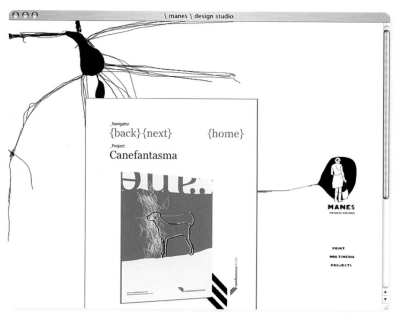

**WWW.UBQ.IT/MANES**
**D:** DOMENICO MANES
**A:** UBQ, **M:** MANES@LIBERO.IT

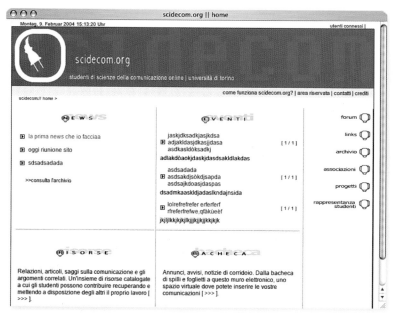

**WWW.CONTEXTO.IT/SCIDECOM/**
**D:** DAVID BOARDMAN, **C:** PAOLO GERBAUDO
**A:** FORMULA ADVERTISING, **M:** FORMULA@TIN.IT

**WWW.NLSTREETS.NL**
**D:** JOACHIM BAAN, **C:** EROEN BEKKER, JOOST OLSTHOORN, **P:** EVA RUIJTE
**A:** OKTOBER VISUELE COMMUNICATIE, **M:** JEROEN@OKTOBER.NL

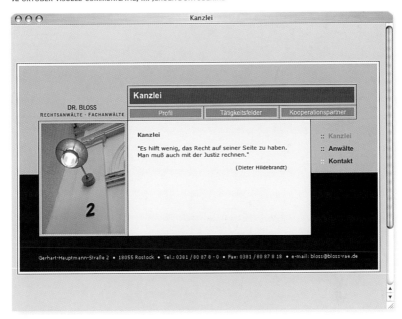

**WWW.BLOSS-RAE.DE**
**D:** JULIA ERBE, **C:** KAI ACKERMANN, **P:** DR. BLOSS RECHTSANWÄLTE - FACHANWÄLTE
**M:** BLOSS@BLOSS-RAE.DE

**WWW.CAFELATINO.IT**
**D:** LORENZO CATTONI
**A:** CREASTILE, **M:** CATTONI@KATAMAIL.COM

**WWW.GIOFORMA.COM**
**D:** DAVIDE MARTELLI, **C: FABRIZIO DANIELI**
**A:** BBJ SRL, **M:** DESIGN@BBJ.IT

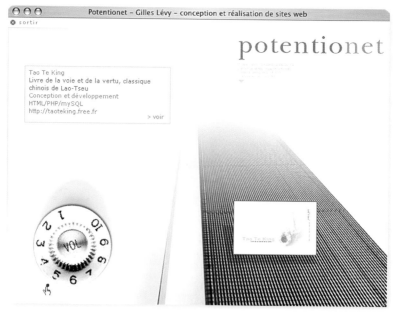

**WWW.POTENTIO.NET**
**D:** GILLES L.
**M:** INFO@POTENTIO.NET

**WWW.MECHAVISION.COM**
**D:** FREDERIC JEAN-JACQUES
**A:** MECHAVISION, **M:** FRED@MECHAVISION.COM

**WWW.RINGBAAN.NL**
**D:** LEO HAMERS
**A:** YAIKZ!, **M:** INFO@YAIKZ.NL

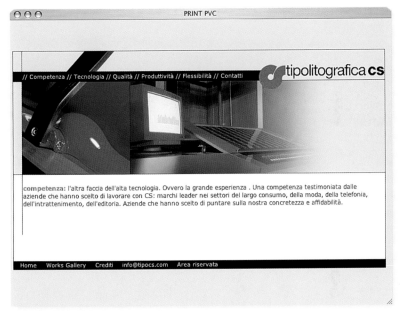

**WWW.TIPOCS.COM**
**D:** STEFANO MARCHI
**A:** XTRAGROOVE-SSG CREATIVE FACTORY, **M:** STEFANO@XTRAGROOVE.COM

**WWW.TRIPDOWN.DE**
**D:** CLEMENS KRACK
**M:** CKRACK@I-Z.DE

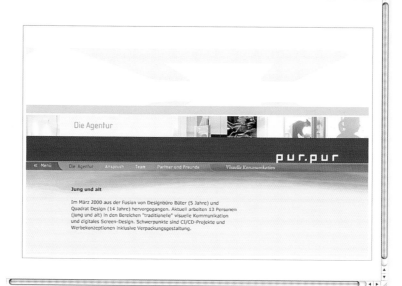

**WWW.PUR-PUR.DE**
**D:** ANJA PETER, KLAUS BIRK
**A:** PUR.PUR - VISUELLE KOMMUNIKATION, **M:** FELIX.WORM@PUR-PUR.DE

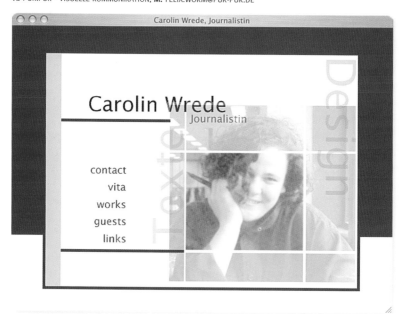

**WWW.CAROLIN-WREDE.DE**
**D:** CAROLIN WREDE, **P:** JOURNALISTEN-ZENTRUM
**M:** WREDE@HAUSBUSCH.DE

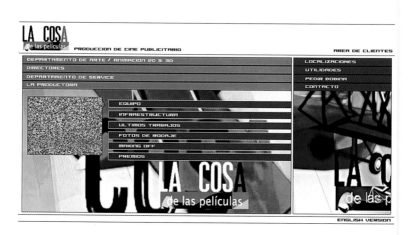

**WWW.LA-COSA.COM**
**D:** RICHARD TALUT
**A:** ESTUDIO ANA MORENO, **M:** RICHARD@ESTUDIOAM.NET

**WWW.FLASH-GARDEN.DE**
**D:** RENE UNRUH, **P:** FLASH-GARDEN
**M:** INFO@FLASH-GARDEN.DE

**WWW.APROPOS.BE**
**D:** LAMMENS DIDIER, **P:** GOOFI
**M:** INFO@GOOFI.BE

**MADEN.FIRENZE.NET**
**D:** JACK, **C:** MARTA LEO
**A:** MADEN, **M:** JACK27@KATAMAIL.COM

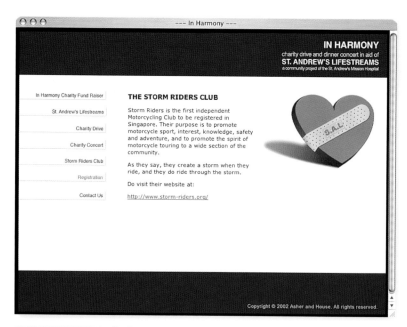

WWW.ASHERANDHOUSE.COM/SAL/INHARMONY.HTM
D: ADELE CHAN, P: ASHER AND HOUSE
M: ADELE@ASHERANDHOUSE.COM

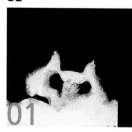

WWW.CSSUDINE.IT/INTRO2.HTM
D: TASSINARI/VETTA, C: SARA PACOR, P: NICOLETTA BENVENUTI
A: INCIPIT SRL, M: INFO@INCIPITONLINE.IT

WWW.EMMEWEB.NET/
D: GIPPO, C: MASSIMO GASTALDELLO
A: GIPPO.TV, M: INFO@GIPPO.TV

**[zubiria]** 1 3

2 Desde 156? → 156? 1587 1629 1668 1705 1736 1770 1793 1824 1862 1892 1923

## 1587
## [Martin Lopez de Zubiri]

Nació en Bakaiku (Navarra). Hijo legítimo de **Joan Lopez de Zubiri** y Gracia de Garate (vecina de Bakaiku).
Fue bautizado el 19 de abril de 1587. Fueron sus padrinos Martin Lopez de Zubiri y Maria de Garate (Vecinos de Arrayoz).
Se casó con Marquesa de Apezechea. Hay constancia de dos hijos:
**Joanes de Zubiri** (Bautizado en Yanci el 27 de julio de 1629) y
Maria de Zubiri (Bautizada en Yanci el 1 de mayo de 1634).

**WWW.ZUBIRIA.COM**
**D:** JORGE ZUBIRIA TOLOSA
**A:** ZUBIRIA DISEÑO, **M:** JORGE@ZUBIRIA.COM

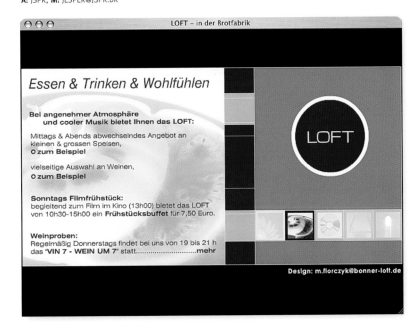

**WWW.EICMF.DK**
**D:** JESPER STEVNHOVED
**A:** JSPR, **M:** JESPER@JSPR.DK

**WWW.BONNER-LOFT.DE**
**D:** MARUSCHKA FLORCZYK
**M:** M.FLORCZYK@BONNER-LOFT.DE

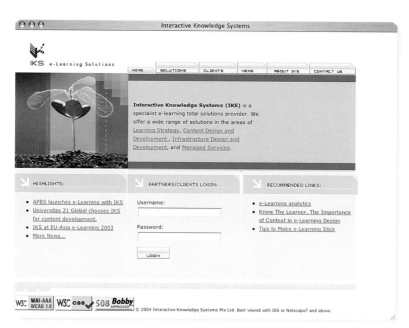

**WWW.IKSONLINE.COM**
**D:** KIM SENG
**A:** INTERACTIVE KNOWLEDGE SYSTEMS, **M:** DUCKFACE74@HOTMAIL.COM

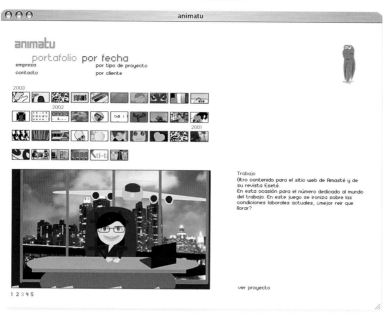

**WWW.ANIMATU.COM**
**D:** JOSÉ MARÍA MARTÍNEZ BURGOS
**A:** ANIMATU, **M:** HAFO@ANIMATU.COM

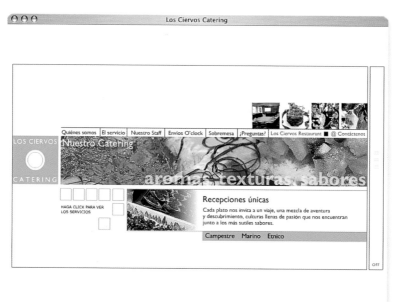

**WWW.LOSCIERVOSCATERING.COM.AR**
**D:** MARIANO GARCIA, **P:** QUINTA LOS CIERVOS
**A:** CRYOLLA DISEÑO, **M:** MARIANOGARCIA@CRYOLLA.COM.AR

**WWW.INSTANTESTORE.COM**
**D:** JASMINE HOR MYN-LI, **C:** CHARLES TANG
**A:** ESOLVED.COM SDN. BHD., **M:** JASZY76@YAHOO.COM

**WWW.POWERSHOT.DE/**
**D:** TOMECZEK, SCHMALER, ENSSLIN, **C:** WAGNER, SCHMALER
**A:** TWMD GMBH, **M:** MT@TWMD.DE

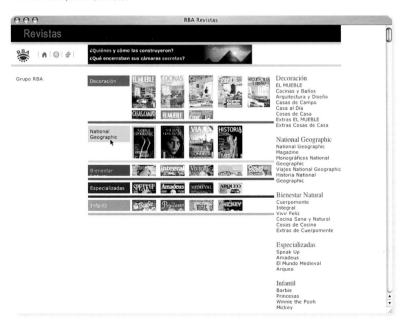

**WWW.RBA.ES**
**D:** PUKKAS WEB'S DESIGN S.L
**A:** PUKKAS WEB'S DESIGN S.L, **M:** INFO@PUKKAS.COM

WWW.DESIGNERSLIFE.COM
**D:** KIKE BESADA FERNANDEZ
**A:** DESIGNERSLIFE*, **M:** KIKE@DESIGNERSLIFE.COM

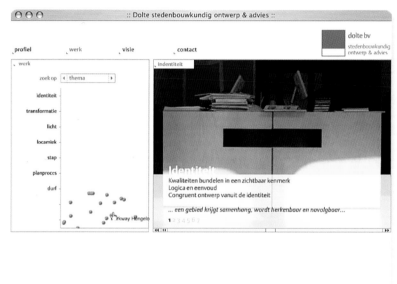

WWW.DOLTE.NL
**D:** DONALD HARTING, **C:** NICK BOLINK, **P:** DOLTE
**A:** FRISMEDIA, **M:** INFO@FRISMEDIA.NL

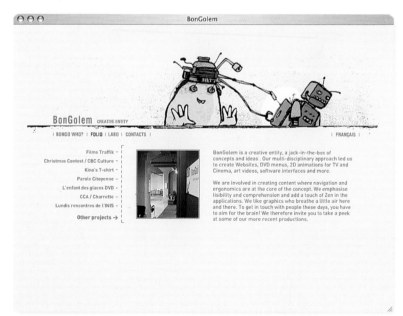

WWW.BONGOLEM.COM
**D:** DOMINIC TURMEL, **C:** VINCENT MORISSET, **P:** PIERRE-MATHIEU FORTIN
**A:** BONGOLEM, ENTITÉ CRÉATRICE, **M:** PMFORTIN@BONGOLEM.COM

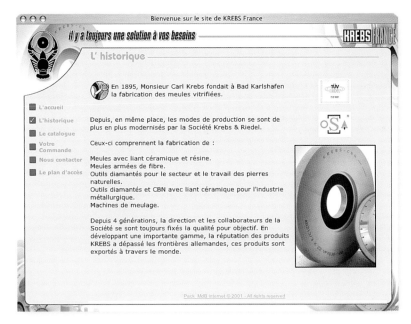

**WWW.KREBSFRANCE.FR**
**D:** JEAN-LUC CHEVALLIER, **P:** MDB INTERNET
**A:** MDB INFORMATIQUE, **M:** JEANLUC.CHEVALLIER@MDBINFORMATIQUE.NET

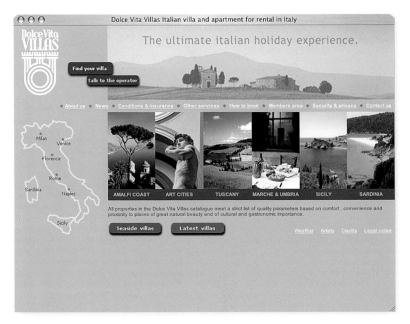

**FAIER.IN-BLEU.COM**
**D:** IMELDA GUNAWAN
**A:** BLE:U, **M:** BLEU@IN-BLEU.COM

**WWW.DOLCEVITAVILLAS.COM**
**D:** VAFIR, **C:** PROW - MILAN, **P:** DOLCEVITAVILLAS
**A:** VAFIR, **M:** G.BRACCI@DOLCEVITAVILLAS.COM

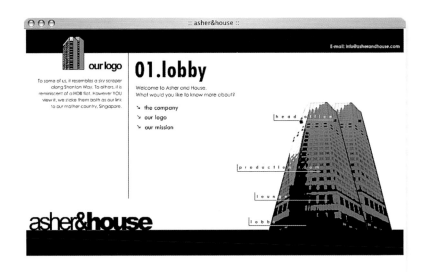

**WWW.ASHERANDHOUSE.COM**
**D:** ADELE CHAN
**A:** ASHER AND HOUSE, **M:** ADELE@ASHERANDHOUSE.COM

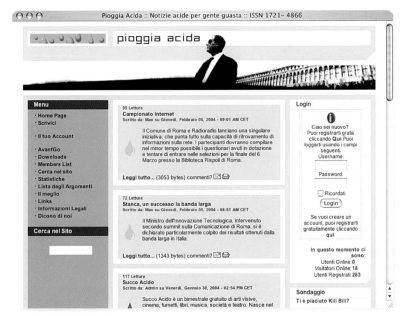

**WWW.MARKETMIND.NL**
**D:** MONIQUE PRIEM, **C:** PETER DEKKER, **P:** GERARD VAN MELIS
**A:** MARKETMIND BV, **M:** GERARD@MARKETMIND.NL

**WWW.PIOGGIACIDA.COM**
**D:** MAX BOSCHINI
**A:** FACCIA DA PIXEL, **M:** IO@MAXBOSCHINI.COM

**WWW.CARLOSCABALLERO.COM**
**D:** CARLOS CABALLERO
**A:** CCBWWWORKS, **M:** CARLOS@CARLOSCABALLERO.COM

**WWW.DEVRIES-VASTGOED.NL**
**D:** JOOST KUIJPERS, **P:** DE VRIES VASTGOED BV
**A:** OIN, **M:** INFO@DEVRIES-VASTGOED.NL

**WWW.WOWINDEX.CO.IL**
**D:** ILAN DRAY - SHARON EHRLICH, **C:** TAMIR MORDEAU - MICHAL COHEN
**P:** BEZEQ ISRAEL TELECOMMUNICATION

WWW.IDEALISTA.COM
D: JESUS ENCINAR, C: PABLO ALVAREZ CASCOS
A: IDEALISTA, M: JENCINAR@IDEALISTA.COM

WWW.2ELEMENTE.DE
D: 2ELEMENTE
A: 2ELEMENTE, M: WINKLER@2ELEMENTE.DE

WWW.DIGISTUDIO.IT
D: SERGIO GIOVANNINI
A: DIGITALSTUDIO, M: SERGIO@DIGISTUDIO.IT

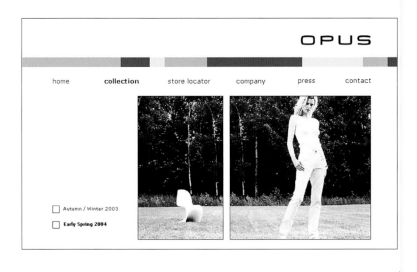

**WWW.OPUS-FASHION.COM**
**D:** STRADA, **C:** MARK LEEWE
**A:** [WERKo1], **M:** MARK@WERKo1.DE

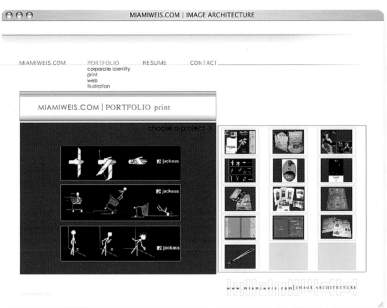

**WWW.MIAMIWEIS.COM**
**D:** LOU WEIS
**A:** MIAMIWEIS, **M:** LOU@MIAMIWEIS.COM

**WWW.DECORO.COM**
**D:** SHARON CHAN, **C:** SAMUEL CHENG, **P:** KELLY SZE
**A:** EUREKA DIGITAL, **M:** KELLY@EUREKA-DIGITAL.COM

WWW.TABACAL.COM.AR
D: JAVIER PEREYRA, P: PROMINENTE S.A.
M: JPEREYRA@PROMINENTE.COM.AR

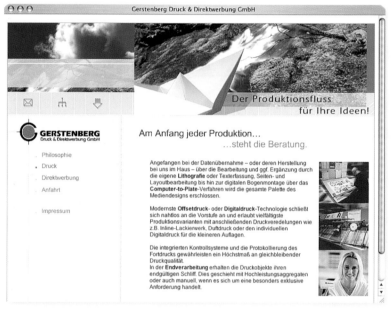

WWW.GERSTENBERG-DRUCK.DE
D: SASKIA VETTER
A: ICONNEWMEDIA, M: SASKIA.VETTER@ICONNEWMEDIA.DE

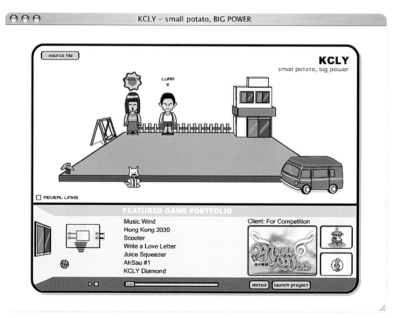

WWW.LUAR.COM.HK/
D: LUAR YEN, C: KELLY CHUNG
A: LUAR'S PRODUCTION, M: LUAR@LUAR.NET

**WWW.SPUMANTISPAGNOL.COM**
**D:** BEATRICE SUSA
**A:** ARTE LAGUNA, **M:** INFO@ARTELAGUNA.IT

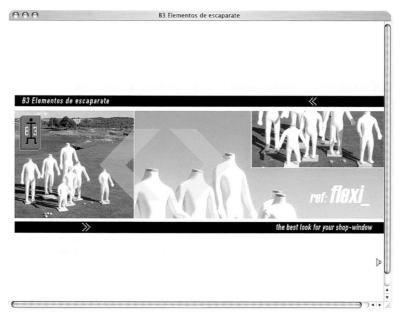

**WWW.B3ESCAPARATE.COM**
**D:** EMILIO GARCIA VAZ
**A:** NOVESCOMUNICACIONS, **M:** INFO@EDISSENY.COM

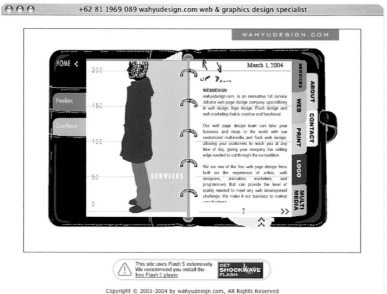

**WWW.WAHYUDESIGN.COM**
**D:** WAHYU DEWANTO, **C:** DENYS
**M:** WAHYU@WAHYUDESIGN.COM

**BESTLAWYERS.COM**
**D:** MARK BARKLEY, **C:** JASON WIDENER, **P:** WOODWARD WHITE, INC.
**A:** LEVINE ASSOCIATES, INC., **M:** MBARKLEY@BESTLAWYERS.COM

**WWW.PLIZO.COM**
**D:** MIGUEL PLIZO
**M:** DESIGN@PLIZO.COM

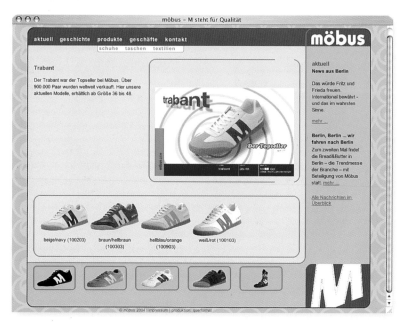

**WWW.MOEBUS.NET**
**D:** MATTHIAS MESSERER, **C:** MATTHIAS MESSERER
**A:** QUERFORMAT - DIE WERBEAGENTUR, **M:** MESSERER@QUERFORMAT.INFO

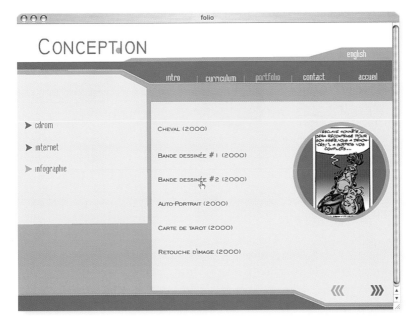

**PAGES.INFINIT.NET/M2M**
**D:** VINCENT DAVID
**A:** M2M : COMMUNICATION INTERACTIVE, **M:** M2M@VIDEOTRON.CA

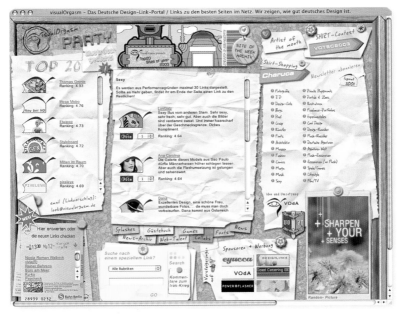

**WWW.VISUALORGASM.DE**
**D:** DANIELA HAGEDORN, MATIAS ROSKOS, **C:** JENS KALUSNIAK, MATIAS ROSKOS
**M:** LOOK@VISUALORGASM.DE

**WWW.ZOOMMULTIMEDIA-ES.COM**
**D:** DAVID SANCHEZ
**A:** ZOOM MULTIMEDIA, **M:** INFO@ZOOMMULTIMEDIA-ES.COM

**WWW.ELEMENTOTERRA.COM**
**D:** ANA GRANJA, **P:** PCW
**M:** PAULA.GRANJA@LABOLIMS.COM

**WWW.FASTVIBE.COM**
**D:** STEVE GAUDER, **C:** CRAIG WELLER, **P:** RICK BROWN
**A:** DESIGN 2.0, **M:** STEVIEG@SYMPATICO.CA

**WWW.DOZHENS.COM**
**D:** CELI SIMONE
**M:** SILEK@DOZHENS.COM

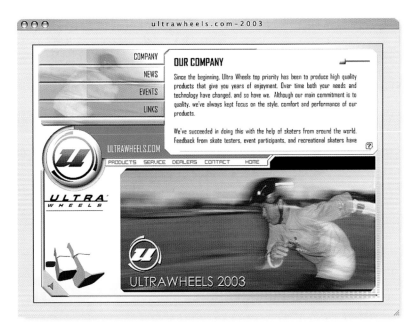

**WWW.ULTRAWHEELS.COM**
**D:** STEVE GABANY, **C:** JOHN GOODWIN
**A:** GAUDER DESIGN, **M:** STEVIEG@SYMPATICO.CA

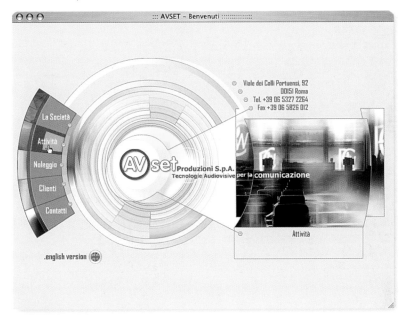

**WWW.AVSET.IT**
**D:** DANIELE GIARDINI / SARAH PENNISI
**M:** DANIELEGIARDINI@HOTMAIL.COM

**WWW.JOAZINTERACTIVE.COM**
**D:** JOAZ AZEVEDO
**A:** JOAZ INTERACTIVE DESIGN, **M:** MAIL@JOAZINTERACTIVE.COM

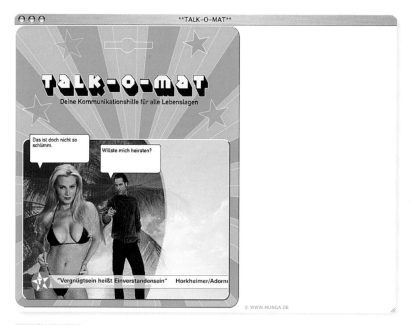

**WWW.TALKOMAT.DE**
**D:** ELKE SCHIEMANN
**M:** ELKE@HUNGA.DE

**WWW.HALCYON.DK**
**D:** GERARD WHELAN, **C:** TOBIAS ANDERSEN, **P:** CASPER HACH
**A:** ENTEGARTE, **M:** WHELAN@BRANDCENTRAL.DK

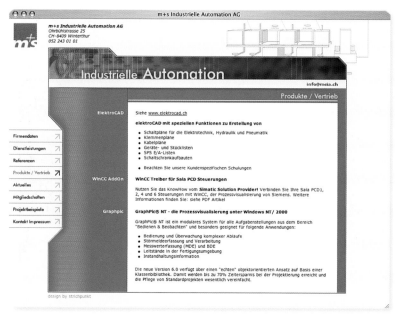

**WWW.MSIA.CH**
**D:** METELSKI, **C:** LANDOLT
**A:** STRICHPUNKT GMBH, **M:** LANDOLT@STRICHPUNKT.CH

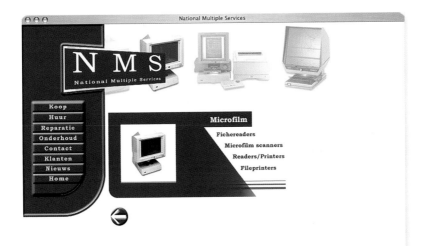

**WWW.NMS.NL**
**D:** MARTIJN SCHOUWE
**A:** WEBWORKZ, **M:** INFO@WEBWORKZ.NL

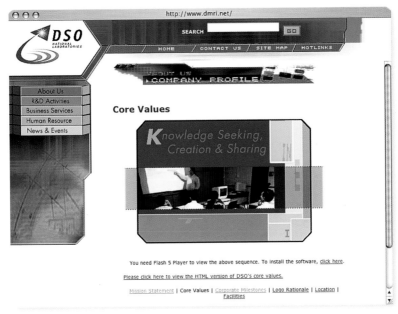

**WWW.DMRI.NET**
**D:** JOANNE ANG, **C:** FOO YANLING, **P:** BAY SIOW WEI
**A:** VOXMEDIA, **M:** JOE@VOXMEDIA.COM.SG

**WWW.FRISMEDIA.NL**
**D:** DONALD HARTING, **C:** NICK BOLINK
**A:** FRISMEDIA, **M:** INFO@FRISMEDIA.NL

**WWW.D-DO.COM**
**D:** GONZALO PEREA
**A:** DEDO MULTIMEDIA

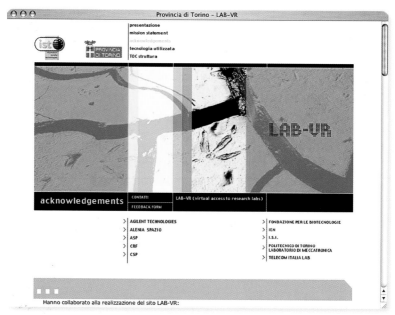

**WWW.FABULAND.DE**
**D:** FABU
**M:** FABU@WAHNSIGNAL.DE

**WWW.FLUIDO.IT**
**D:** ANTONIO GIACOMIN FLUIDO
**A:** ZOOVISIVO, **M:** FLUIDO@FLUIDO.IT

**WWW.VIAKATALYX.COM**
**D:** LAURA CASTILLO, SERGIO SEGOVIA
**A:** SYNAPSIS DIGITAL, **M:** LAURA@SYNAPSISDIGITAL.COM

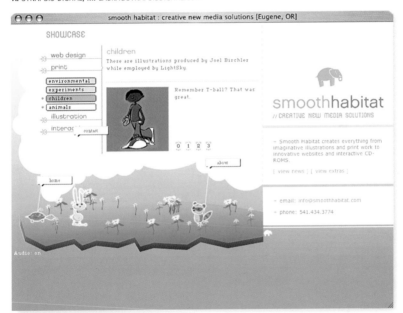

**WWW.SMOOTHHABITAT.COM**
**D:** JOEL BIRCHLER, **P:** SMOOTH HABITAT
**M:** JOEL@SMOOTHHABITAT.COM

**TOOL.COM.MK**
**D:** ALEKSANDAR KOLOV
**A:** TOOL DESIGN, **M:** EON@SONET.COM.MK

**WWW.SLOGANS.DE**
**D:** INGA WERMUTH, ALEXANDER HAHN, **C:** PHILIP SIMON/ALEXANDER HAHN
**A:** SATELLITEN MEDIA DESIGN, **M:** IWERMUTH@SATELLITEN.DE

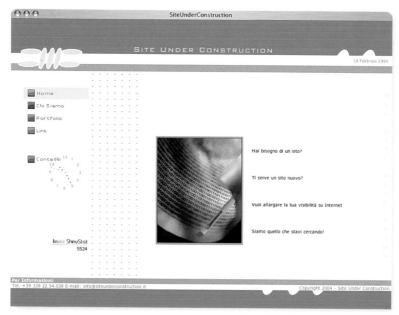

**WWW.SITEUNDERCONSTRUCTION.IT**
**D:** ROBERTO F., **C:** ANDREA B.
**A:** SITEUNDERCONSTRUCTION, **M:** GIOGALMA@EMAIL.IT

**WWW.EASYBRICK.COM/**
**D:** VICTOR PEDERSEN
**A:** AD INFINITUM DESIGN, **M:** VIC@INFINITUM.DK

**WWW.EASYMULTIMEDIA.IT**
**D:** FABIO BRUNELLO
**M:** FABIO.BRUNELLO@INWIND.IT

**WWW.DRALCALA.COM**
**D:** LOURDES MOLINA
**A:** SPAINCREATIVE, **M:** LOURDESMOLINA@SPAINCREATIVE.COM

**WWW.25G.DE**
**D:** ROMAN BASILIUS BRAEMER
**M:** ROMAN@14H.DE

AGENCE**NANCY**             AGENCE**METZ**

© PROJETP40 - juin 2000 - réalisation I-spheres webdesign - illustrations Thierry Badet

**WWW.PROJETP40.COM**
**D:** JEAN-LOUIS BUR, **C:** OLIVIER KAUTZ
**A:** I-SPHERES, **M:** WWW.PROJETP40.COM

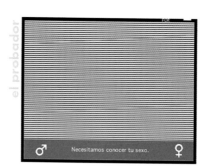

**WWW.FOR.ES**
**D:** HAIKU MEDIA TEAM,
**A:** HAIKU MEDIA TEAM, **M:** A@HAIKU-MEDIA.COM

Metrovacesa

**WWW.E-INDICA.COM**
**D:** MANUEL ESTRADA DISEÑO GRÁFICO
**A:** MANUEL ESTRADA DISEÑO GRÁFICO, **M:** DIGITAL@MANUELESTRADA.COM

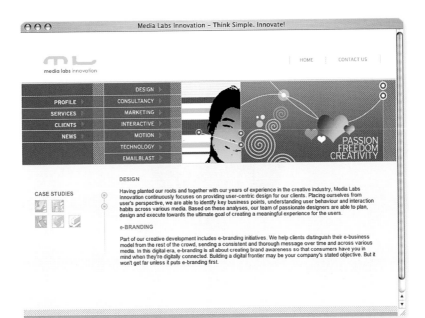

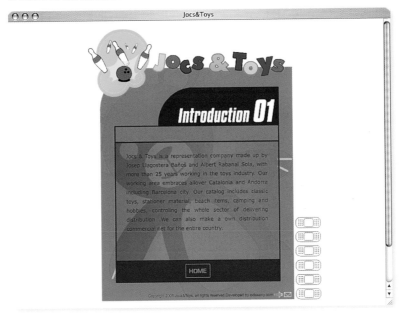

**WWW.ALESSIOGUARINO.IT**
**D:** ALESSIO GUARINO
**M:** INFO@ALESSIOGUARINO.IT

**WWW.GRAPHIX.AT/**
**D:** MARTIN FUCHS
**M:** MARTIN.FUCHS@GRAPHIX.AT

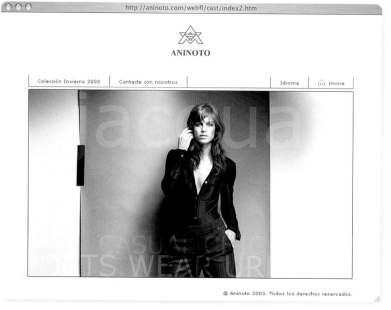

**ANINOTO.COM**
**D:** PUKKAS WEB'S DESIGN S.L.
**A:** PUKKAS WEB'S DESIGN S.L., **M:** INFO@PUKKAS.COM

**WWW.LOCODROM.DE**
**D:** CLAUDIA SIEPER, CHRISTOPH PACKHIESER
**A:** KALT8 KONZEPT, **M:** WIR@KALT8.DE

**WWW.GALLARDO-LLOPIS.COM**
**D:** COTE GALLARDO LLOPIS
**M:** COTE@GALLARDO-LLOPIS.COM

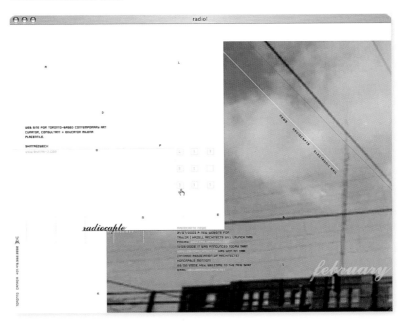

**WWW.RADIOCAPTE.NET**
**D:** SARAH FERGUSON
**A:** RADIOCAPTE, **M:** SARAH@RADIOCAPTE.NET

$f/22$   ◀ PREVIOUS    Porto, 1991
Zenit XP12    NEXT ▶    menu

**WWW.AFLYINTHEWEB.COM/F22/INDEX.ASP**
**D:** OSCAR ALVES
**M:** AFLYINTHEWEB@AFLYINTHEWEB.COM

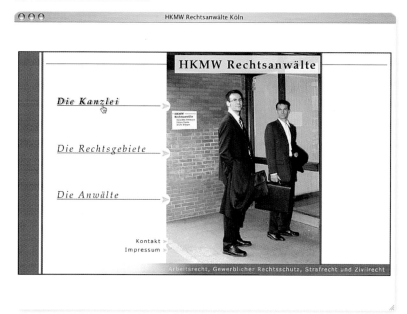

**WWW.HKMW.DE**
**D:** SONJA RADKE
**A:** RADKE INTERAKTIV, **M:** INFO@RADKE-INTERAKTIV.DE

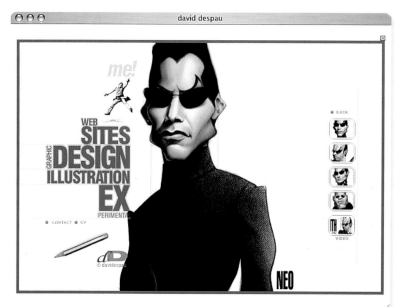

**WWW.DESPAU.COM**
**D:** DAVID DESPAU
**M:** SPBERMEJO@YA.COM

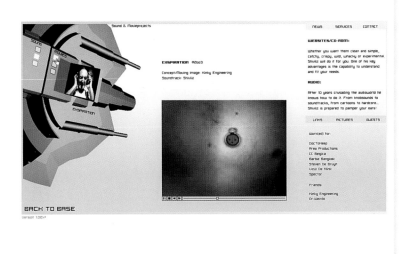

**WWW.SHIVLIZ.COM**
**D:** TOM MAEBE
**A:** SHIVLIZ, **M:** INFO@SHIVLIZ.COM

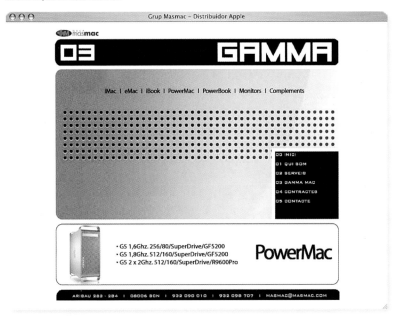

**WWW.GRUPMASMAC.COM**
**D:** JACINTO LANA TORROBA, **P:** GRUP MASMAC
**M:** JACINTOSH@MASMAC.COM

**DANILAB.NET**
**D:** D:E:M
**A:** D:E:M, **M:** DANIEL@DANILAB.NET

**WWW.DAVEHASLAM.COM**
**D:** TAYO ABIODUN, **C:** GUY KILTY
**A:** 44MEDIA LTD., **M:** TY@44MEDIA.COM

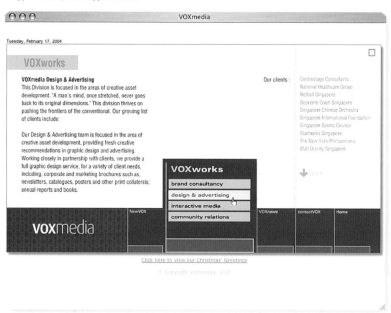

**WWW.VOXMEDIA.COM.SG**
**D:** TAN MANN CHUAN
**A:** VOXMEDIA, **M:** JOE@VOXMEDIA.COM.SG

**AN.THONY.NET**
**D:** CHING KEE HO
**M:** AN@THONY.NET

**WWW.LONGEDESIGN.COM/818**
**D:** HERIC LONGE ABRAMO
**M:** 818@LONGEDESIGN.COM

**WWW.HOMELESS.DE**
**D:** ANNE WITTHAKE
**M:** AWITTHAKE@WEB.DE

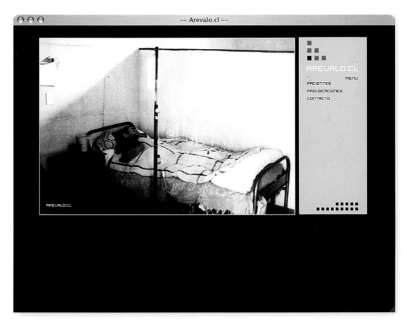

**WWW.AREVALO.CL**
**D:** THINK PROJECT
**A:** THINK PROJECT, **M:** FELIPEALVARADO@MANQUEHUE.NET

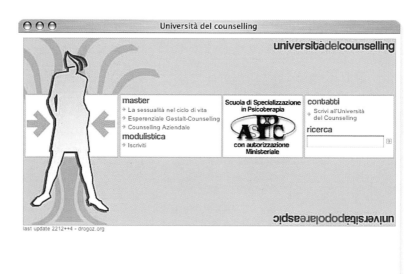

WWW.UNICOUNSELLING.ORG
**D:** MATTEO FAIT
**A:** DROGOZ, **M:** IMAD@DROGOZ.ORG

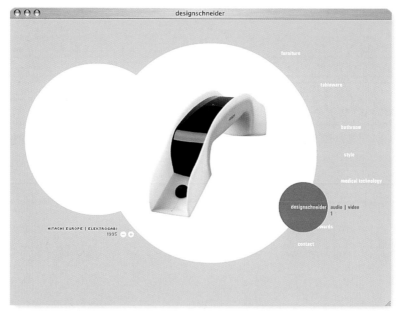

WWW.DESIGNSCHNEIDER.DE
**D:** JOERG WASCHAT, **C:** ANDREAS KUBANEK
**A:** DEFINIT, **M:** INFO@DEFINIT.ORG

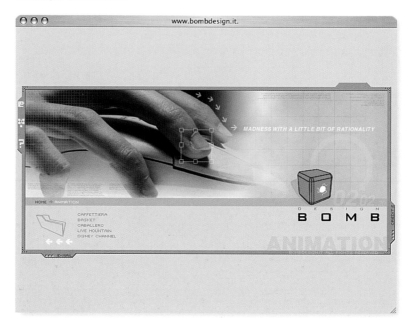

WWW.BOMBDESIGN.IT
**D:** LUCIANO LIMOLI
**A:** BOMBDESIGN, **M:** INFO@BOMBDESIGN.IT

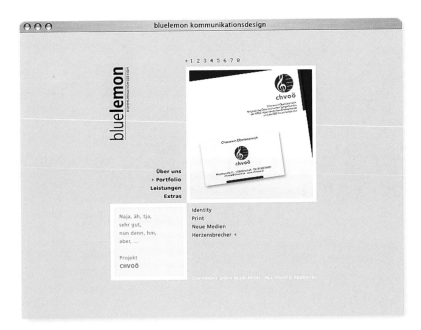

**WWW.BLUELEMON.AT**
**D:** BLUELEMON
**A:** BLUELEMON, **M:** OFFICE@BLUELEMON.AT

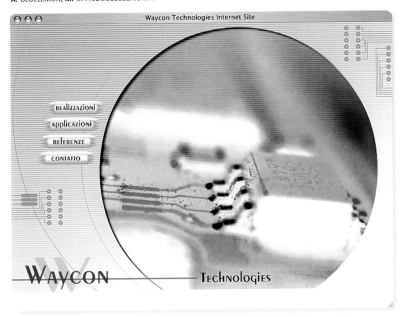

**WWW.WAYCON.IT/**
**D:** MIRCO PECORARI
**A:** DYNAMICAD, **M:** M.PECORARI@DYNAMICAD.IT

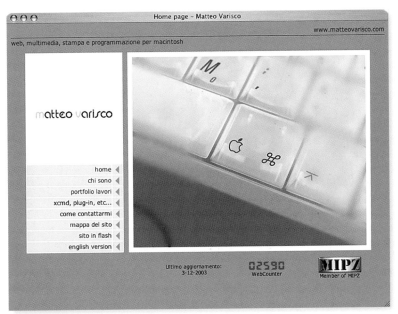

**WWW.MATTEOVARISCO.COM**
**D:** MATTEO VARISCO
**M:** INFO@MATTEOVARISCO.COM

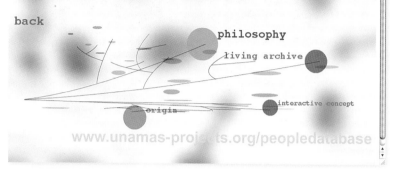

A lot of people have already participated in this ongoing project. They were asked to pick one or more photographs and then write, draw, paint, compose, photograph... their personal reaction to them. They used the pictures as a mirror  to write their own story, to articulate their own thoughts, desires, philosophies and dreams. All the contributions share the focus on the narrative, and are derived from a particular consciousness or situation. They are fragments and private histories from the contributors' collection of personal experiences.
I ask each participant  to go beyond the cold, aesthetic representation of these people. Each face triggers a memory, a sentiment, a sensation, an emotion.Take a look at another person, and attempt to represent yourself. From this web of self-representations, expressed by people from around the world, a human narrative that is constantly in progress will begin to take shape.

back

philosophy

living archive

origin

interactive concept

www.unamas-projects.org/peopledatabase

**WWW.PINKER.BE**
**D:** INES VAN BELLE
**A:** PINKER, **M:** INFO@PINKER.BE

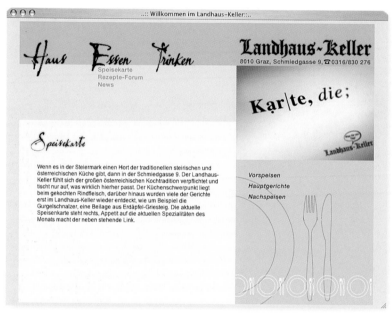

**WWW.LANDHAUS-KELLER.AT**
**D:** NICOLE ZAISER, **C:** HARALD ZETTLER
**A:** DER I-PUNKT., **M:** N.ZAISER@IPU.AT

**WWW.OSCARCABALLERO.NET**
**D:** OSCAR CABALLERO
**M:** OSCAR@OSCARCABALLERO.NET

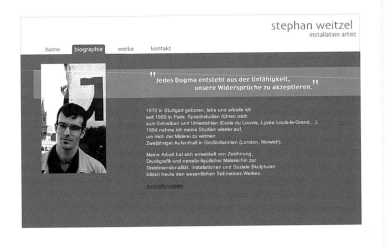

**WWW.STEPHANWEITZEL.COM**
**D:** THOMAS WEITZEL
**A:** WEITZELDESIGN, **M:** INFO@STEPHANWEITZEL.COM

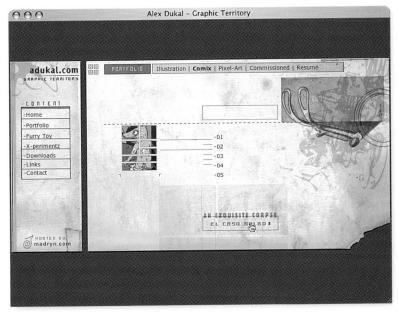

**WWW.ADUKAL.COM**
**D:** ALEX DUKAL, **P:** JOSÉ PAREJA
**A:** MEKANO DIGITAL, **M:** ADUKAL@ADUKAL.COM

**NURBS.MTGC.NET**
**D:** ANDREA SCIARRETTA
**M:** ANDREA@MTGC.NET

**WWW.SPATIUM-NEWSLETTER.DE**
**D:** PETER REICHARD/CHRISTOPHER LINDLOHR
**A:** TYPOSITION, **M:** TEAM@TYPOSITION.DE

**WWW.CEMICHOC.COM**
**D:** EMILIO GARCIA VAZ
**A:** NOVESCOMUNICACIONS, **M:** INFO@EDISSENY.COM

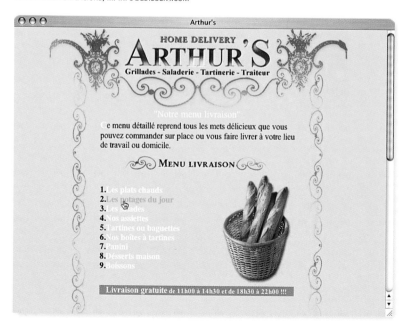

**WWW.ARTHURS.BE**
**D:** SÉBASTIEN DECORNÉ
**M:** SEB@BELBONE.BE

WWW.ITALIAHOUSES.IT
D: ILARIA BOZ
M: ILA74@LIBERO.IT

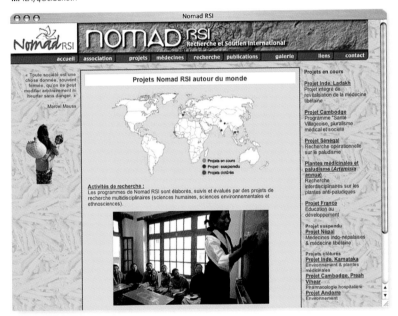

WWW.NOMADRSI.ORG
D: FRANCOIS MORIN
M: FRANKOY@SYMPATICO.CA

WWW.MYFASHION.CO.KR
D: HYERI KIM
A: MYFASHION, M: HR21@MYFASHION.CO.KR

# franca minardi
### artista

opere

biografia   photos   opere   esposizioni   opinioni   contatto

**WWW.FRANCAMINARDI.IT**
**D:** LUCA BARTOLINI
**A:** EQUILIBRISOSPESI, **M:** LUCA@EQUILIBRISOSPESI.COM

---

Consell Català de la Música

### CONSELL CATALÀ DE LA MÚSICA

## Presentació

(▶) Qui som?
(▶) Activitats
(▶) Socis
(▶) Enllaços

NOVETAT

*L'INSTRUMENT LEGAL NECESSARI PER VIURE DE LA MÚSICA.*

El Consell Català de la Música és una entitat privada sense ànim de lucre que aplega des de l'any 1990 la major part d'associacions catalanes relacionades directa o indirectament amb el fet musical.

Les nostres línies d'actuació sorgeixen de l'establiment de punts de confluència entre els interessos i necessitats dels diferents col·lectius que es troben en la nostra associació d'associacions. Així doncs, els interessos d'un sector seran defensats a partir del moment en què aquestes reivindicacions responguin a reivindicacions que puguin ser compartides amb la resta d'associacions, amb la intenció que l'interès general superi el possible corporativisme que pugui tenir una entitat o conjunt d'entitats d'imposar les seves opinions.

Ens trobem, doncs, davant un model associatiu flexible, amatent a la realitat de l'activitat musical del país i que, en petit, seria susceptible, en canvi, de projectar-se com a model de gestió per al tractament de les grans qüestions que les diferents administracions tenen, en relació a la música, l'obligació de tractar i sobretot de solucionar.

En fi, des del CCM hem de dir que la nostra voluntat és promocionar i enfortir el diàleg constructiu i permanent entre les diferents institucions públiques, i entre aquestes i el conjunt de ciutadans vinculats d'alguna manera amb la música.

✉ CONTACTA AMB NOSALTRES

**WWW.CCMUSICA.ORG**
**D:** PEP SANABRA
**A:** EDISSENY.COM*, **M:** EMILIO@EDISSENY.COM

---

Schmuck Börse Hidir

**WWW.SCHMUCKBOERSE-HIDIR.DE**
**D:** KAI GREIM
**A:** GRAFIKAI, **M:** INFO@GRAFIKAI.DE

**WWW.LEEDUNGAREES.COM**
**D:** TRAVIS BECKHAM / LUKE KNOWLES, **P:** CHARLIE O'SHIELDS
**A:** LOOKANDFEEL NEW MEDIA, **M:** COSHIELDS@LOOKANDFEEL.COM

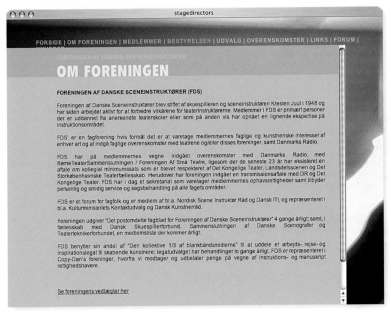

**WWW.STAGEDIRECTORS.DK/**
**D:** JAKOB BRANDT-PEDERSEN
**A:** SPACECONTROLLER, **M:** JBRANDTP@GET2NET.DK

**WWW.LOOPLOOPLOOP.COM**
**D:** TANDA FRANCIS
**A:** LOOP, **M:** ANDA@LOOPLOOPLOOP.COM

WWW.PREODE.COM
**D:** ANDREW BAASCH
**A:** PREODE, **M:** ANDREW@PREODE.COM

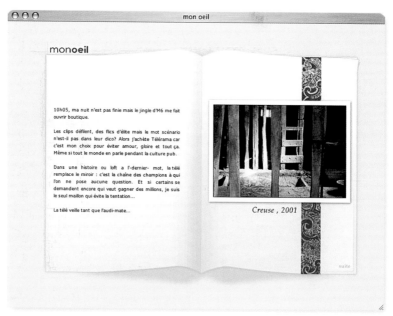

GEONEO.FREE.FR/MONOEIL/
**D:** GEONEO
**M:** THEGEONEO@YAHOO.FR

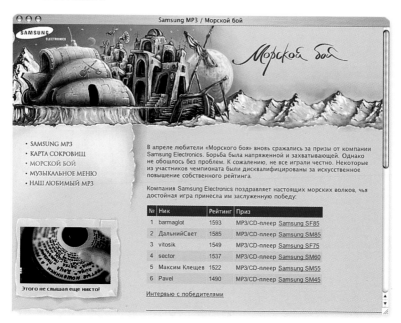

MP3.SAMSUNG.RU/
**D:** OLEG TISCHENKOV, **C:** IGOR SHERGIN, **P:** ANDREY VORONKOV
**A:** ART LEBEDEV STUDIO, **M:** OLEG@DESIGN.RU

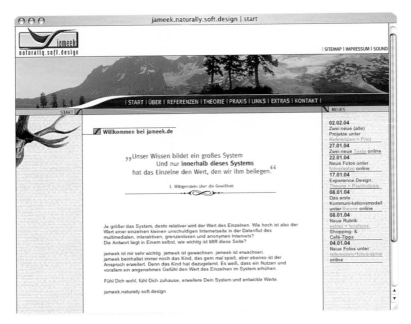

**WWW.JAMEEK.DE**
**D:** CHRISTOPHE PAPKE
**M:** CHRISTOPHE@JAMEEK.DE

**WWW.VSTGROUP.COM.MY/**
**D:** ADRIN SHAMSUDIN
**M:** ADRIN@SPECTRELABS.COM

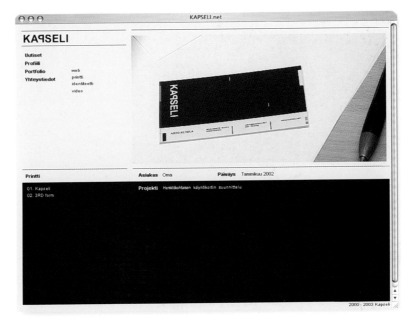

**WWW.KAPSELI.NET**
**D:** ARTO KETOLA
**A:** KAPSELI, **M:** ARTO@KAPSELI.NET

**PERSO.WANADOO.ES/PE2000/HOME.HTML**
**D:** IVAN BLANCO LORENZO
**A:** MISIVA, **M:** IVANBLANCO@IESPANA.ES

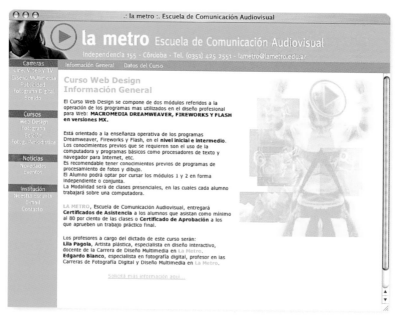

**WWW.LAMETRO.EDU.AR**
**D:** EMANUEL LONGO
**A:** PUNTA Y HACHA, **M:** LONGO.E@PUNTAYHACHA.COM.AR

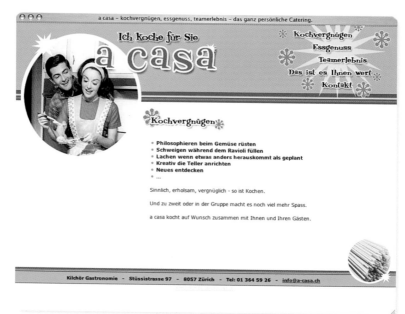

**WWW.A-CASA.CH**
**D:** METELSKI, **C:** MARTIN LANDOLT
**A:** STRICHPUNKT GMBH, **M:** LANDOLT@STRICHPUNKT.CH

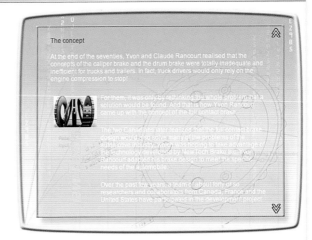

WWW.NEWTECH-IBS.COM
**D:** VINCENT DAVID
**A:** M2M : COMMUNICATION INTERACTIVE, **M:** M2M@VIDEOTRON.CA

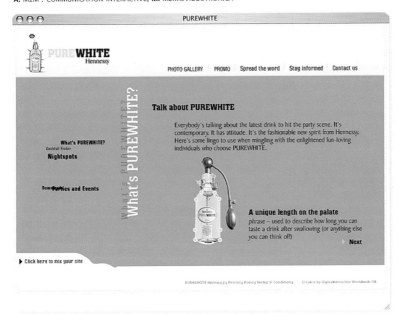

WWW.PUREWHITE.COM.HK
**D:** GARY CHAN **C:** KENNY TSANG, FAI, **P:** CONNIE HO
**A:** OGILVY INTERACTIVE WORLDWIDE (HK), **M:** FLETCH.WONG@OGILVY.COM

WWW.TWENTYSEVEN.IT
**D:** CLAUDIO AUTERI
**A:** TWENTYSEVEN FACTORY, **M:** INFO@TWENTYSEVEN.IT

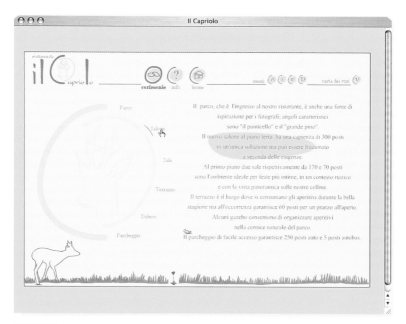

WWW.ILCAPRIOLO.IT
**D:** DANIELE PODDA
**A:** LINEACURVA, **M:** INFO@LINEACURVA.IT

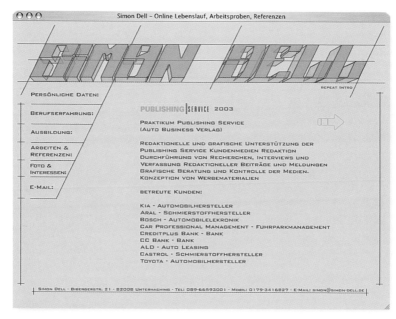

WWW.SIMON-DELL.DE
**D:** SIMON DELL
**M:** SIMON@SIMON-DELL.DE

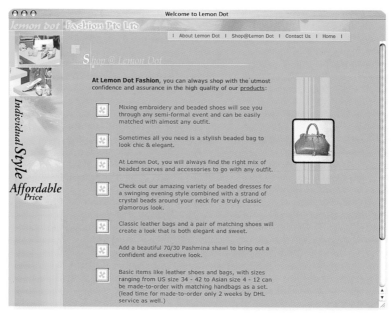

WWW.LEMONDOT.COM.SG/
**D:** VOXMEDIA, **C:** FOO YANLING, **P:** JASBIR
**A:** VOXMEDIA, **M:** JOE@VOXMEDIA.COM.SG

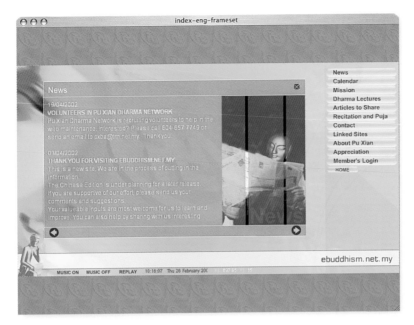

**WWW.EBUDDHISM.NET.MY**
**D:** HENRY YAP SWEE CHENG
**M:** SC.YAP@CARDOS.COM.MY

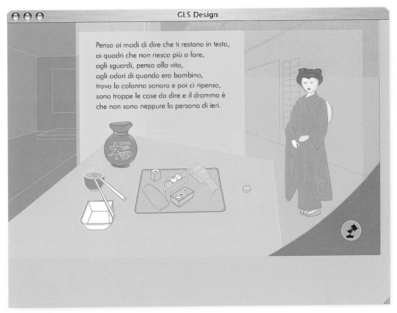

**WWW.GLSDESIGN.IT**
**D:** GIUSEPPE LA SPADA
**A:** GLS DESIGN, **M:** INFO@GLSDESIGN.IR

**WWW.A-LTERNATIVO.CL**
**D:** SYLVIA PEÑA PONCE, **C:** RODRIGO ROJAS DÍAZ
**A:** A-LTERNATIVO, **M:** INFO@A-LTERNATIVO.CL

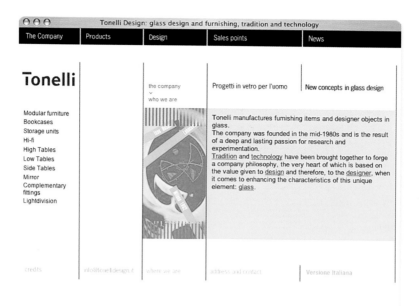

**WWW.TONELLIDESIGN.COM**
**D:** NICOLA SANCISI, **C:** WALTER DEL PRETE
**A:** E-LEVA, **M:** INFO@E-LEVA.COM

**WWW.BRITTYNDEWERTH.COM**
**P:** BRITTYN DEWERTH
**M:** BRITTYN@BRITTYNDEWERTH.COM

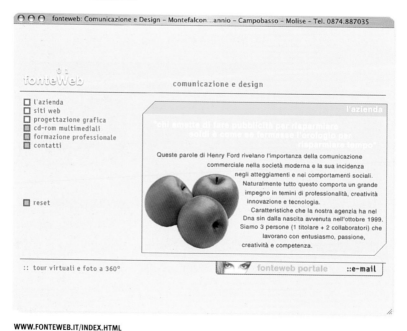

**WWW.FONTEWEB.IT/INDEX.HTML**
**D:** GABRIELE MOSCUFO
**A:** FONTEWEB, **M:** INFO@FONTEWEB.IT

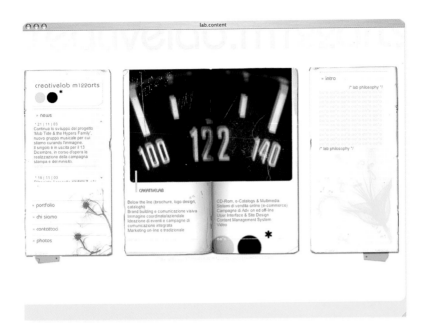

**WWW.M122ARTS.COM**
**D:** CHRISTIAN MELE, **P:** M122ARTS
**M:** CIEMME@190975.COM

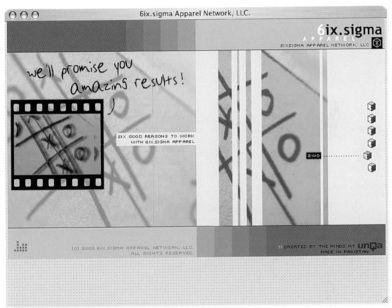

**WWW.SIXSIGMA-APPAREL.COM**
**D:** TANYA ELAHI
**A:** UNQA, **M:** AIYAZ@HOTMAIL.COM

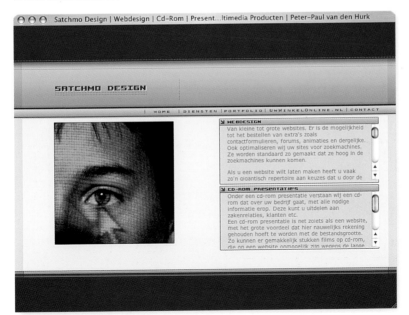

**WWW.SATCHMO-DESIGN.NL**
**D:** PETER-PAUL VAN DEN HURK
**A:** SATCHMO DESIGN, **M:** INFO@SATCHMO-DESIGN.NL

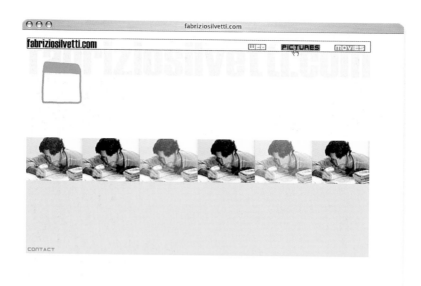

**WWW.FABRIZIOSILVETTI.COM**
**D:** FABRIZIO SILVETTI
**A:** NEXUS DIGITAL SOLUTIONS, **M:** FABRIZIOSILVETTI@NEXUS-DS.COM

**WWW.JUNKFLEA.COM**
**D:** GERARD AGNES
**A:** JUNKFLEA, **M:** ATGT@PACIFIC.NET.SG

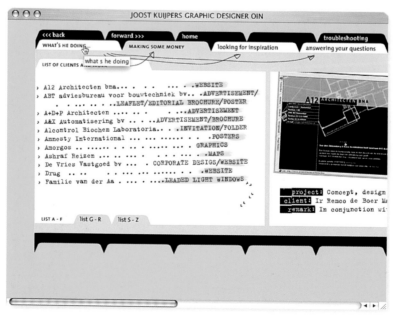

**WWW.JOINK.NL/**
**D:** JOOST KUIJPERS
**A:** OIN, **M:** INFO@JOINK.NL

**WWW.FASHIONFUGITIVE.NL**
**D:** FABRICE KOOPMAN + SANDER PLUG, **C:** FABRICE KOOPMAN
**A:** MEDIUMRARE ID, **M:** FABRICE@MEDIUMRARE.NL

**WWW.PORENTIEF100.DE**
**D:** ELKE SCHIEMANN KATRIN LAHR
**M:** ELKE@HUNGA.DE

**WWW.SOODA.COM**
**D:** HANNA NISKANEN / JANI RUUSKANEN, **C:** JUSSI VIITANIEMI, **P:** HANNA PURO
**A:** NICEFACTORY LTD., **M:** HANNA.NISKANEN@NICEFACTORY.COM

153

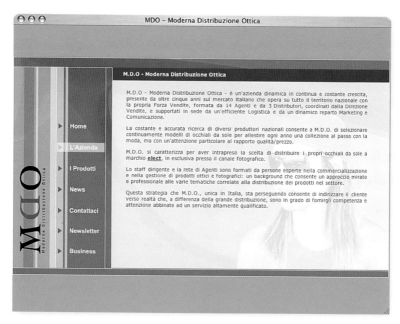

**WWW.MDOSRL.IT**
**D:** VALENTINA BESOZZI, **C:** MARCO CALLEGARI
**A:** MEDIAGRAFICA SRL, **M:** INFO@MEDIAGRAFICA.IT

**WWW.BAROLO.NET**
**D:** DANIELE ACCORNERO
**A:** GRPPO MULTIMEDIA, **M:** DANIELE@ARTESTUDIO.COM

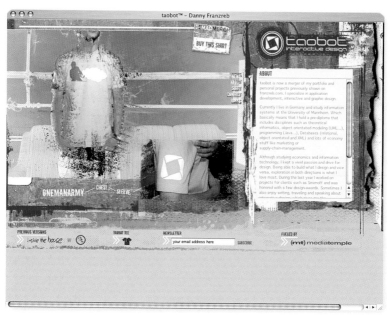

**WWW.TAOBOT.COM**
**D:** DANNY FRANZREB
**A:** TAOBOT, **M:** DANNY@TAOBOT.COM

**WWW.KARBSTEIN.DE**
**D:** ALEX KARBSTEIN
**A:** ALEX KARBSTEIN GBR, **M:** INFO@KARBSTEIN.DE

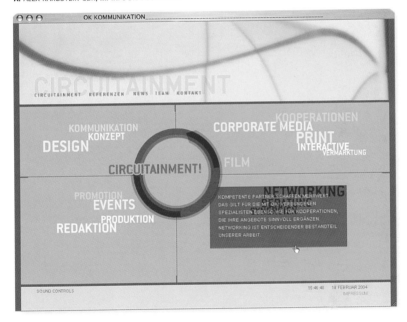

**WWW.OK-KOM.DE**
**D:** LARS WOEHNING,
**A:** V2A**NETFORCE**RUHR, **M:** LW@V2A.NET

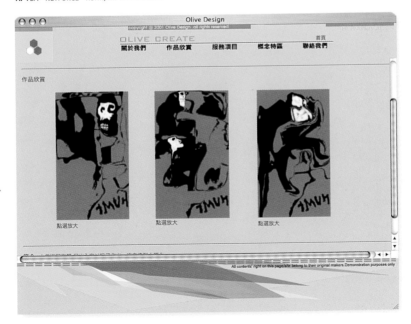

**WWW.OLIVECREATE.COM**
**D:** CHIALIANG LIN, **C:** OLIVE'S PAGES, **P:** OLIVE GROUP
**A:** OILVECREATE, **M:** CHIALIANG@OLIVECREATE.COM

WWW.NIMMERGRUEN.CH
**D:** RETO SANTSCHI, MICHAEL BÄHNI, **C:** MICHAEL BÄHNI, **P:** APPROX. MEDIA
**A:** UPART KOMMUNIKATIONS DESIGN, **M:** BAEHNI@APPROX.CH

WWW.GCITY.BE
**D:** FRÉDÉRIC JOIRIS - LAC NHAN PHAN MAI
**A:** GCITY, **M:** FREDERIC@LKNET.COM

**champs**

Archives

WWW.CONSPI.COM
**D:** GHILIONE VINCENT
**M:** CONSPI@CONSPI.COM

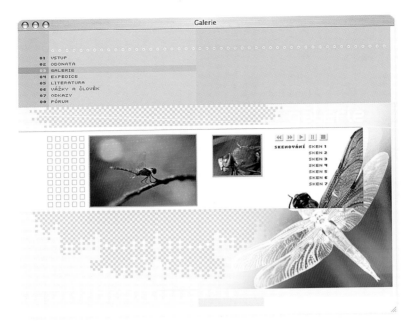

**WWW.ODONATA.CZ**
**D:** BARBORA KUKLÍKOVÁ, **C:** RADEK BALKOVSK
**A:** D-SIGN, **M:** KUKLIKOVA@D-SIGN.CZ

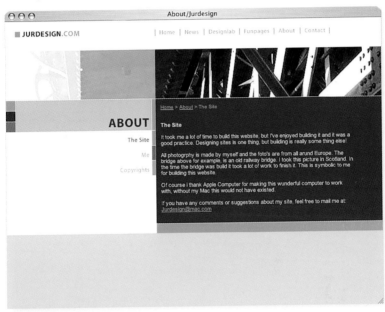

**WWW.JURDESIGN.COM**
**D:** JURRIAAN VAN BOKHOVEN
**A:** JURDESIGN, **M:** JURDESIGN@HETNET.NL

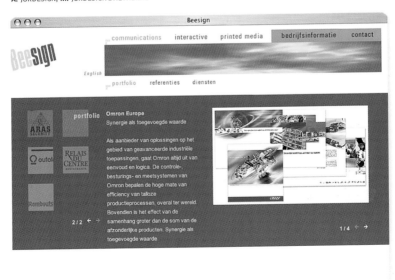

**WWW.BEESIGN.NL**
**D:** JEROEN VAN DER HAM, **C:** MARCEL BEEKMANS, ROB MULDER, **P:** HUGO RAAIJMAKERS
**A:** BEESIGN INTERACTIVE, **M:** JOEBOB@HETNET.NL

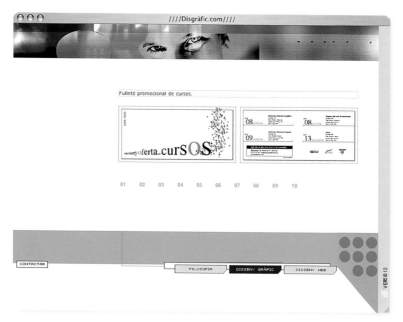

**WWW.DISGRAFIC.COM**
**M:** INFO@DISGRAFIC.COM

**WWW.ZIMMERMANN-IMMOBILIEN.CH**
**D:** SANDRA BAUMANN, MICHAEL BÄHNI, **C:** MICHAEL BÄHNI, **P:** APPROX. MEDIA
**A:** UPART, **M:** BAEHNI@APPROX.CH

**WWW.RAUMZWO.DE**
**D:** MISCHA LANDWEHR
**A:** RAUMZWO GMBH, **M:** INFO@RAUMZWO.DE

**WWW.CROSSMIND.DE**
**D:** KIRILL BRUSILOVSKY DIMITRI EICHHORN, **C:** DIMITRI EICHHORN
**A:** CROSSMIND COMMUNICATIONS GMBH, **M:** KB@CROSSMIND.DE

**WWW.DSPKOMM.DE**
**D:** LUTZ ESSERS
**A:** DER SPRINGENDE PUNKT KOMMUNIKATION GMBH, **M:** ESSERS@DSPKOMM.DE

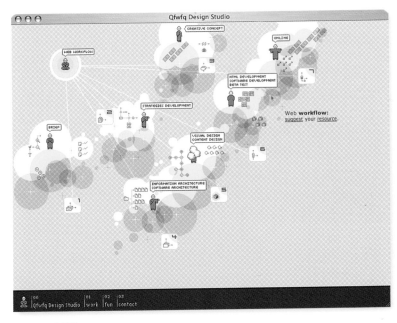

**WWW.QFWFQ.COM**
**D:** FRANCESCO MISERERE
**A:** QFWFQ DESIGN STUDIO, **M:** CICCIO@QFWFQ.COM

159

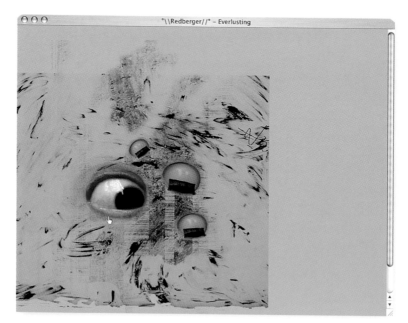

**WWW.REDBERGER.COM**
**D:** JOSE ILLENBERGER, **P:** REDBERGER
**A:** REDBERGER

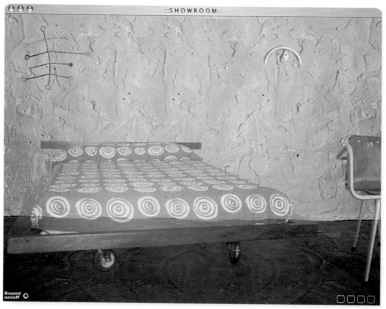

**WWW.TRIBALE.NET**
**D:** GIACOMO GIANCARLO, GIUSEPPE TOLO
**A:** KYNETOS, **M:** INFO@KYNETOS.COM

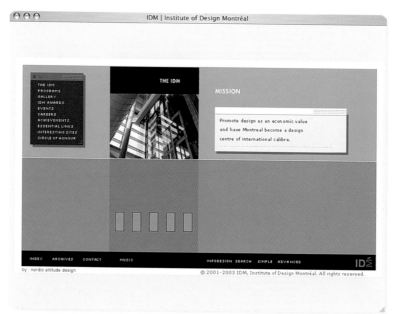

**WWW.INFO-DESIGN.QC.CA**
**D:** RONALD FILION MALLETTE / SALOMÉ ÉLIBERT, **P:** NELU WOLFENSOHN
**A:** NORDIC ATTITUDE DESIGN, **M:** RON@NORDICATTITUDE.COM

160

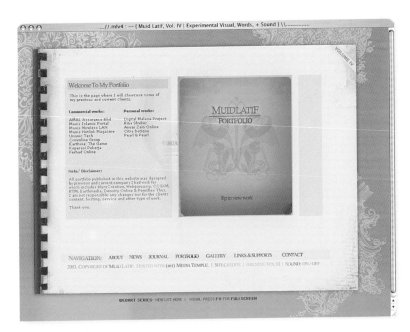

**WWW.MUIDLATIF.COM**
**D:** MUID LATIF
**A:** MUID LATIF, **M:** MUID@DIGITALMALAYA.COM

**WWW.BILLABONG-USA.COM/STORE**
**D:** TODD PURGASON, **C:** PHIL SCOTT, BRIAN DRAKE, JEFF KEYSER
**A:** JUXT INTERACTIVE, **M:** TODDHEAD@JUXTINTERACTIVE.COM

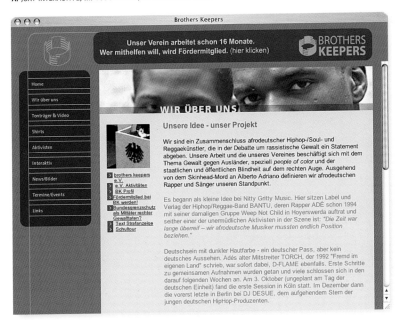

**WWW.BROTHERS-KEEPERS.DE/**
**D:** ROLAND PECHER, **C:** ROLF KRÜGER / NILS NOHNWALD, **P:** NITTY GRITTY MUSIC
**A:** KINGMEDIA / PECHER UND SOIRON, **M:** SCHMIDT@UNIT-MEDIENHAUS.DE

WWW.BUEROBARTELT.DE
**D:** BRITTA BARTELT,
**A:** BUEROBARTELT, **M:** BRITTABARTELT@BUEROBARTELT.DE

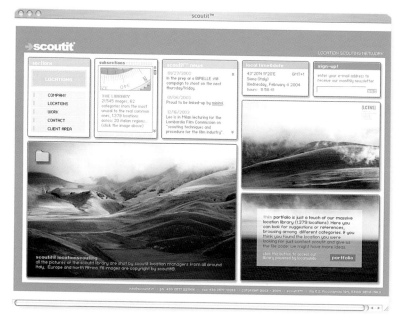

WWW.SCOUTIT.IT
**D:** STEFANO TINTI, **P:** FRISCA
**A:** FLEISCHMANN&PONS, **M:** BANTE@SCOUTIT.IT

WWW.INSEKT01.FR.ST
**D:** AURÉLIEN TERRADE
**M:** INSEK01@FR.ST

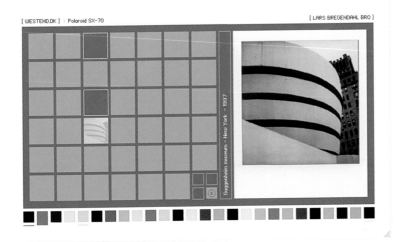

**WWW.WESTEND.DK**
**D:** LARS BREGENDAHL BRO
**A:** WESTEND, **M:** LBB@WESTEND.DK

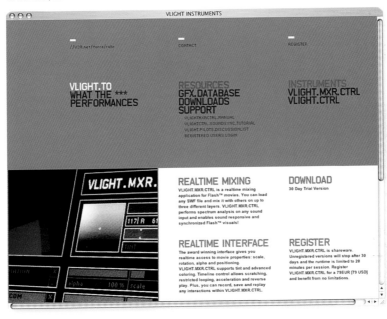

**WWW.VLIGHT.TO**
**D:** LARS WOEHNING
**A:** V2A**NETFORCE**RUHR, **M:** LW@V2A.NET

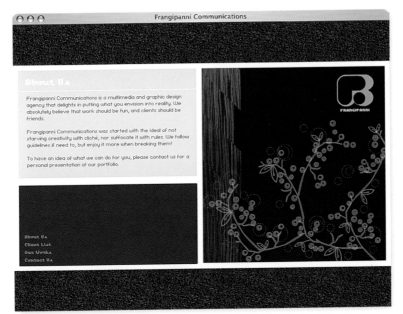

**WWW.FRANGIPANNI.COM.SG**
**D:** GERARD TAN
**A:** JUNKFLEA, **M:** INFO@JUNKFLEA.COM

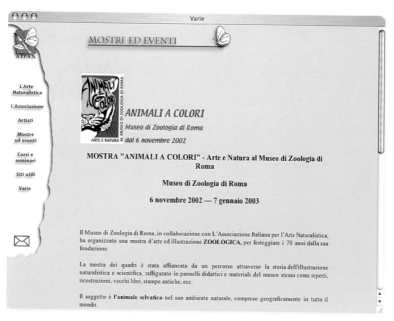

WWW.AIPAN.IT
D: FEDERICO GEMMA
M: F.GEMMA@TISCALINET.IT

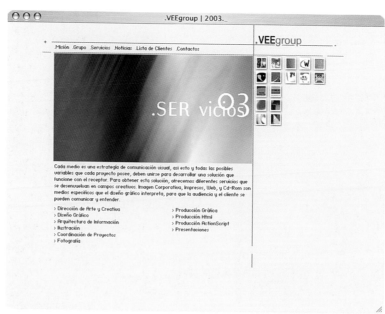

WWW.VEE.CL
D: FELIPE AGUILERA / CRISTIAN ORDÓÑEZ, P: VEEGROUP
M: CRISTIAN@VEE.CL

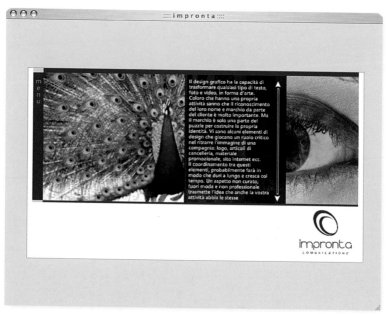

WWW.IMPRONTACOMUNICAZIONE.COM
D: NANDO SERPICO
A: IMPRONTA COMUNICAZIONE, M: MAIL@IMPRONTACOMUNICAZIONE.COM

**WWW.GREVE-MODEN.DE**
**D:** CHRISTIAN KLEIN
**M:** CEKA81@HOTMAIL.COM

**WWW.BLASFEM.COM**
**D:** BLASFEM INTERACTIF
**A:** BLASFEM INTERACTIF, **M:** SGROLEAU@BLASFEM.COM

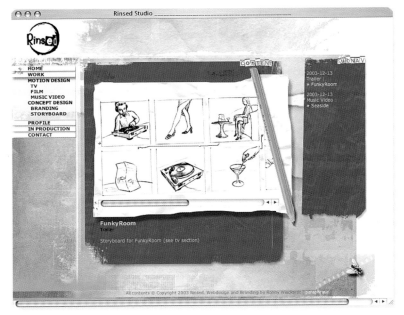

**WWW.RINSED.NET**
**D:** RONNY WIECKARDT
**A:** PARAPHRASE, **M:** ME@PARAPHRASE.NL

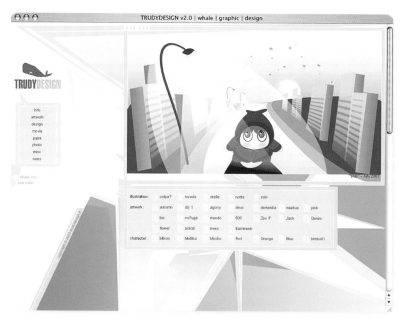

**WWW.TRUDYDESIGN.IT**
**D:** RUDY BENEDETTI
**M:** INFO@TRUDYDESIGN.IT

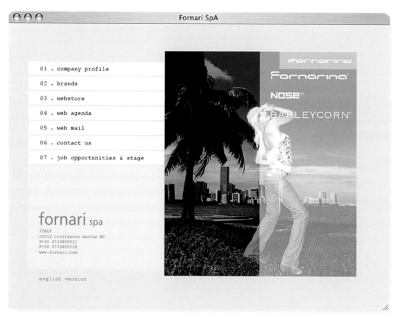

**WWW.FORNARI.COM**
**D:** ANGELO BANDINU, **P:** DROP
**A:** RE-LOAD.IT, **M:** ANGELO@DROP.IT

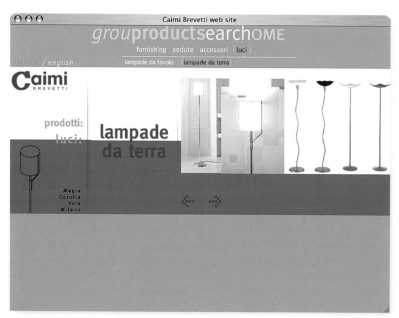

**WWW.CAIMI.IT**
**D:** CHIARA MUSSINI - LUCA BUSCAGLIA, **C:** PAOLO CHIESA
**A:** FACTORY WEB, **M:** INFO@FACTORYGROUP.IT

WWW.EVIAN.COM
D: ALFREDO TADIAR, C: JOSE GUEVARA, P: IRENE CHEUNG
A: NURUN, M: IRENE.CHEUNG@NURUN.COM

WWW.GIGIGRASSO.COM
D: JAC, P: ERIKA MARQUEZ, GIGI GRASSO
M: ERIKA_MARQUEZ_99@YAHOO.IT

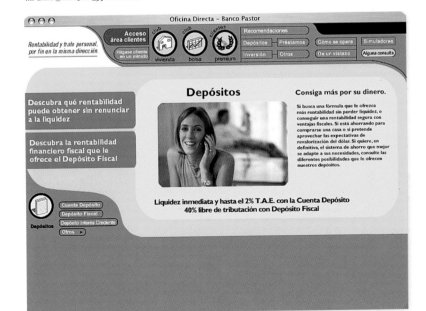

WWW.OFICINADIRECTA.COM
D: LEIRE MAZIZIOR, C: ENTREWEBS, P: IGNACIO RODRIGÁLVAREZ SANZ
A: DIMENSIÓN_INTERACTIVA, M: INFO@DIMENSIONINTERACTIVA.COM

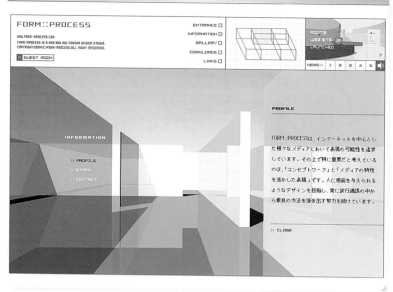

**WWW.FORM-PROCESS.COM**
**D:** TAKAAKI YAGI
**A:** FORM::PROCESS, **M:** INFO@FORM-PROCESS.COM

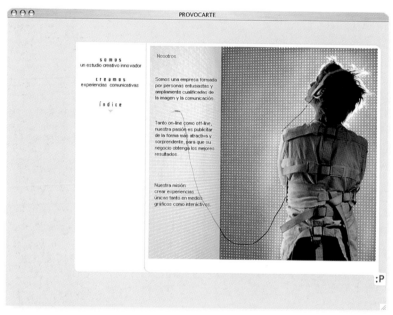

**WWW.PROVOCARTE.COM**
**D:** CARLOS NIETO, **P:** PROVOCARTE
**M:** QUIERO@PROVOCARTE

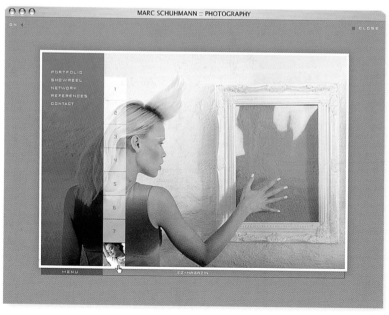

**WWW.MARCSCHUHMANN.DE**
**D:** ALFRED SCHNEIDER, **C:** ALEXANDER SCHÄFER
**A:** D2S, **M:** INFO@MARCSCHUHMANN.DE

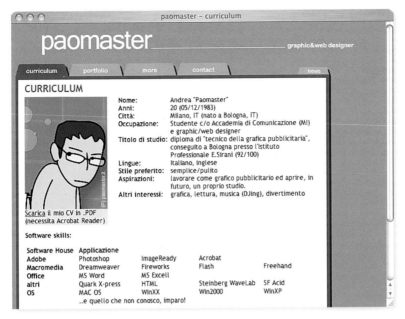

WWW.PAOMASTER.IT
**D:** ANDREA BAIETTI
**A:** PAOMASTER:DESIGN, **M:** ANDRE@PAOMASTER.IT

WWW.MEZANIN.CZ
**D:** BARBORA KUKLÍKOVÁ, **C:** RADEK BALKOVSK
**A:** D-SIGN, **M:** KUKLIKOVA@D-SIGN.CZ

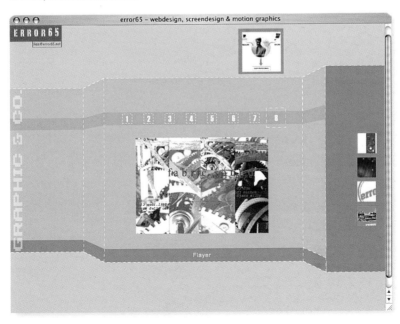

WWW.ERROR65.NET
**D:** LIDA PERIN
**M:** LIDA@ERROR65.NET

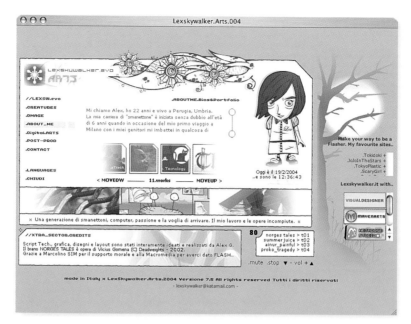

**WWW.LEXSKYWALKER.IT**
**D:** ALEX GIUSTOLISI
**A:** LEXSKYWALKER.ARTS, **M:** LEXSKYWALKER@KATAMAIL.COM

**WWW.GLOBAL-PACKAGING-ALLIANCE.COM**
**D:** ROGER HASSLER, **C:** TIM SCHATTKOWSKY, **P:** GLOBAL PACKAGING ALLIANCE
**A:** NEW ART, **M:** ROGER.HASSLER@NEWART.DE

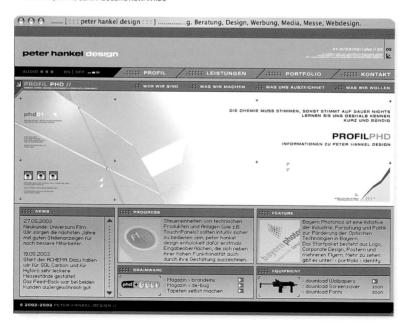

**WWW.PETER-HANKEL-DESIGN.DE**
**D:** PETER HANKEL, **C:** CHRISTIAN ITTNER
**A:** PETER_HANKEL DESIGN, **M:** INFO@PETER-HANKEL-DESIGN.DE

**WWW.KADOS.ES**
**D:** CHRISTIAN RUGE, **C:** LUIS DORADO
**A:** ESPACIO DIGITAL, **M:** CRUGE@EDIGITAL.ES

**WWW.ERTHAL.COM**
**D:** WERNER M.KÖRTELT, **C:** WOLFGANG BRAUNSCHWEIG
**A:** MAXX-MEDIA GMBH, **M:** INFO@MAXX-MEDIA.TV

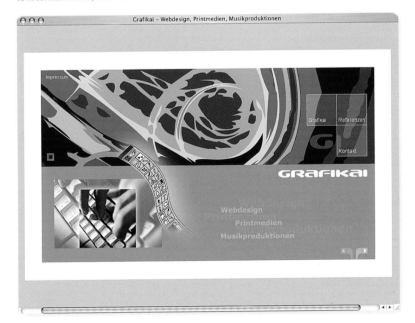

**WWW.GRAFIKAI.DE**
**D:** KAI GREIM
**A:** GRAFIKAI, **M:** INFO@GRAFIKAI.DE

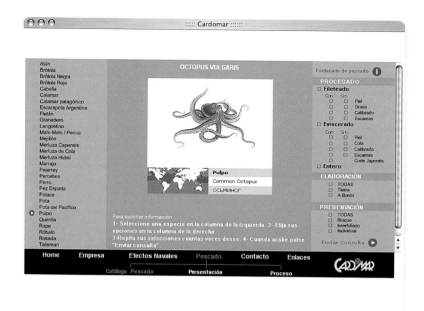

**WWW.CARDOMAR.COM**
**D:** DESOÑOS, **C:** ALBERTO GONZALEZ PEÑA
**A:** DESOÑOS, **M:** MULTIMEDIA@DESONHOS.NET

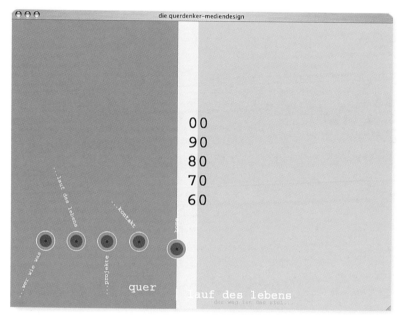

**WWW.DIE-QUER-DENKER.DE**
**D:** ANTJE WEBER / HANNO DENKER
**A:** DIE QUERDENKER, **M:** QUERDENKER2000@GMX.DE

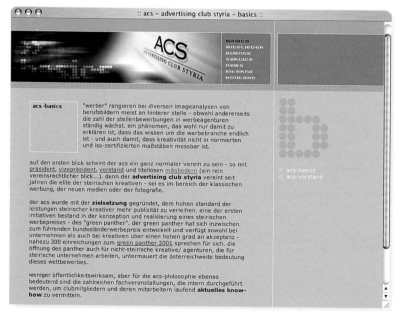

**WWW.ACS.OR.AT/**
**D:** JOERG WUKONIG
**A:** WUKONIG, **M:** OFFICE@WUKONIG.COM

VINS2K.FREE.FR/TAKE2/
D: VINCENT PUCHEUX
M: VINS2K@FR.ST

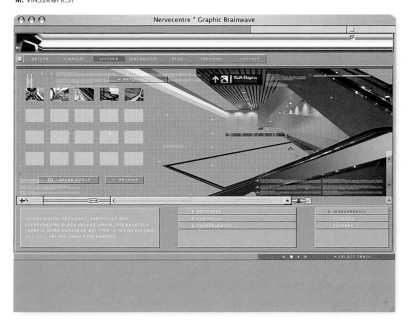

WWW.S8N.CJB.NET
D: SYAMLY RUSHDI
A: GRAPHIC BRAINWAVE, M: SYAMLY@MILLENNIUM-INTEGRA.COM

ALVEZEXPRESIONES.CJB.NET
D: ANNA MARIA LOPEZ, A: ANNA-OM-LINE INTERNATIONAL MULTIMEDIATIC DESIGNS
M: ANNANET@NAVEGALIA.COM

**WWW.CHATEAU-HAUT-BAILLY.COM/FRANCAIS/INDEX.HTML**
**D:** LAURENT CHARTIER
**A:** DUC - DISTANCE ULTRA COURTE, **M:** INFOS@D-U-C.COM

**ZYWORX.COM**
**D:** JULIA ERBE, **C:** KAI ACKERMANN
**A:** ZYWORX, **M:** D.ZEIDLER@ZYWORX.COM

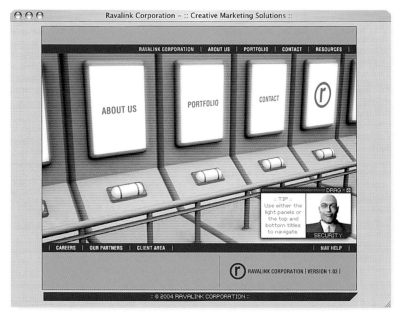

**WWW.RAVALINK.COM**
**D:** DANIEL FERKUL, **P:** RAVALINK CORPORATION
**M:** DAN@RAVALINK.COM

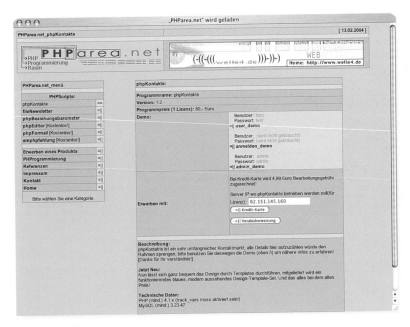

**WWW.PHPAREA.NET**
**D:** NIKO SCHOTTE, **C:** MATIS SCHOTTE
**M:** INFO@PHPAREA.NET

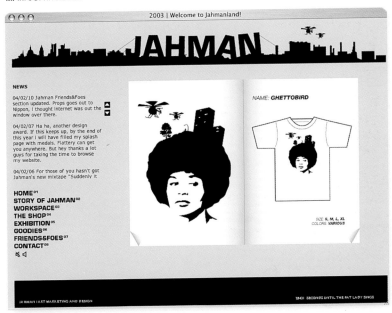

**WWW.JAHMAN.NU**
**D:** JOHAN ANNERSTEDT
**A:** JAHMAN, **M:** JOHAN@JAHMAN.NU

**WWW.RAPOSOPHOTO.COM**
**D:** SACHA RAPOSO
**M:** SACHA@DANGERKIDS.COM

accueil   actualité   le groupe   liens   le disque   télécharger

**WWW.ANGELFIRE.COM/INDIE/ROGOJINE/SOMMAIRE.HTML**
**D:** NICOLAS BARNABÉ
**A:** WSCOM, **M:** ANJIE@NY.COM

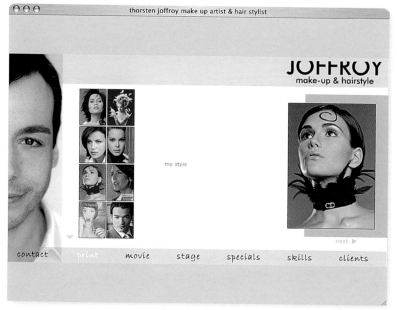

**WWW.THORSTENJOFFROY.COM**
**D:** SYLVIA TRAUTMANN
**A:** DAS TAGEWERK, **M:** SYLVIA.TRAUTMANN@DAS-TAGEWERK.DE

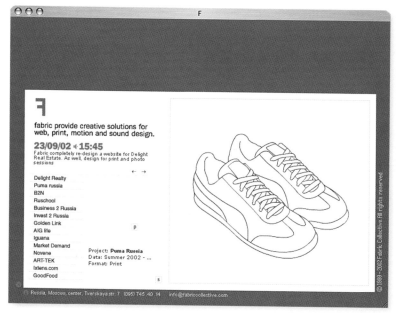

**WWW.FABRICCOLLECTIVE.COM**
**D:** ANDREY PELENKOV
**A:** FABRICCOLLECTIVE, **M:** ONDRIK@NOVENE.COM

Kompania jonë posedon më tepër se 4,000 artikuj që do të thot se çdonjëra prej tyre janë pjesë për makinën tuaj, por gjithashtu kompania bën shitjen e produkteve tjera siç janë: ngjyrra për vetura, vajra dhe shumë artikuj tjerë.

Këto produkte janë të prodhuara prej kompanive më të shquara të këtij sektori, pra vetëm marka e tyre mjafton që të vërtetoheni nga kualiteti. OTO NETKO ariti që ti sjellë të gjitha këto marka më afër jush. Vizitoni neve, shpresojmë se njera prej 4,000 artikujve është ajo që ju nevojitet juve.

OTO NETKO është distributor gjeneral për Maqedoni të markave vijuese: Kuttenkeulrr, Swag, Frenlas, Mahle, Ferbe, Ajusa dhe Aes.

**WWW.OTONETKO.COM.MK**
**D:** FLORIN HASANI, **P:** NEDMIRAN IBRAIMI
**A:** LED DESIGN, **M:** CERCI@MT.NET.MK

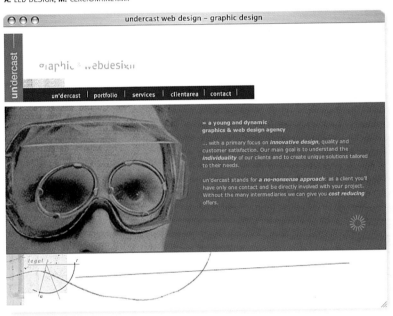

» a young and dynamic
graphics & web design agency

... with a primary focus on *innovative design*, quality and customer satisfaction. Our main goal is to understand the *individuality* of our clients and to create unique solutions tailored to their needs.

un'dercast stands for *a no-nonsense approach*: as a client you'll have only one contact and be directly involved with your project. Without the many intermediaries we can give you *cost reducing* offers.

**WWW.UNDERCAST.COM**
**D:** REG HERYGERS, **C:** CHRISTIAN AMMAN
**A:** UNDERCAST GRAPHIC, **M:** REG@UNDERCAST.COM

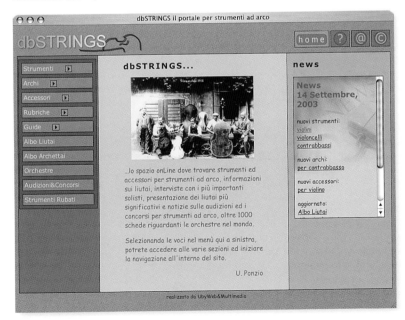

dbSTRINGS...

news

News
14 Settembre, 2003

nuovi strumenti:
violini
violoncelli
contrabbassi

nuovi archi:
per contrabbasso

nuovi accessori:
per violino

aggiornato:
Albo Liutai

...lo spazio onLine dove trovare strumenti ed accessori per strumenti ad arco, informazioni sui liutai, interviste con i più importanti solisti, presentazione dei liutai più significativi e notizie sulle audizioni ed i concorsi per strumenti ad arco, oltre 1000 schede riguardanti le orchestre nel mondo.

Selezionando le voci nel menù qui a sinistra, potrete accedere alle varie sezioni ed iniziare la navigazione all'interno del sito.

U. Ponzio

realizzato da UbyWeb&Multimedia

**WWW.DBSTRINGS.COM**
**D:** UBALDO PONZIO
**A:** UBYWEB&MULTIMEDIA, **M:** UBALDO@PONZIO.IT

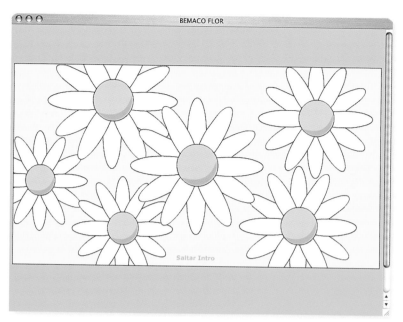

**WWW.BEMACO.COM**
**D:** ABRAHAM ROIG, **C:** EZEQUIEL, **P:** CARLES FONTSERRE
**M:** ABRAHAM@ROIG.NET

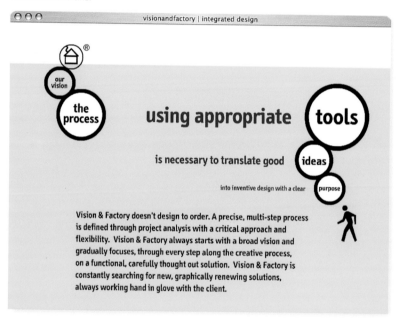

**WWW.VISIONANDFACTORY.COM**
**D:** KIM MATTHÉ, **P:** VISION, **A:** THE KNOWLEDGE FACTORY FOR DATABASE DRIVEN PART
**M:** MARCEL@VISIONANDFACTORY.COM

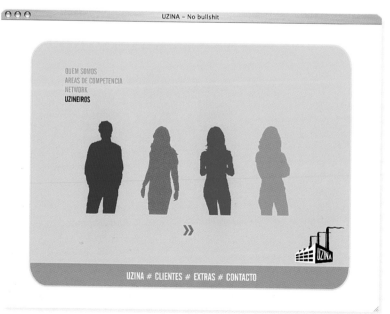

**WWW.UZINA.COM**
**D:** GUSTAVO ROSCITO
**A:** CGR DESIGN, **M:** CGR@CGRDESIGN.COM

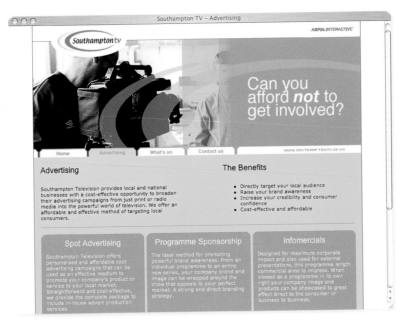

**WWW.SOUTHAMPTONTV.CO.UK**
**D:** NATHAN KINGSTONE, **C:** ADAM GORSE, **P:** MARCUS PULLEN
**A:** ASPIN INTERACTIVE, **M:** MARCUSP@ASPIN.CO.UK

**WWW.DOUBLEDESIGN.IT**
**D:** BRUNO TRAVAGLIONE / GERMANO ALBANO
**A:** DOUBLE DESIGN, M: BRUNO@DOUBLEDESIGN.IT

**WWW.DESIGNAMANOVELLA.COM**
**D:** DANIELE TABELLINI
**M:** DT@DESIGNAMANOVELLA.COM

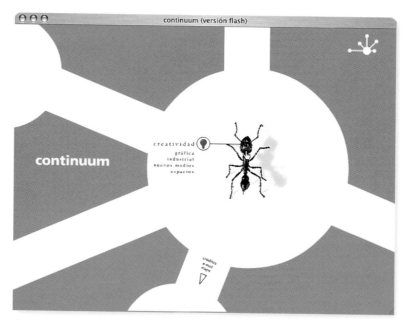

**WWW.CONTINUUM.ES**
**D:** CONTINUUM
**A:** CONTINUUM, **M:** CONTINUUM@CONTINUUM.ES

**WWW.NORDICATTITUDE.COM**
**D:** RONALD FILION MALLETTE  SALOMÉ ÉLIBERT, **C:** RONALD FILION MALLETTE
**A:** NORDIC ATTITUDE DESIGN, **M:** RON@NORDICATTITUDE.COM

**WWW.SPLENDID-CREW.COM**
**D:** GLENN LEMING, RIVELINO PANKA, STEVE TIRBENI, **C:** JEROME DE KONING
**A:** DIGITAL TRAFFIC, **M:** S.R.TIRBENI@CHELLO.NL

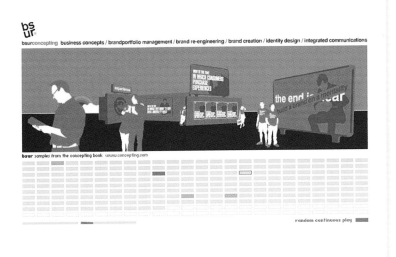

**WWW.BSUR.COM**
**D:** PASCAL DUVAL, **C:** RICHARD GROENENDIJK / MERIEN KUNST
**A:** BSUR, **M:** RICHARD@BSUR.COM

**WWW.PANDACOMIX.BIZ**
**D:** LUCA BARTOLINI
**A:** EQUILIBRISOSPESI, **M:** LUCA@EQUILIBRISOSPESI.COM

**WWW.PINSELSPRUENGE.DE**
**D:** LINDA RUMBACH, **P:** PINSELSPRÜNGE
**M:** INFO@PINSELSPRUENGE.DE

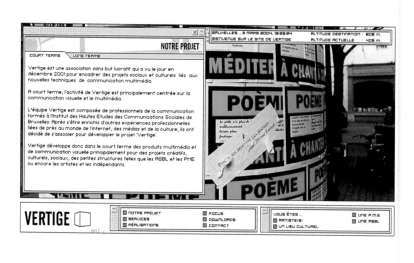

**WWW.VERTIGE.ORG**
**D:** VERTIGE
**A:** VERTIGE ASBL, **M:** VERTIGE@MAIL.BE

**WWW.SHERIDANWEB.COM**
**D:** DAVID ARROYO, **C:** JORGE ATICA
**A:** SHERIDAN, **M:** DAVID@NO-AGE.ORG

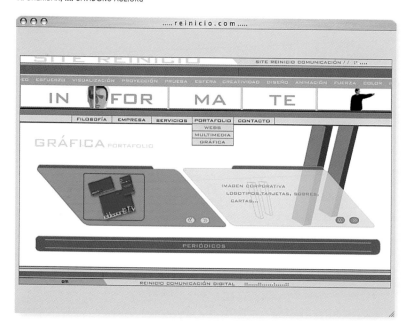

**WWW.REINICIO.COM**
**D:** CAROL CABREJAS
**A:** REINICIO, **M:** CAROLCABREJAS@HOTMAIL.COM

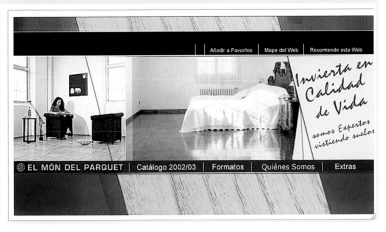

WWW.ELMONDELPARQUET.COM
D: FÈLIX RAMOS PEDROL, C: IDEM
A: EKUSE, M: FELIXRAMOSP@HOTMAIL.COM

WWW.LAUFSTEG-LAHR.DE
D: JENS MEIER
A: MEIER GRAFIKDESIGN, M: J.MEIER@GRAFIKANGELEGENHEITEN.DE

WWW.SITESFACTORY.IT/HOME.ASP
D: EMILIO GIANVENUTI, C: PAOLO
A: SITESFACTORY, M: INFO@SITESFACTORY.IT

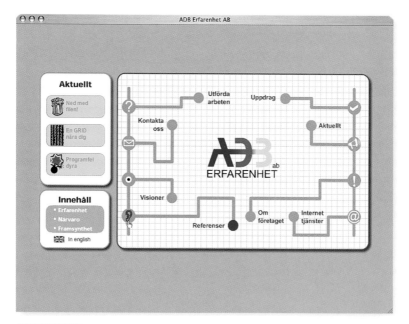

**ADBERFARENHET.SE**
**D:** MAGNUS AGARD / FÉLIX GARCÍA
**A:** ARKIPO, **M:** FELIX@ARKIPO.COM

**WWW.YOUR-MISSING-LINK.COM**
**D:** JOERN TOELLNER
**M:** JOERN_TOELLNER@WEB.DE

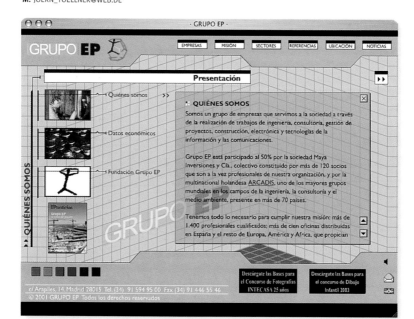

**WWW.GRUPOEP.ES**
**D:** JUAN JOSÉ PALACIOS VALDECANTOS, **C:** DIEGO PINILLA
**A:** BINDAR, **M:** JUANJO_P@YAHOO.COM

**WWW.OBJEKTAGENTUR.DE**
**D:** SASCHA C. SCHALTHÖFER
**A:** SCS::DESIGN, **M:** SCHALTHOEFER@WEB.DE

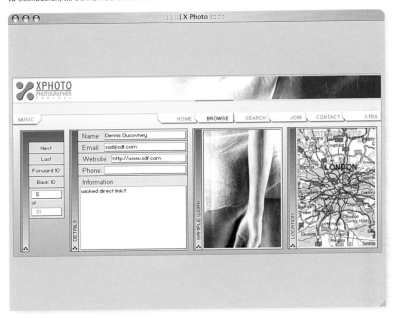

**WWW.XPHOTO.CO.UK/HEXICA/NICK/MAP/INDEX2.HTM**
**D:** NICK BRETT
**M:** JAMIESITH45@HOTMAIL.COM

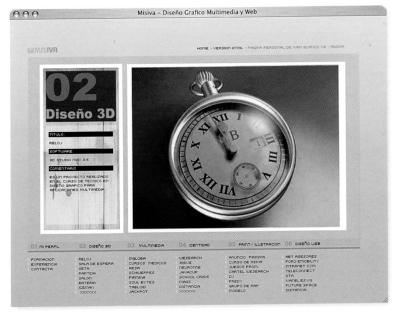

**WWW.MISIVA.NET/MISIVA_FLASH**
**D:** IVAN BLANCO LORENZO
**A:** MISIVA, **M:** IVANBLANCO@IESPANA.ES

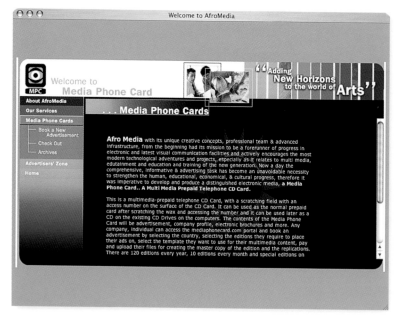

**WWW.MEDIAPHONECARD.COM**
**D:** VOXMEDIA, **C:** RAY, **P:** JULIANA GOH
**A:** VOXMEDIA, **M:** JIMMY@DCSSOLUTIONS.NET

**WWW.LESMETIERS.NET**
**D:** CAPARIF, **P:** CONSEIL RÉGIONAL ILE-DE-FRANCE
**A:** CAPARIF, **M:** CLIBERT@CAPARIF.ASSO.FR

**WWW.ZAKI.IT**
**D:** STEFANO PAMPALONI
**M:** ZAKI@ZAKI.IT

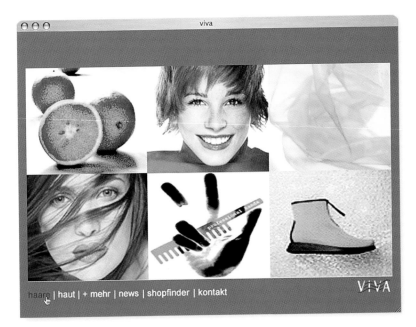

**WWW.VIVA-IHR-FRISEUR.DE**
**D:** ANTJE WEBER
**A:** DIE QUERDENKER, **M:** ANTJEWEBER2000@GMX.DE

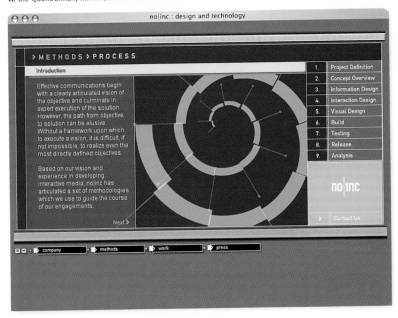

**WWW.NOINC.COM**
**D:** NO|INC
**A:** NO|INC, **M:** MARK@NOINC.COM

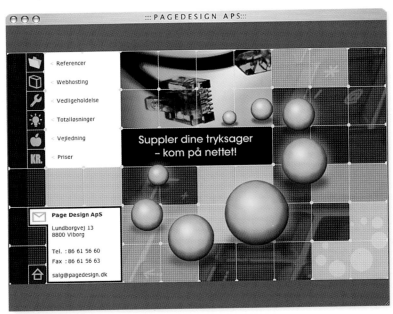

**WWW.PAGEDESIGN.DK**
**D:** MICHAEL ELKJÆR
**A:** PAGE DESIGN, **M:** MICHAEL@PAGEDESIGN.DK

**WWW.FIGOO.NET**
**D:** DIDIER LAMMENS
**A:** GOOFI, **M:** DIDZ@FIGOO.NET

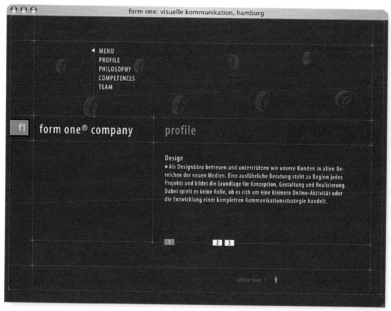

**WWW.FORM-ONE.DE**
**D:** CARLO KRÜGER / NIELS BÜNEMANN, **C:** HOLGER PLOCH
**A:** FORM ONE, **M:** INFO@FORM-ONE.DE

**WWW.JACQUES-MUELLER.CH**
**D:** SANDRO FISCHER
**A:** VITAMIN2, **M:** FISCHER@VITAMIN2.CH

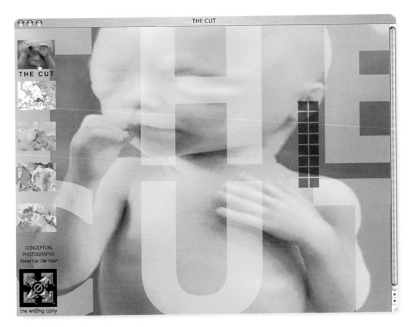

**WWW.NOWRONGWAY.COM/**
**D:** JAKOB BRANDT-PEDERSEN, **P:** THE WRØNG CPNY
**A:** SPACECONTROLLER, **M:** JBRANDTP@GET2NET.DK

**WWW.PAPERDESIGN.NET**
**D:** ANNACHIARA FIGLIA, **P:** PAPER DESIGN SNC
**A:** ANNACHIARA FIGLIA, **M:** INFO@PAPERDESIGN.NET

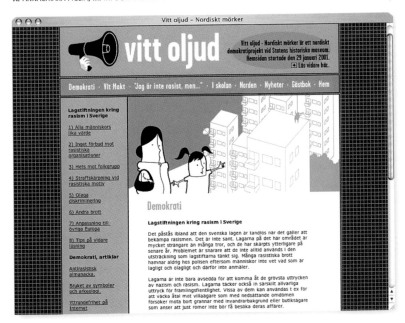

**WWW.HISTORISKA.SE/VITTOLJUD/**
**D:** SAM SOHLBERG
**A:** LÖNEGÅRD, **M:** SAM@LONEGARD.SE

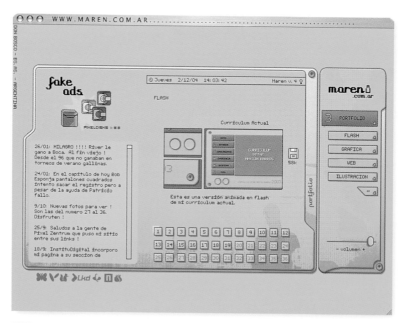

**WWW.MAREN.COM.AR**
**D:** MARTIN BARRÓS
**M:** INFO@MAREN.COM.AR

**WWW.CALEIDOS.ES**
**D:** CARLOS JIMENO GONZÁLEZ
**A:** CALEIDOS/WEB DESIGN DEPT., **M:** CARLOS.JIMENO@CALEIDOS.ES

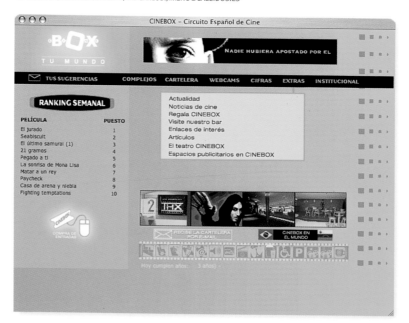

**WWW.CINEBOX.ES**
**D:** BEGOÑA MIGUEL, **C:** DAVID GARCÍA
**A:** EL TALLER DIEÑO GRAFICO, **M:** ELTALLER@ELTALLERDIGITAL.COM

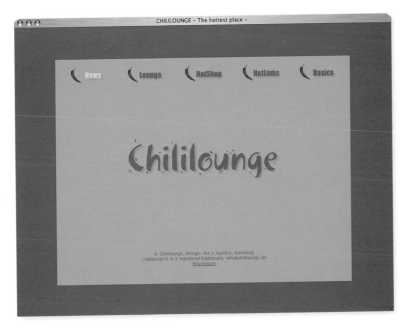

**WWW.CHILILOUNGE.DE**
**D:** FSA
**A:** ART.5 TEXTKONTOR INTERNET SUPPORT, **M:** FSA@ART5AGENTUR.DE

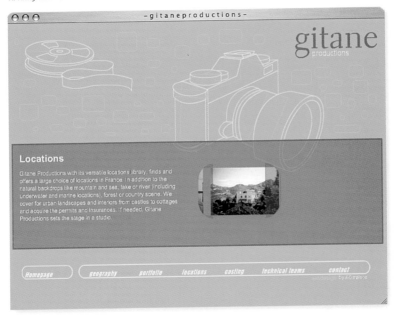

**WWW.GITANEPRODUCTIONS.COM**
**D:** KIMMO KUUSISTO
**A:** AC-MAINOS, **M:** KIMMO@ACMAINOS.FI

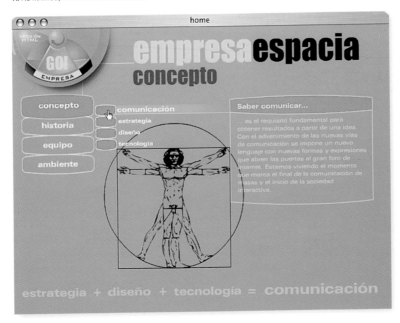

**WWW.ESPACIA.NET**
**D:** MIGUEL ARENCIBIA, **C:** ORLANDO PERDOMO, **P:** MILA GONZÁLEZ
**A:** ESPACIA NETWORKS, S.L., **M:** MIGUEL@ESPACIA.NET

WWW.HOTELVILLAGLORIA.IT
D: ILARIA BOZ
M: IBOZ@VILLAGE.IT

WWW.OST-KOMBINAT.DE
D: WEITIROMM, C: BENJAMIN WEISS
A: WEITIROOM, M: BENJAMIN@OST-KOMBINAT.DE

WWW.MRENO.COM
P: MAXIME NEMOURS
A: IN EXTENSO MEDIA, M: ADMIN@IE-M.COM

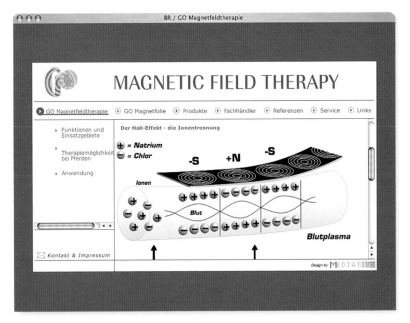

**WWW.GO-MAGNET.DE**
**D:** SONJA RADKE, **P:** MEDIATIVE
**A:** RADKE INTERAKTIV, **M:** INFO@RADKE-INTERAKTIV.DE

**WWW.BELLINI-RISTORANTE.DE**

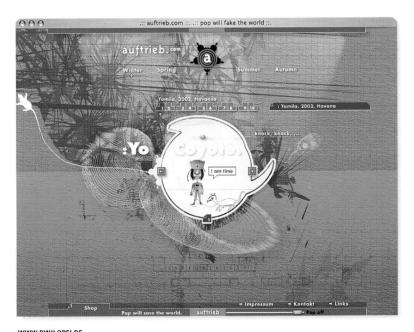

**WWW.PINILOPEI.DE**
**D:** TOMAS GARCIA GODINES
**A:** 3W4U, **M:** TOMAS@3W4U.DE

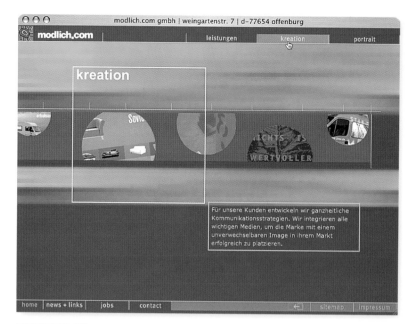

**WWW.MODLICH.COM**
**D:** GERD MODLICH, JEAN MIERECKE, **C:** JEAN MIERECKE, **P:** MODLICH.COM GMBH
**M:** INFO@MODLICH.COM

**WWW.THEBOX-ADV.COM**
**D:** MAITE CAMACHO PÉREZ, **C:** MARIO GUTIÉRREZ
**A:** ESTUDIO MAMÁS, **M:** MAITE@ESTUDIOMAMAS.COM

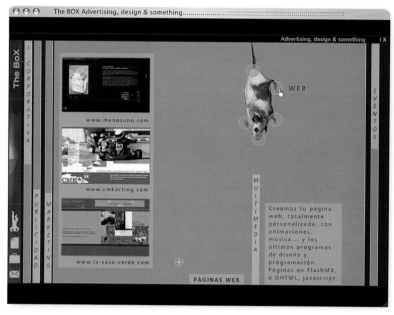

**WWW.CLOSAS-ORCOYEN.COM**
**D:** FRANCISCO PIEDRA CRUZ, **C:** JORGE AGUADO, **P:** CLOSAS-ORCOYEN
**A:** TEN FLOWERS ADVERTISING, **M:** INFO@TENFLOWERS.COM

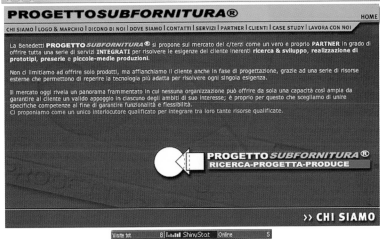

WWW.PROGETTOSUBFORNITURA.IT
**D:** ALESSANDRO CAPPELLETTI
**M:** CAPPELLETTI@INFINITO.IT

WWW.QUIT.PT.VU
**D:** CARLOS QUITERIO
**M:** CARLOS@RE-SEARCHER.COM

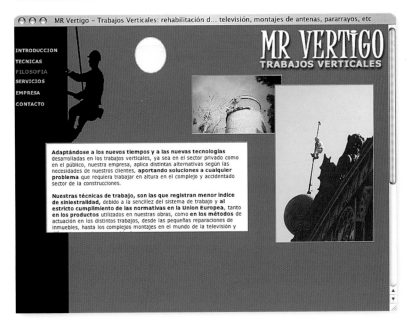

WWW.MISTER-VERTIGO.COM
**D:** JAVIER DONOSO
**M:** JDONOSO@IMPRODEX.COM

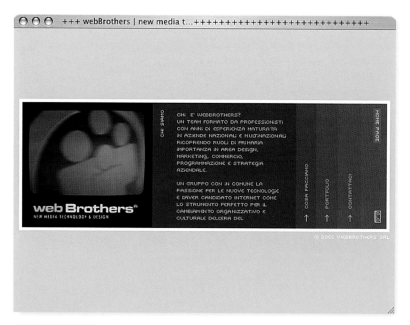

**WWW.WEBBROTHERS.IT**
**D:** STEFANO BALDUINI, **C:** MARCO DORONI
**A:** WEBBROTHERS, **M:** DESIGN@WEBBROTHERS.IT

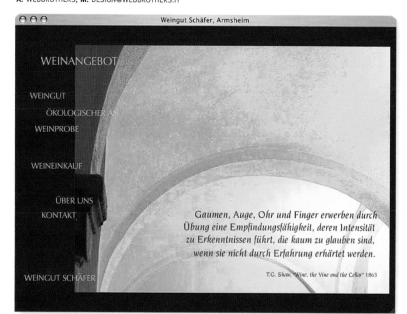

**WWW.WEINGUT-SCHAEFER.DE**
**D:** KLAUDIA SCHÄFER, **C:** SCHÄFER, JUNKER
**A:** AGENTUR SCHÄFER PARTNER, **M:** INFO@GRAFIKAGENTUR-SCHAEFER.DE

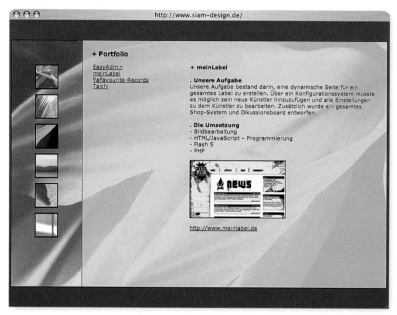

**WWW.SIAM-DESIGN.DE**
**D:** JULIUS VON BISMARCK, **C:** PAUL SPIEKER
**A:** SIAM-DESIGN, **M:** BERLIN-GRAFF@GMX.DE

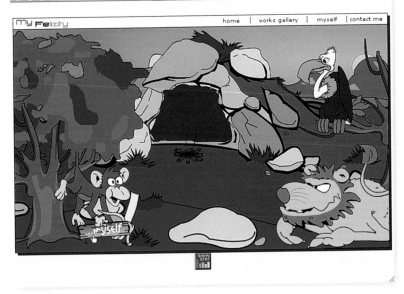

WWW.MYFELIZITY.COM
D: FABIO DI DIO
A: MYFELIZITY, M: INFO@MYFELIZITY.COM

WWW.1844DESIGN.COM
D: DAN
A: DGRAPHIKS.NET, M: DANHUNTERH@HOTMAIL.COM

WWW.EVAGARDE.IT
D: FEDERICO ROCCO, C: DAVIDE RUSSO, P: KETTYDO | BEAUTYFARM
M: FEDERICO@KETTYDO.COM

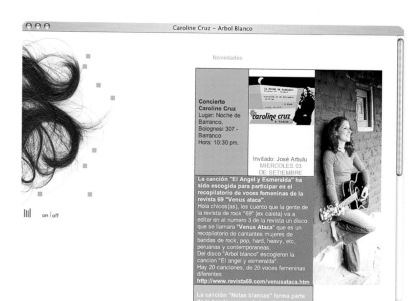

WWW.LA-ROJA.COM
D: FABRIZIO SOTELO JIRON
A: KAKTUS, M: FSOTELO@CORREO.ULIMA.EDU.PE

WWW.PRINSENKIND.NL
D: NIENKE DIRKSE, C: MARCEL KLOMP, P: MARK MARTENS
A: IF/THEN, M: HELLO@IFTHEN.NL

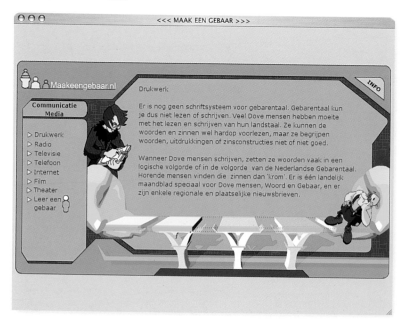

WWW.MAAKEENGEBAAR.NL
D: EMMA HKU, C: SANDER VERHOF, P: EMMA TEAM HKU
A: HKU, M: S.VERHOF@CHELLO.NL

**WWW.OVERNOISE.NET**
**D:** ALBINO TONNINA
**A:** NETQPS PSC, **M:** INFO@OVERNOISE.NET

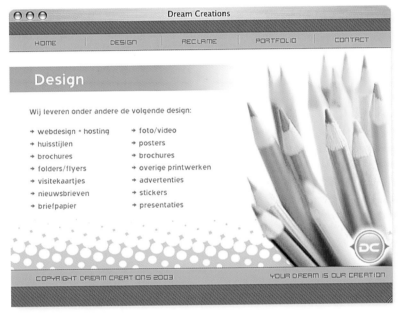

**WWW.DREAM-CREATIONS.NL**
**D:** SAM GERKE

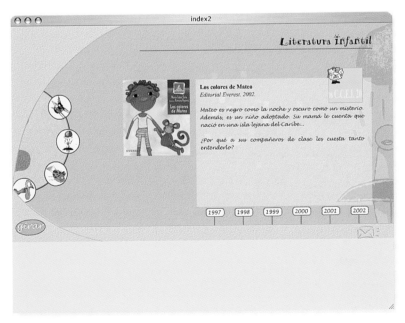

**WWW.MARISALOPEZSORIA.COM**
**D:** LUIS LARBEC
**M:** LLARBEC@HOTMAIL.COM

**WWW.DRAG-AND-DROP.NET**
**D:** ALEJANDRO SÁNCHEZ GÓMEZ, **C:** JUAN MANUEL GOMEZ CASTRO
**A:** DROP MEDIA LAB S.L., **M:** INFO@DRAG-AND-DROP.NET

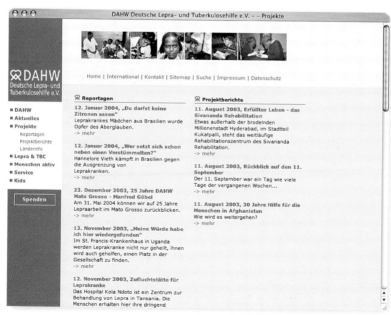

**WWW.ENSECO.IT**
**D:** ALESSANDRO TOFANI
**M:** A.TOFANI@CENTERWEB.IT

**WWW.DAHW.DE**
**D:** ZELLTEILUNG, **C:** DIGRAMM MEDIA GMBH
**A:** ZELLTEILUNG, **M:** INFO@ZELLTEILUNG.DE

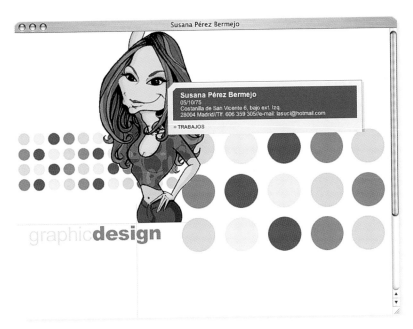

**WWW.JUNCIONA.NET/SUSIA**
**D:** SUSANA PÉREZ BERMEJO, **C:** LUIS NAVALPOTRO
**M:** SPBERMEJO@YA.COM

**WWW.DRINGSTATION.COM**
**D:** VERONIQUE HOULET, **C:** PROBBES, **P:** UTEL
**M:** VHOULET@UTEL.FR

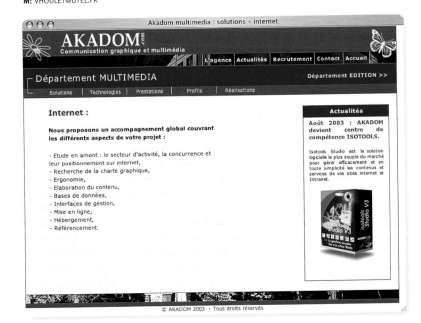

**WWW.AKADOM.FR**
**D:** MATHIEU SAUDEL, **P:** AKADOM
**M:** MATHIEU.SAUDEL@WANADOO.FR

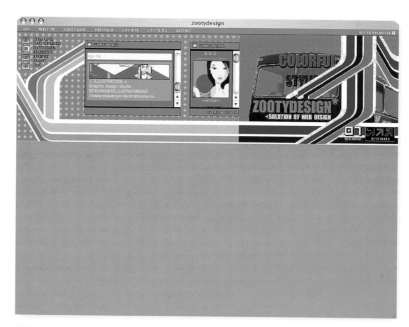

**WWW.ZOOTYDESIGN.COM**
**D:** SUNGSU-YOO
**M:** INFO@ZOOTYDESIGN.COM

**BLENDER70.COM**
**D:** JASMIN SCHNEIDER, **C:** SVEN SCHMEIER, **P:** ASMIN SCHNEIDER
**A:** BLENDER70, **M:** SHE@BLENDER70.COM

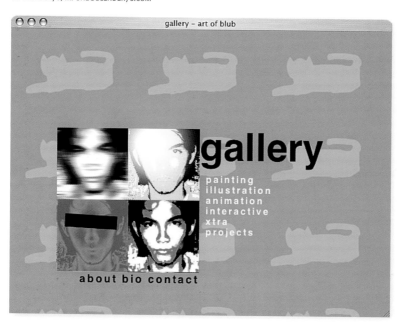

**WWW.GEOCITIES.COM/ARTOFBLUB**
**D:** KRIST MENINA
**M:** PALE_BLUE@LINUXMAIL.ORG

**WWW.SARKANNIEMI.FI/SAHKIS**
**D:** HANNA NISKANEN, **C:** JUSSI VIITANIEMI, **P:** HANNA PURO
**A:** NICEFACTORY LTD., **M:** HANNA.NISKANEN@NICEFACTORY.COM

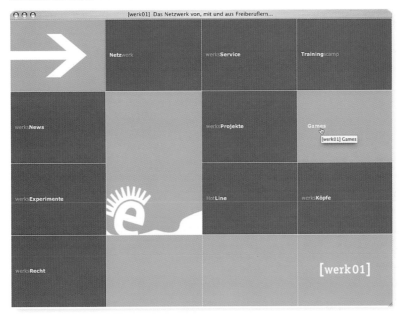

**WWW.WERK01.DE**
**D:** HANNO DENKER / BORIS RÖMER / OLIVER MICHALAK
**A:** [WERK01], **M:** HANNO@WERK01.DE

**WWW.ICONIQUE.COM**
**D:** CJ VAN GORSEL
**M:** JOOST@ICONIQUE.COM

**WWW.HAJOPLOETZ.DE**
**D:** BRITTA BARTELT
**A:** BUEROBARTELT, **M:** BRITTABARTELT@BUEROBARTELT.DE

**WWW.THEREDARMY.JP**
**D:** LEN LIM, **C:** TERENCE ANG
**A:** 9QUBE, **M:** JEROME@9QUBE.NET

**WWW.WAHSIGNAL.DE**
**D:** FABU
**M:** FABU@WAHNSIGNAL.DE

**AMSMULTIMEDIA.COM**
**D:** ALBERT MARTÍNEZ SERRACLARA
**A:** AMSM, **M:** ALBERTMARTINEZS@YAHOO.ES

**WWW.KITKATCITY.COM**
**D:** SERGIO SEGOVIA / LAURA CASTILLO, **C:** DANIEL SEGOVIA
**A:** SYNAPSIS DIGITAL, **M:** LAURA@SYNAPSISDIGITAL.COM

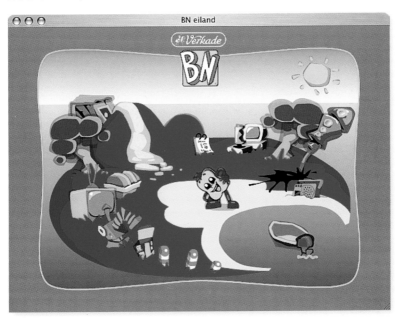

**WWW.BNKIDS.NL**
**D:** GIJS VAN DER SCHOOT, **C:** FORTUNATO GEELHOED, **P:** GERARD DE BOER
**A:** DBK OGILVY, **M:** MARK@WEBINZICHT.COM

**HOME.SINGTEL.COM/PREMIUM/**
**D:** IVAN MP TAN, **P:** ARETAE LTD
**A:** ARETAE LTD, **M:** IVAN.TAN@ARETAE.COM

**WWW.MARIALBISTUR.COM.AR**
**D:** MAGALI PITERMAN
**A:** MAGA WEB GRAFICA, **M:** MARIALBISTUR@HOTMAIL.COM

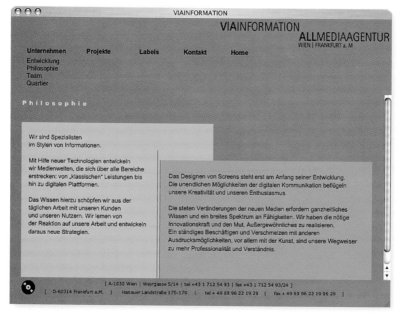

**WWW.VIAINFO.COM**
**D:** OLGA MARTSCHITSCH, JULIA FINEDER, REGINA SZALAY,
**A:** VIAINFORMATION ALLMEDIAAGENTUR, **M:** INFO@VIAINFO.COM

WWW.UQAM.CA/CRIN
**D:** RONALD FILION MALLETTE **C:** RONALD FILION MALLETTE, **P:** NELU WOLFENSOHN
**A:** NORDIC ATTITUDE DESIGN, **M:** RON@NORDICATTITUDE.COM

WWW.DARBOTZ.COM
**D:** DARMA ADHITIA
**M:** ME@DARBOTZ.COM

WWW.POINTPIXEL.COM
**D:** DEMIAN CONRAD
**A:** POINTPIXEL, **M:** INFO@POINTPIXEL.COM

**WWW.AVELINOGONZALEZ.COM**
**D:** DESOÑOS
**A:** DESOÑOS, **M:** MULTIMEDIA@DESONHOS.NET

**WWW.SITARATEXTILE.COM**
**D:** FOUAD RIAZ BAJWA FADIB
**A:** CYGENTECHMULTIMEDIA, **M:** FOUADBAJWA@HOTMAIL.COM

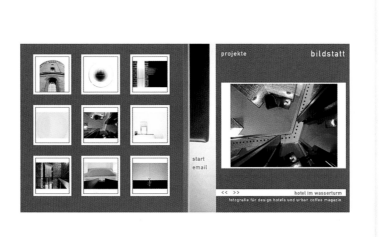

**WWW.BILDSTATT.DE**
**D:** CHRISTIAN BÜTTNER, MARKUS TEBBERT
**A:** TEMA MEDIEN GMBH, **M:** CB@TEMA-MEDIEN.DE

**WWW.HERWORLD.COM**
**D:** HAIKAL LIM

**WWW.LINEABASE.COM**
**P:** LINEABASE
**M:** INFO@LINEABASE.COM

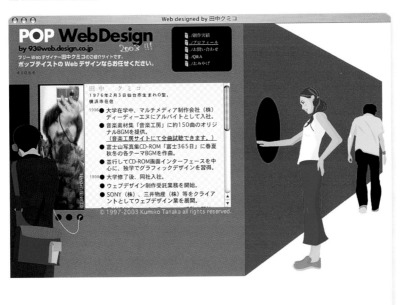

**WWW.19760203.COM/**
**D:** KUMIKO TANAKA
**M:** TANAKA@19760203.COM

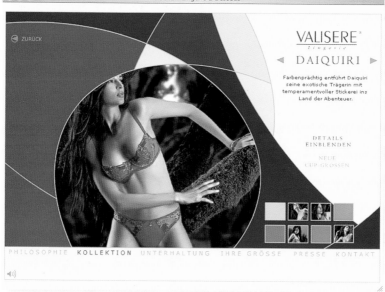

**WWW.VALISERE.COM**
**D:** COMA2 · COLLECTIVE OF MEDIA ARTISTS
**M:** COLLIN@COMA2.COM

**WWW.IL-LIBERTY.IT**
**D:** DAVIDE ALDRIGHETTI
**A:** INTERPOP DIGITAL MEDIA AGENCY, **M:** SERVIZI@INTERPOP.IT

**LILO.KREBERNIK.AT**
**D:** LILO KREBERNIK
**M:** LILO@KREBERNIK.AT

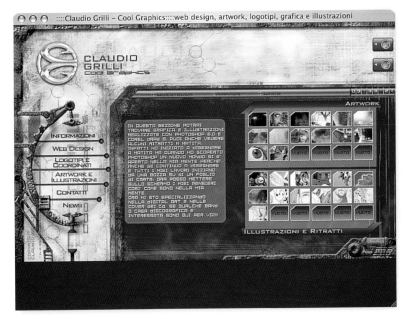

**WWW.COOLGRAPHICS.IT**
**D:** CLAUDIO GRILLI
**M:** INFO@COOLGRAPHICS.IT

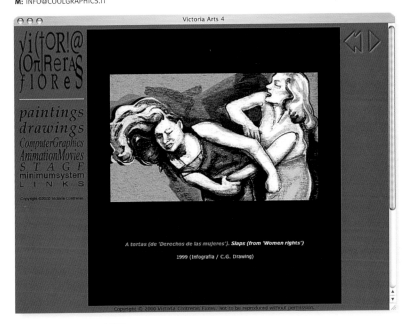

**WWW.VICTORIACONTRERAS.COM**
**P:** VICTORIA CONTRERAS

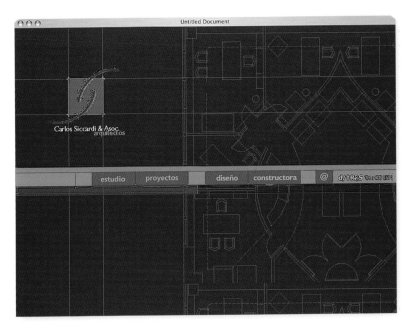

**WWW.SICCARDI.COM**
**D:** DAINA BAGURSKAS / LUCÍA BRITO DEL PINO / ANA INÉS DÍAZ
**A:** D/TRES, **M:** DTRES@ADINET.COM.UY

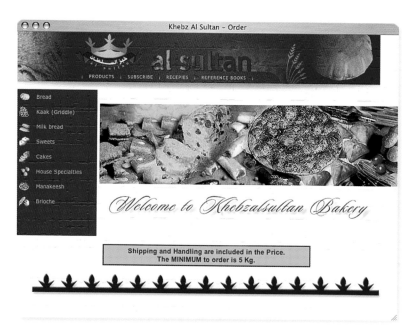

**WWW.KHEBZALSULTAN.COM**
**D:** GRAFIUM
**A:** GRAFIUM, **M:** INCOTEL@CYBERIA.NET.LB

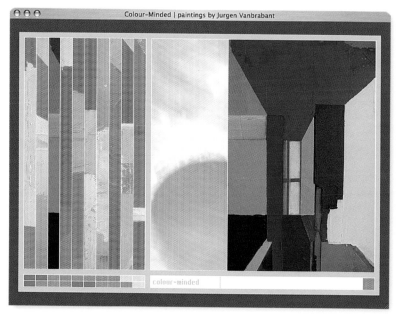

**WWW.COLOUR-MINDED.COM**
**D:** HIPATRIP
**M:** BRANT@COLOUR-MINDED.COM

**WWW.PUERTASSANRAFAEL.COM**
**D:** JAVIER DÍAZ
**A:** ARANEA DIGITAL, S.R.L., **M:** WEBMASTER@ARANEADIGITAL.COM

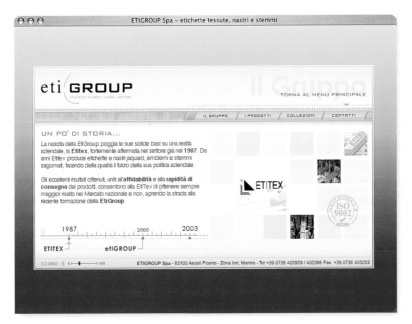

**WWW.ETIGROUP.IT**
**D:** GABRIELE DI LORENZO
**A:** ALFA MULTIMEDIA, **M:** GRAFICA@ALFAMULTIMEDIA.IT

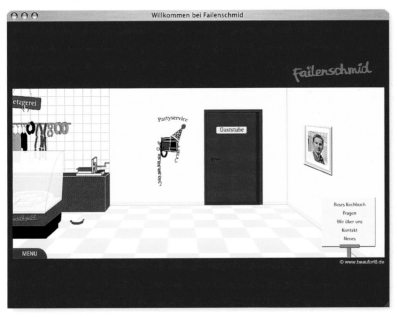

**WWW.FAILENSCHMID.DE**
**D:** JENS HENNINGS
**A:** BEAUFORT 8, **M:** HENNINGS@BEAUFORT8.DE

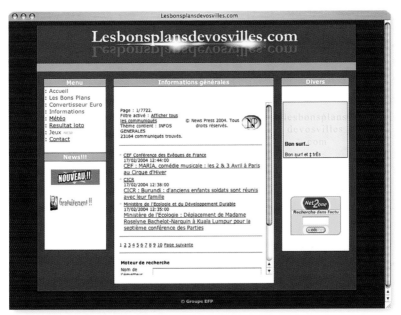

**WWW.LESBONSPLANSDEVOTREVILLE.COM**
**D:** CESAR MASRI, **P:** CMC ADVERTISING
**A:** WSCOM, **M:** JHASS@NY.COM

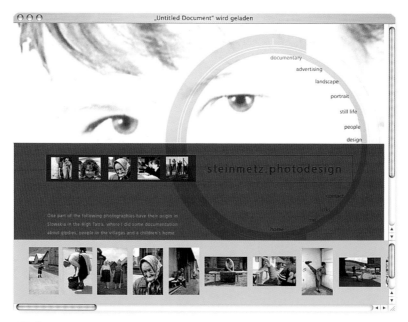

**WWW.STEINMETZ-PHOTODESIGN.COM**
**D:** VERONIKA STEINMETZ
**M:** VS@STEINMETZ-PHOTODESIGN.COM

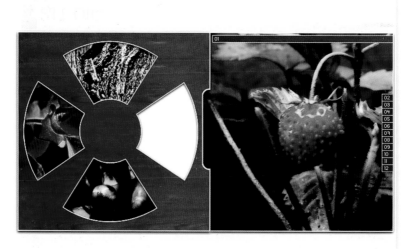

**WWW.CFSTUDIO.NET**
**D:** CARLOS ALBERTO FERREIRA MARTINEZ
**A:** CF STUDIO, **M:** DESIGN@CFSTUDIO.NET

**WWW.CLANDESTINA.COM**
**D:** JUAN LLAMOSAS, FRANCISCO LEMOS
**A:** LA VERTICAL, **M:** JUAN@CLANDESTINA.COM

**WWW.PRIMERAPERSONA.COM**
**D:** ANNA MARIA LOPEZ LOPEZ
**A:** ANNA-OM-LINE MULTIMEDIATIC DESIGNS, **M:** ANNA@FASHIONMAS.COM

**WWW.ARS3.COM**
**D:** FERRAN SENDRA, **C:** MIQUEL ANGLARILL
**A:** ARS3, **M:** FERRAN@ARS3.COM

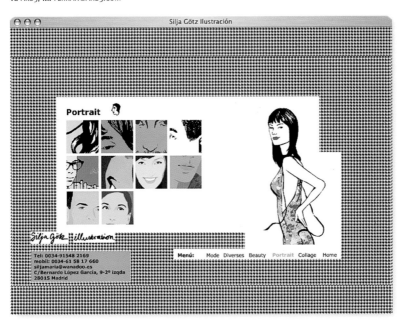

**WWW.SILJAGOETZ.COM**
**D:** SILJA GOETZ
**A:** SILJA GOETZ ILLUSTRATION, **M:** SILJAMARIA@WANADOO.ES

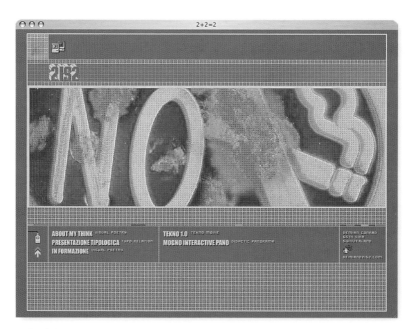

**WWW.2IS2.COM**
**D:** DEMIAN CONRAD
**A:** POINTPIXEL | COMMUNICATION DESIGN, **M:** INFO@POINTPIXEL.COM

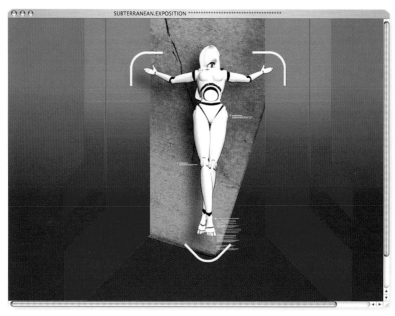

**WWW.INGEN.NU**
**D:** BEN, **C:** RICH CROFT
**M:** PILOTC@INGEN.NU

**WWW.CAFFECOSMAI.COM**
**D:** ANGELA D'AMELIO, **C:** ANNA COMINAZZINI, **P:** COSMAI CAFFÈ -FABRIZIO COSMAI
**A:** CARTA E MATITA, **M:** UDEGASPARI@CARTAEMATITA.IT

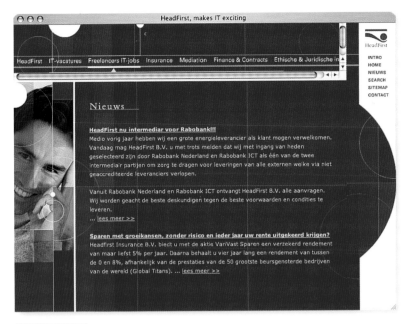

WWW.HEADFIRST.NL/
**D:** JEROEN HERMES
**A:** BOOLEANPARK, **M:** JEROEN.HERMES@BOOLEANPARK.COM

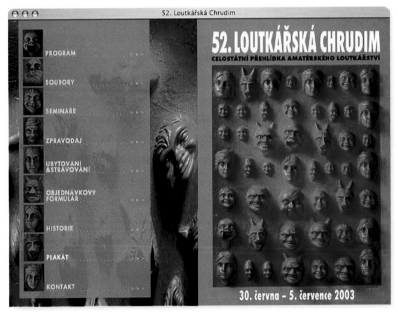

WWW.LOUTKARSKA-CHRUDIM.CZ
**D:** JAN BABORÁK
**A:** STUDIO-BABORÁK, **M:** JANACEK.JEBE@SEZNAM.CZ

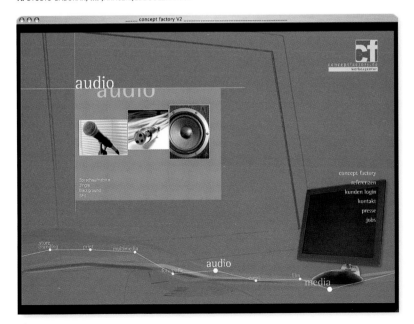

WWW.CONCEPTFACTORY.DE
**D:** SASA STOJANOVIC
**A:** CONCEPTFACTORY, **M:** DERWEL@CONCEPTFACTORY.DE

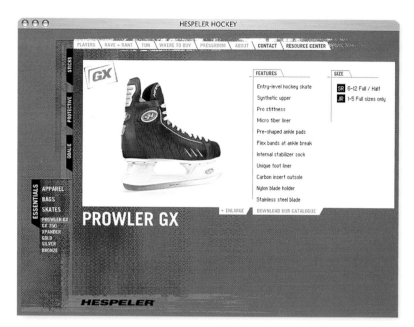

**WWW.HESPELER.COM**
**D:** STEVE GAUDER, **C:** JOHN GOODWIN, **P:** STEVE GABANY
**A:** GAUDER DESIGN, **M:** STEVIEG@SYMPATICO.CA

**WWW.SIMSNS.AT**
**D:** ROBERT ONDROVICS
**A:** WATCHOUT, **M:** R.ONDROVICS@VIENNA.AT

**WWW1.TTCN.NE.JP/~TOSHIFUMI/**
**D:** TOSHIFUMI TANABU
**M:** T_TANABU@YBB.NE.JP

**WWW.RUTADELAPLATA.COM**
**D:** LUIS ENRIQUE RAMOS, **P:** CARMEN BOUZAS CORTINA
**M:** CARMEN@ASTURIAS.COM

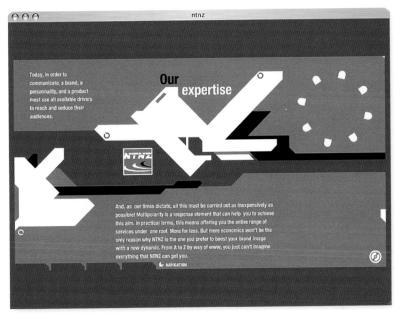

**WWW.NTNZ.COM**
**D:** NTNZ
**A:** NTNZ, **M:** O.MAERNHOUT@NTNZ.COM

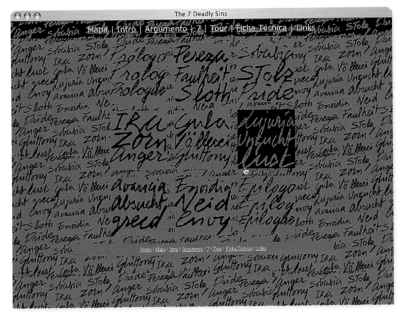

**WWW.7PECADOS.COM**
**P:** VICTORIA CONTRERAS

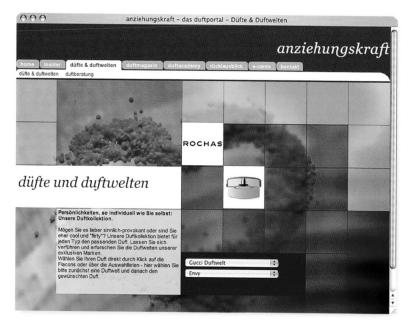

WWW.ANZIEHUNGSKRAFT.DE
C: FRANK MÜLLER, THOMAS HERRMANN, P: DIETMAR SCHMIDT
A: KINGMEDIA, M: SCHMIDT@UNIT-MEDIENHAUS.DE

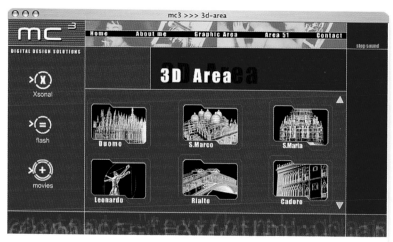

WWW.MC3.IT
D: MATTEO A. COLOMBO
M: MATTEO_COLOMBO@HOTMAIL.COM

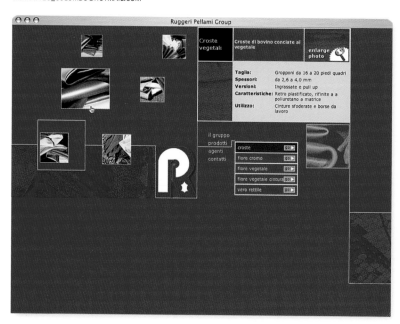

WWW.RUGGERIPELLAMI.COM
D: GIANLUCA RECALCATI, P: MODEPOQUE
A: MAGNETIKA DI GIANLUCA RECALCATI, M: GREKA@MAGNETIKA.IT

**WWW.DIEKUECHE-LIVE.DE**
**D:** SIMONE HEISSEL, JAN KÜNZEL, **P:** MAXIMILIAN DÜRST
**M:** MAX@DUERST.DE

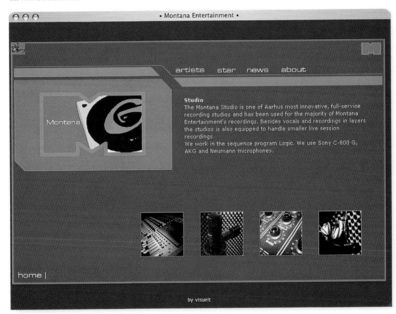

**WWW.MONTANA-ENTERTAINMENT.COM**
**D:** THOMAS BRIXEN
**A:** MONTANA ENTERTAINMENT, **M:** BRIXEN@ONCABLE.DK

**WWW.WEBAGENT007.COM**
**D:** JAMES BEGERA
**A:** WEBAGENT007, **M:** INFO@WEB

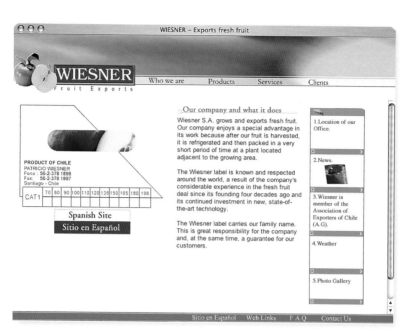

**WWW.WIESNER.CL**
**D:** PAULO LEYTON, **P:** ALVARO CANALES
**A:** IWCORP, **M:** PLEYTON@IWCORP.COM

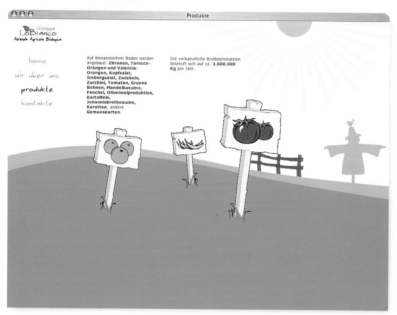

**WWW.AGRIBIOLOBIANCO.IT**
**D:** STAXOFT
**A:** STAXOFT, **M:** INFO@STAXOFT.IT

**WWW.APICE.INF.BR**
**D:** LUCIANO GUEDES
**A:** ÁPICE TECNOLOGIA, **M:** LU75BR@YAHOO.CO.UK

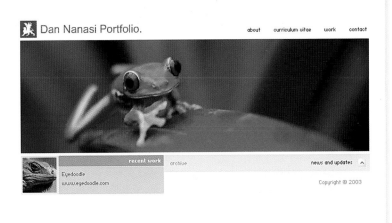

**DAN.INKO.CA**
**D:** DAN NANAS
**A:** DANINKO, **M:** DAN@INKO.CA

**WWW.RICEBAY.COM**
**P:** GARY CHUNG
**A:** PLUS ONE OFFICE, **M:** MYLC3@YAHOO.COM

**WWW.FAKIESHOP.COM**
**D:** MARCO FORNASIER / ANDREA TRONCHIN, **C:** RUDY PIO LOCO BOSCARIOL
**A:** NEA07.ORG, **M:** TTRONKO@NEA07.ORG

SNOW IS DRIVEN BY PASSION AND AN UNYIELDING DEDICATION TOWARDS QUALITY DESIGN, PROFESSIONAL SERVICES AND PRODUCTION EXCELLENCE.

DESIGN IS DEFINED IN ITS TIME. WE BELIEVE THAT CERTAIN FUNDAMENTAL REMAINS ALTHOUGH PERCEPTION ARE CONSTANTLY CHANGING. IT TAKES A GOOD DESIGNER TO RECOGNISE WHAT IS FUNDAMENTAL AND A BETTER DESIGNER TO PUSH THE BOUNDARIES OF THAT DEFINITION.

**WWW.SNOW.COM.SG**
**D:** JR, **C:** JEAN
**A:** SNOW DESIGN, **M:** JR@SNOW.COM.SG

**WWW.VIRTUALTEAM.WS**
**D:** TONI SANCHEZ, **C:** JORDI AMENGUAL
**A:** VIRTUALTEAM, **M:** TSANCHEZ@VIRTUALTEAM.WS

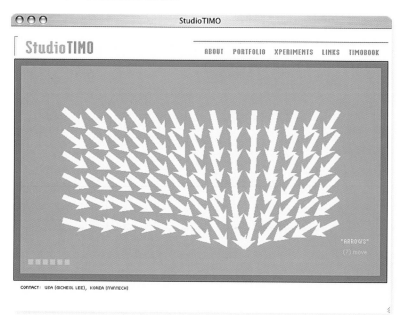

**WWW.STUDIOTIMO.COM**
**D:** GICHEOL LEE
**A:** STUDIOTIMO, **M:** CAMEO@STUDIOTIMO.COM

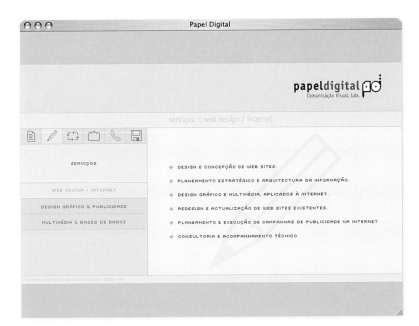

**WWW.PAPELDIGITAL.PT**
**D:** RUI PINTO
**A:** PAPEL DIGITAL, **M:** RPINTO@PAPELDIGITAL.PT

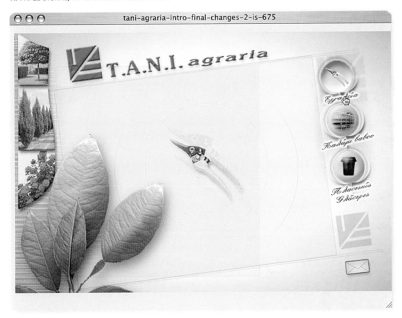

**WWW.TANI.GR**
**D:** STEFANOS STEFANIDIS
**A:** WEB RELATION DESIGN, **M:** INFO@E-INFO.GR

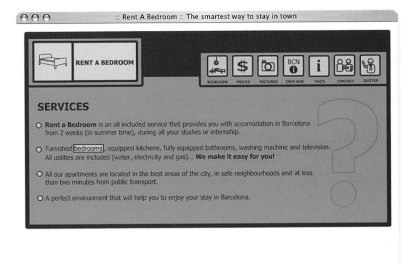

**WWW.RENTABEDROOM.COM**
**D:** EDGAR FERDEZ
**M:** INFO@RAGDE.NET

01 02 03 04 **05**

**WWW.PHASEZERO.DE**
**D:** KARSHAN PATEL AND ALESSANDRA TAGLIABUE
**A:** PHASEZERO, **M:** KARSHAN@PHASEZERO.DE

**WWW.CREATIVEBEHAVIOR.COM**
**D:** YOEL BURMAN KAREL
**M:** CREATIVE@CREATIVEBEHAVIOR.COM

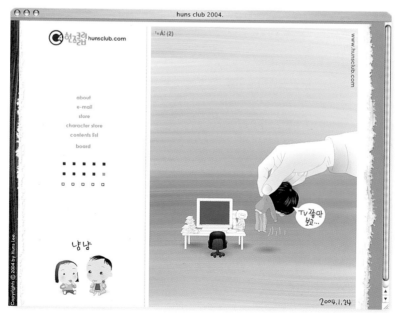

**WWW.HUNSCLUB.COM**
**D:** MYUNG-HUN LEE
**M:** GREGHUNS@LYCOS.CO.KR

226

**WWW.CONECTA.COM.UY**
**D:** PABLO MERESHIAN, **C:** LEONARDO SANCHEZ
**A:** SOLUZIONA SI, **M:** PMERESHIAN@SOLUZIONA-SI.COM

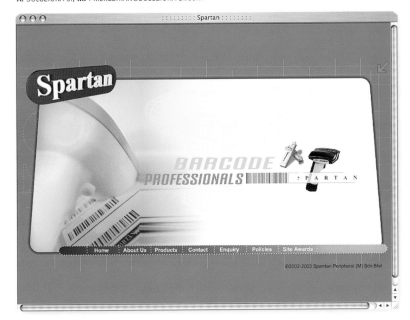

**WWW.SPARTAN.COM.MY**
**D:** YEVA CHOW LAI WAN
**M:** LW.CHOW@CARDOS.COM.MY

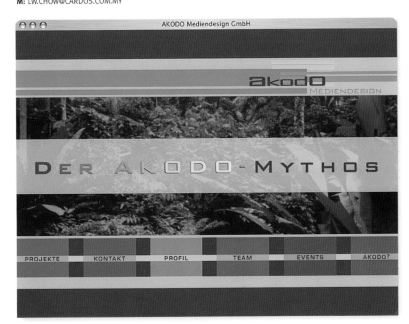

**WWW.AKODO.DE**
**D:** EVA RAST, **C:** INGO ILLBRUCK
**A:** AKODO MEDIENDESIGN GMBH, **M:** I.ILLBRUCK@AKODO.DE

WWW.CLP-POWERWISE.COM.HK
**D:** SHARON CHAN, **C:** SAMUEL CHENG, **P:** KELLY SZE
**A:** EUREKA DIGITAL, **M:** KELLY@EUREKA-DIGITAL.COM

WWW.KRONREIF.COM
**D:** KATE KRONREIF
**M:** KATE@CHELLO.AT

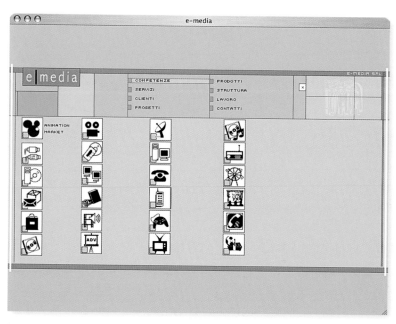

WWW.E-MEDIA.IT
**D:** CATERINA AGUECI
**A:** CATECF, **M:** CATE@MARKINO.NET

**WWW.ELRASILLO.COM**
**D:** GUILLERMO RIVILLAS SORIA
**A:** LEITMOTIV MEDIA S.L., **M:** INFO@LEITMOTIVMEDIA.COM

**WWW.SILENZIO.AT**
**D:** KATE KRONREIF, **C:** ANTONINA DIMITROVA
**M:** KATE@CHELLO.AT

**WWW.HARTPLASTIK.COM**
**D:** HARTPLASTIK
**A:** HARTPLASTIK, **M:** HOME@HARTPLASTIK.COM

# What Engineering Consultants do

**The engineering consultant**

Engineering consultancy services embrace more than purely technical advice and design. A technical proposal is the basis of each project to which a whole array of services are to be added. These services can be summarised in 7 points. He/she :

- advises on procurement and funding of projects
- assumes the tasks of both project and construction management;
- studies the feasibility of projects;
- conceives the design;
- executes the design in detail;
- procures contractors and suppliers;
- administers contracts and supervises construction and installation.

Engineering consultancy services are market or client driven. Clients increasingly require the full range of project related services from the consultancies, e.g. economic, legal, accountancy, financial and other ad hoc services. However, one should bear in mind that a well-engineered project can be improved by a sophisticated legal and financial framework, but clever financing can never make a badly designed project feasible.

Engineering consultancy and related services are by nature intellectual services and therefore intangible. That is why engineering consultants are not seen in the street scene whereas everyone will know the name of e.g. road maintenance companies or contractors who materialise the thinking behind a project.

**WWW.EFCA.BE/**
**D:** KAAT FLAMEY, **C:** KOEN KEMSEKE, **P:** VANDEN BROELE
**A:** VANDEN BROELE, **M:** JODY.DUYCKP@VANDENBROELE.BE

**WWW.TRIMAXMOWERS.COM/**
**D:** RONALD STALLMACH
**A:** TEXTUS DESIGN, **M:** INFO@TEXTUSDESIGN.CO.NZ

**SHANSHUI.DE**
**D:** CLAUDIA STEIN
**A:** CLAUDIA STEIN | DESIGN, **M:** INFO@CLAUDIA-STEIN-DESIGN.COM

**WWW.ASTROHILL.NET/**
**D:** ADRIN SHAMSUDIN
**A:** MINDPLAY STUDIOS, **M:** ADRIN@MINDPLAYSTUDIOS.COM

**WWW.GPTNET.COM**
**D:** CHILO RIVERO, **P:** MAÑANAMAS
**A:** GPT COMUNICACIONES, **M:** JAIMER10@HOTMAIL.COM

**WWW.PHOTON.LU**
**D:** TOM LUCAS
**M:** PHOTON@PHOTON.LU

WWW.ANYMO.COM/PORTFOLIO/SHOWCASE/NESTLE/
**D:** CHAN ADAM, CLAY
**A:** MULTI.D, **M:** ADAM@MULTID.COM.HK

WWW.ANYMO.COM
**D:** ADAM CHAN
**A:** MULTI.D, **M:** ADAM@MULTID.COM.HK

WWW.PEPPERMIND.DE
**D:** MARIA LUISA VALLEJO
**M:** ML.V@GMX.DE

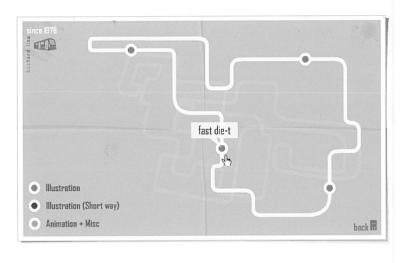

**WWW.MOOPORAMA.COM**
**D:** FRANCESCA MAGLIANI, **C:** FRANCESCA MAGLIANI / ROB ROOS
**A:** MOOPORAMA, **M:** MOOP@MOOPORAMA.COM

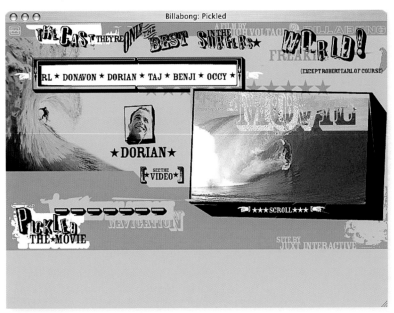

**WWW.PICKLED.TV**
**D:** TODD PURGASON, **C:** PHIL SCOTT, BRIAN DRAKE, JEFF KEYSER
**A:** JUXT INTERACTIVE, **M:** TODDHEAD@JUXTINTERACTIVE.COM

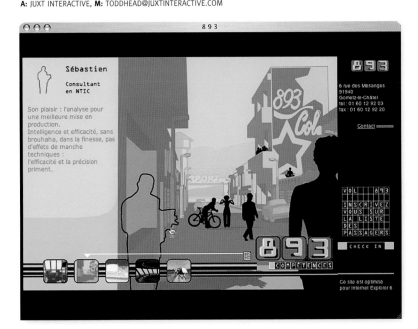

**WWW.893EXPERIENCE.COM**
**D:** 893
**A:** 893, **M:** CONTACT@893EXPERIENCE.COM

**WWW.JANAKIRSCHNER.COM**
**D:** PAVEL SUROVY, **C:** MARTIN KALIS, **P:** JOZKO SEBO
**A:** S-DESIGN, **M:** KALIS@NEXTRA.SK

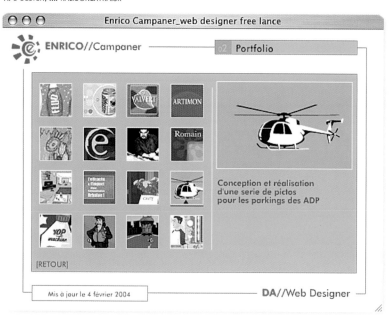

**WWW.ENRICOCAMPANER.IT**
**D:** ENRICO CAMPANER, **P:** CUBENET
**A:** IDE@WEB, **M:** ECAMPANER@HOTMAIL.COM

**WWW.MESCOLANZA.BIZ**
**D:** MARCO MARINI, **C:** STEFANO COSENTINO
**A:** MESCOLANZA, **M:** MARCO@MESCOLANZA.BIZ

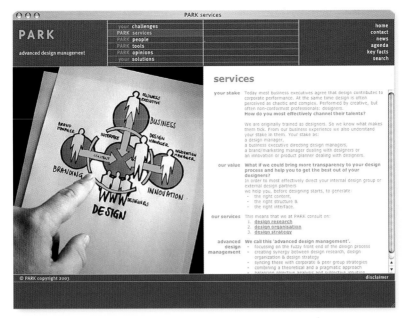

**WWW.PARK.BZ**
**D:** ELPHINSTONE, **C:** J. ROL
**A:** ELPHINSTONE, **M:** INFO@ELPHINSTONE.NL

**WWW.GEOCITIES.COM/ELMORO1979**
**D:** JORGE MORENO
**M:** ELMORO1979@HOTMAIL.COM

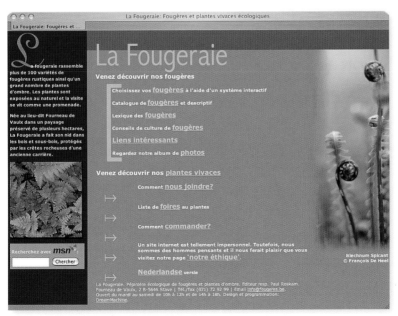

**WWW.FOUGERES.BE**
**D:** GERDA VAN DAMME, **C:** GUIDO JANSSENS
**A:** DREAMMACHINE, **M:** INFO@DREAMMACHINE.BE

**WWW.PORQUELAVIDAESAHORA.COM**
**D:** ERNESTO RINALDI, **C:** SABRINA EFLER, **P:** VISA
**A:** 451, **M:** JAVIER8M@HOTMAIL.COM

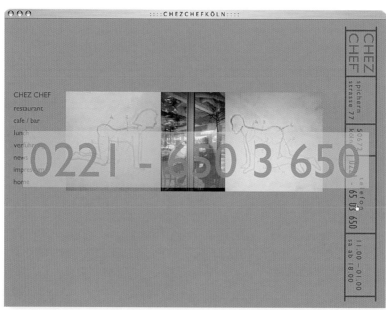

**WWW.CHEZ-CHEF.DE**
**D:** WALTER MÖSSLER
**A:** BAMBOO-PRODUKTION.COM, **M:** MAIL@TOUCHEE.DE

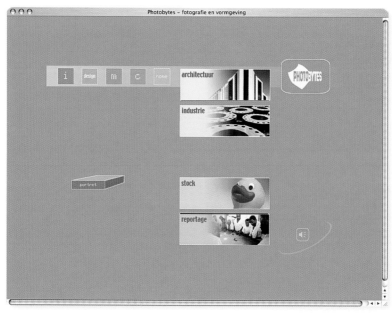

**WWW.PHOTOBYTES.BE**
**D:** ERWIN CLOETENS
**A:** PHOTOBYTES, **M:** INFO@PHOTOBYTES.BE

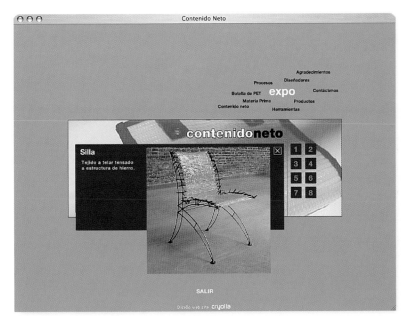

WWW.XK.COM.AR/CONTENIDONETO/
**D:** MARIANO GARCIA, **P:** MIKI FRIEDENBACH
**A:** CRYOLLA DISEÑO, **M:** MARIANOGARCIA@CRYOLLA.COM.AR

MASH.PE.KR
**D:** JEAHO.PARK
**M:** ACAC900@HANMAIL.NE

WWW.BACARDI.DE
**D:** KONSTANTIN MINSTER, **P:** WWW.ARGONAUTEN.DE
**M:** INFO@RUSSENTREFF.COM

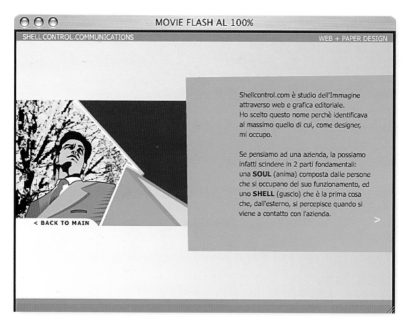

**WWW.SHELLCONTROL.COM**
**D:** LUCA ORLANDINI
**A:** SHELLCONTROL.COM, **M:** INFO@SHELLCONTROL.COM

**WWW.BODAMUSICA.COM**
**D:** JORGE ZUBIRIA TOLOSA, **P:** BODA MÚSICA
**M:** JORGE@ZUBIRIA.COM

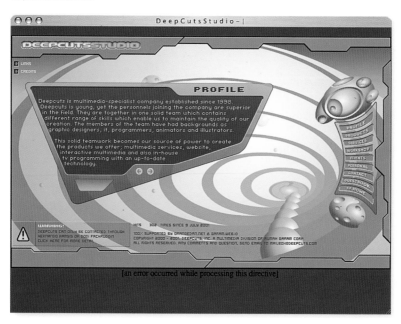

**DEEPCUTS.COM**
**D:** HERNANDO RAMSIS
**A:** NINA GALE, **M:** GALENINA@YAHOO.COM

**WWW.ARTEYPAISAJE.COM**
**D:** BORJA BELLOD, **P:** ARTE Y PAISAJE
**A:** IMAGEN CONSULTING, **M:** INFO@ARTEYPAISAJE.COM

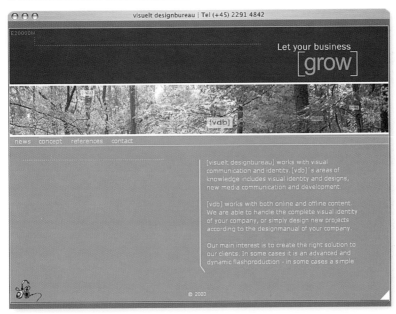

**WWW.VISUELT.DK**
**D:** THOMAS BRIXEN
**A:** ISUELT DESIGNBUREAU, **M:** BRIXEN@VISUELT.DK

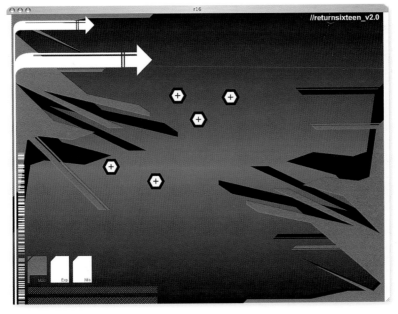

**WWW.RETURNSIXTEEN.COM**
**D:** ROBERTO STOCCO
**M:** INFO@RETURNSIXTEEN.COM

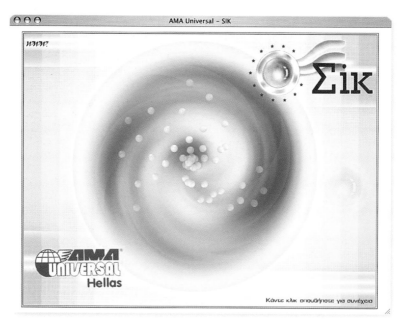

**WWW.AMA-CLEANING.GR**
**D:** STEFANOS STEFANIDIS
**A:** WEB RELATION DESIGN, **M:** INFO@E-INFO.GR

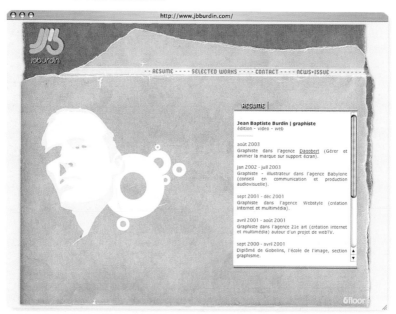

**WWW.JBBURDIN.COM**
**D:** JBBURDIN
**M:** JB@JBBURDIN.COM

**WWW.CAMPER.ES/WEB/EN/BASICA.ASP?FLSID=27**
**D:** LAURA CASTILLO, SERGIO SEGOVIA
**A:** SYNAPSIS DIGITAL, **M:** LAURA@SYNAPSISDIGITAL.COM

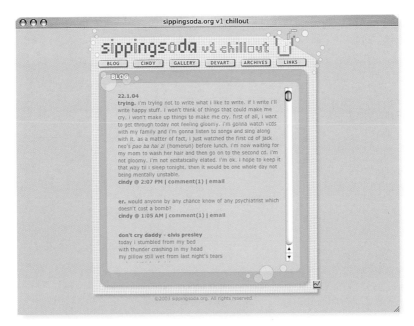

**SIPPINGSODA.ORG/**
**D:** CINDY KHOO
**A:** TAU-EW.COM, **M:** INDY@SIPPINGSODA.ORG

**WWW.AIRBAGCRAFTWORKS.COM**
**D:** LARS WOEHNING
**A:** V2A**NETFORCE**RUHR, **M:** LW@V2A.NEV

**WWW.TRANKILA.COM**
**D:** A-T-N, **C:** RNOZ
**A:** TRANKILA, **M:** TRANKILA@FREE.FR

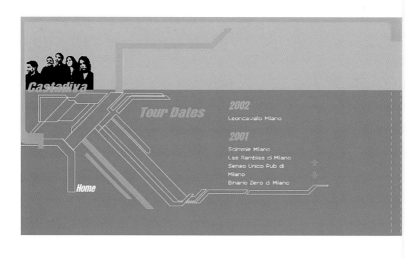

WWW.MISSION.NO
**D:** ALLE@MISSION
**A:** MISSION DESIGN AGENCY, **M:** EVA@MISSION.NO

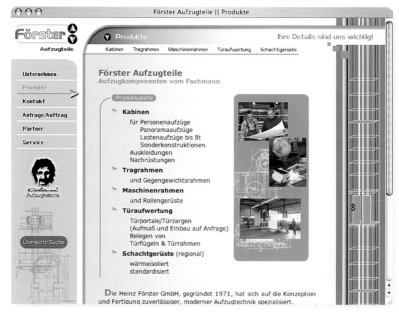

WWW.FOERSTER-AUFZUGTEILE.DE
**D:** BIRGIT VON DER WENSE, **C:** PATRICK WOLF
**A:** IN PUNCTO DESIGN, **M:** WOLF@INPUNCTODESIGN.DE

WWW.TRAVELADVISOR.GR
**D:** STEFANOS STEFANIDIS
**A:** WEB RELATION DESIGN, **M:** INFO@E-INFO.GR

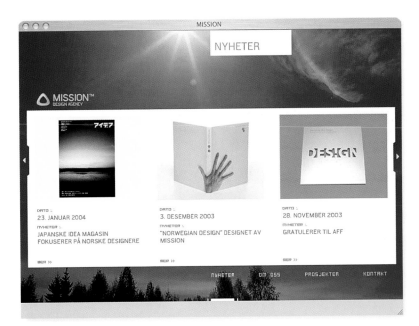

**WWW.MISSION.NO**
**D:** ALLE@MISSION
**A:** MISSION DESIGN AGENCY, **M:** EVA@MISSION.NO

**WWW.POCKETPM.IT**
**D:** ROBERTO AIELLO
**A:** NOTANGLE, **M:** JAMAI@TIN.IT

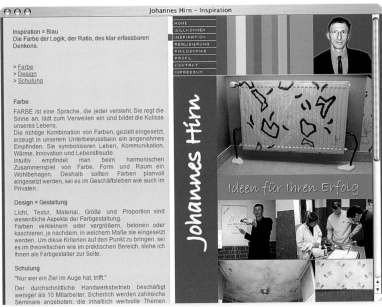

**WWW.DASHIRN.COM/**
**D:** ALEX KARBSTEIN
**A:** IKOFRA NEUE MEDIEN GMBH, **M:** INFO@IKOFRA.DE

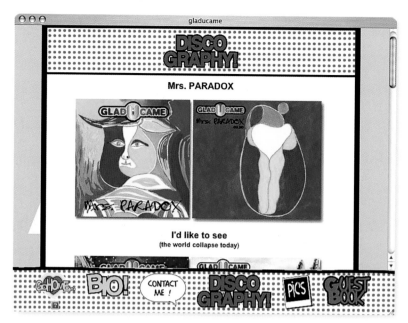

WWW.GLADUCAME.W3.TO
**D:** SVEN GODIJN, **C:** JAN BOLS
**A:** ENCOUNTERS MEDIASCIENCE, **M:** INFO@ENCOUNTERS.BE

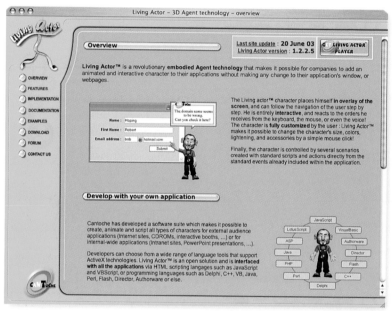

WWW.LIVINGACTOR.COM
**D:** JEAN-LUC CHEVALLIER
**A:** MDB INTERNET, **M:** JEANLUC.CHEVALLIER@MDBINFORMATIQUE.NET

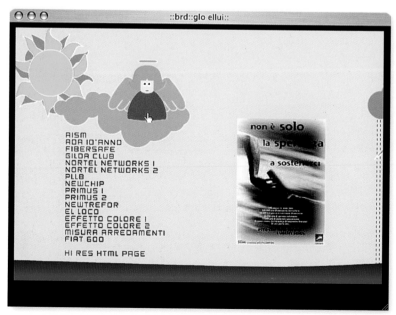

WWW.RASPADESIGN.IT/GLO.HTML
**D:** RASPAGLIESI GIULIO
**A:** BYRASPADESIGN, **M:** HAIR@RASPADESIGN.IT

**WWW.TEOTATO.COM**
**D:** ALESSANDRA TAGLIABUE
**A:** PHASEZERO.DE, **M:** ALESSANDRA@PHASEZERO.DE

**WWW.ASPAL.IT**
**P:** ILARIA BOZ
**M:** ILA74@LIBERO.IT

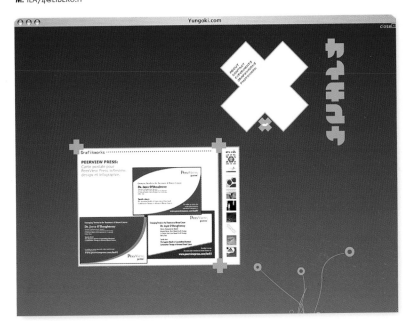

**WWW.YUNGOKI.COM**
**D:** DANY KWINTNER
**A:** YUNGOKI DOT COM, **M:** DANY@YUNGOKI.COM

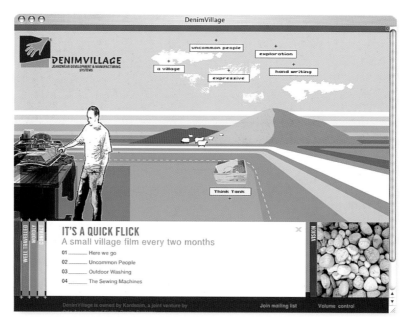

**WWW.DENIMVILLAGE.COM**
**D:** GÜL GÜRDAMAR, **C:** OYGAR ERDAL, **P:** CA©£LAR AKP NAR, ASL AK N,
**A:** MAKEFRESHMEDIA, **M:** BURAKA@MAKEFRESHMEDIA.COM

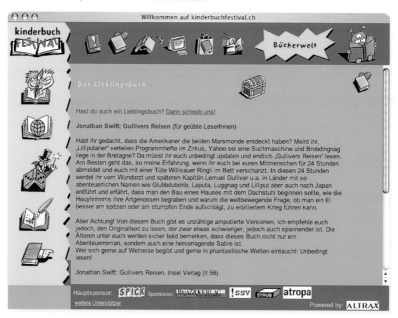

**WWW.KINDERBUCHFESTIVAL.CH**
**D:** ROBERT MASSE
**A:** SP-MULTIMEDIA, **M:** INFO@SP-MULTIMEDIA.CH

**WWW.THE-MCCORMICKS.DE**
**D:** F. DIEDERICH
**M:** SALAMI@UNI-MUENSTER.DE

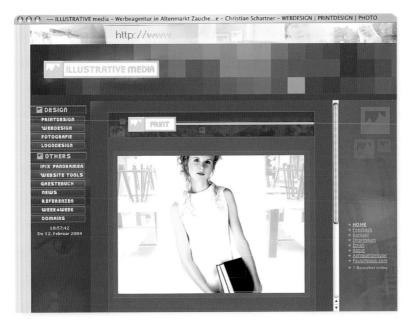

**WWW.ILLUSTRATIVE.AT**
**D:** CHRISTIAN SCHARTNER
**A:** ILLUSTRATIVE MEDIA, **M:** INFO@ILLUSTRATIVE.AT

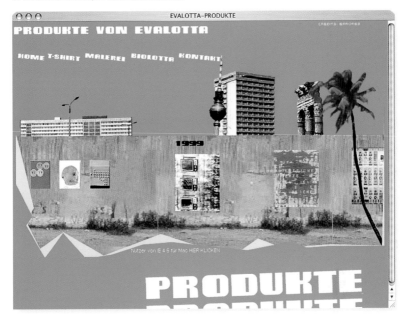

**WWW.EVALOTTA-PRODUKTE.DE**
**D:** LIDA PERIN
**M:** LIDA@ERROR65.NET

**WWW.KILLERLOOP.COM**
**D:** JIM MORGAN, **P:** RICCARDO ZAMURRI
**A:** DEEPEND ROMA

**WWW.MATERIO.COM**
**D:** AMY KILLOREN CLARK, **C:** KOHEI NAGANUMA; GABRIEL LEROY
**A:** CLARK&CLARK, **M:** CLARK@MONDORONDO.COM

**WWW.AMWEB.IT**
**D:** MARCO BOLLETTINI, **C:** AMERICO TRAINI
**A:** ARCHIMEDIA SNC, **M:** STAFF@AMWEB.IT

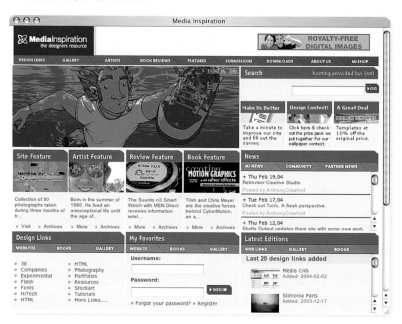

**WWW.MEDIAINSPIRATION.COM**
**D:** PHIL DE PAULIS
**A:** MEDIA INSPIRATION, **M:** PHIL@MEDIAINSPIRATION.COM

**WWW.BENFRANKDESIGN.COM**
**D:** BENFRANK
**A:** BENFRANK{DESIGN}, **M:** BENFRANK@BENFRANKDESIGN.COM

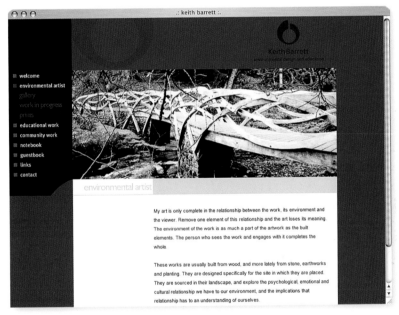

**WWW.KEITHBARRETT.CO.UK**
**D:** ONEBESTWAY, **C:** PHELIM CAVLAN, **P:** JUSTIN COCKBURN
**A:** ONEBESTWAY, **M:** MIKE@ONEBESTWAY.COM

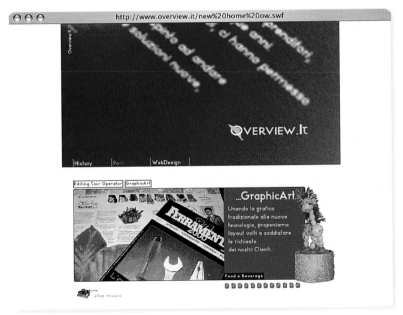

**WWW.OVERVIEW.IT**
**D:** GIANLUCA RECALCAT
**A:** MAGNETIKA DI GIANLUCA RECALCATI, **M:** GREKA@MAGNETIKA.IT

**WWW.DATAXPERT.DE**
**D:** KAI GREIM, **P:** ANDREAS KÜRSCHNER
**A:** GRAFIKAI, **M:** INFO@GRAFIKAI.DE

**WWW.JP-GONTHIER.NET**
**D:** IVAN LAMMERANT
**A:** LAMMERANT.NET, **M:** IVAN@LAMMERANT.NET

**WWW.EUROWIND.COM**
**D:** SAM SOHLBER
**A:** LÖNEGÅRD, **M:** SAM@LONEGARD.SE

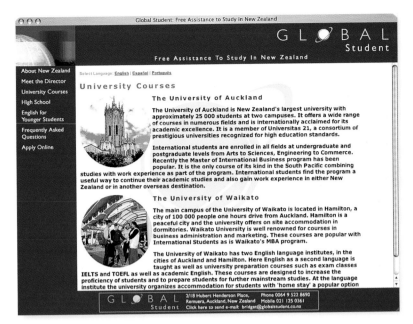

**WWW.GLOBALSTUDENT.CO.NZ/**
**D:** RONALD STALLMACH
**A:** TEXTUS DESIGN, **M:** INFO@TEXTUSDESIGN.CO.NZ

**WWW.IMPRODEX.COM**
**D:** JAVIER DONOSO
**A:** IMPRODEX S.L., **M:** JDONOSO@IMPRODEX.COM

**WWW.CANON.DE/EOS300**
**D:** OMECZEK / ENSSLIN, **C:** WAGNER / SCHUETZE
**A:** TWMD GMBH, **M:** MT@TWMD.DE

**WWW.STUDIOCMD.COM**
**D:** J CHESEBROUGH
**A:** STUDIO:CMD [ACTIVEMEDIA], **M:** INFO@STUDIOCMD.COM

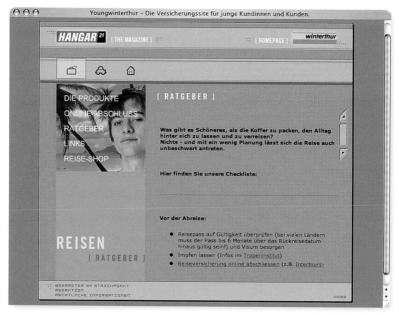

**WWW.YOUNGWINTERTHUR.CH**
**D:** METELSKI, **C:** LANDOLT
**A:** STRICHPUNKT GMBH, **M:** LANDOLT@STRICHPUNKT.CH

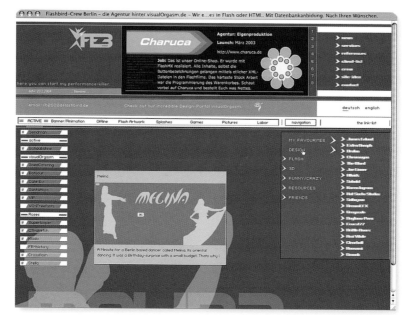

**WWW.FLASHBIRD.DE**
**D:** MATIAS ROSKOS
**M:** WEBDESIGNINDEX@FLASHBIRD.DE

**WWW.LILITHWORLD.COM**
**D:** NICOLA CAPPELLETTI
**A:** APOSTROPHE, **M:** N.CAPPELLETTI@APOSTROPHE.IT

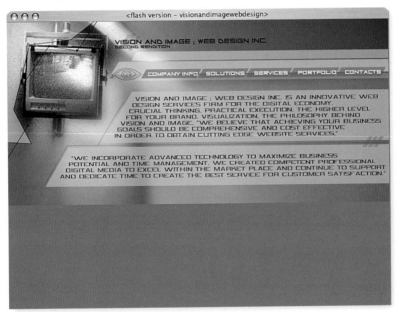

**WWW.VISIONANDIMAGE.COM**
**D:** YAP FREDERICK, **P:** RIO ALFORTE
**A:** VISION AND IMAGE WEB DESIGN INC, **M:** EYAPPERS@VISIONANDIMAGE.COM

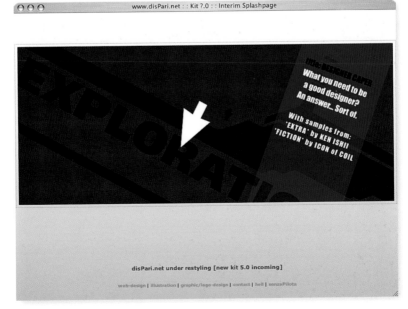

**WWW.DISPARI.NET**
**D:** DANILO MORETT
**A:** DISPARI.NET, **M:** PARI@DISPARI.NET

**WWW.EURONOLEGGI.IT**
**D:** GIUDICI LUCA
**A:** INTENSO.IT, **M:** INFO@INTENSO.IT

**WWW.HYPERIONBLU.COM**
**D:** STANLEY COLOMA
**A:** CREATIVE SYNERGY INC., **M:** STANLEY@CREATIVE-SYNERGY.COM

**WWW.THEDIGITALVISUALIST.COM**
**D:** DAN
**A:** CYBER SOLUTIONS, **M:** DAN@DANHARPER.COM

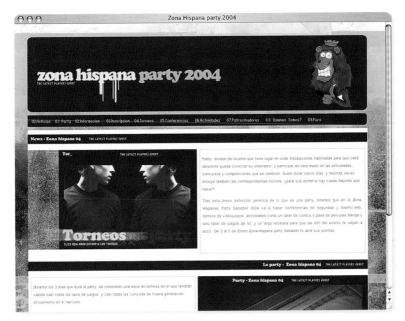

**WWW.ZONA-HISPANA.COM/PARTY**
**D:** KIKE BESADA FERNANDEZ
**A:** DESIGNERSLIFE*, **M:** KIKE@DESIGNERSLIFE.COM

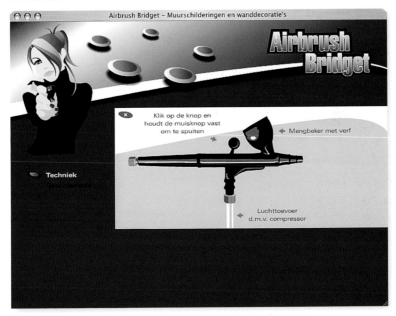

**WWW.AIRBRUSH-BRIDGET.NL**
**D:** DEBBY VAN DONGEN
**A:** CONK, **M:** INFO@CONK.NL

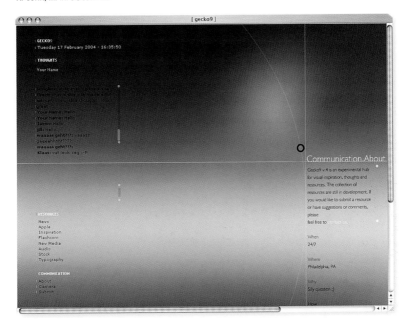

**WWW.GECKO9.COM**
**D:** JON MONTENEGRO
**A:** VARIOUSWAYS, **M:** JONM@VARIOUSWAYS.COM)

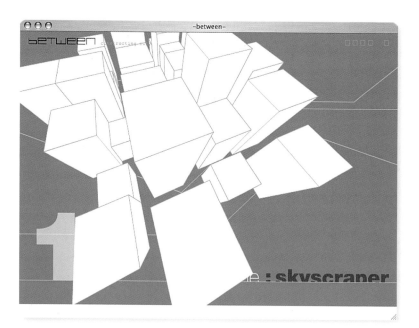

WWW.BETWEENDESIGN.COM
**D:** STANLEY LEUNG
**A:** -BETWEEN-, **M:** STANLEY@BETWEENDESIGN.COM

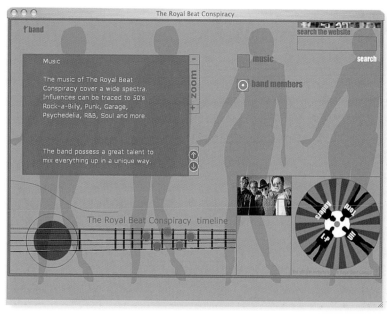

WWW.TRBC.DK
**D:** ANNE HAASTRUP HANSEN
**A:** DOLPHIN_DESIGN, **M:** DOLPHIN@OFIR.DK

WWW.GIANKY.COM
**D:** DAVIDE BIANCHINI
**M:** GIANKY@GIANKY.COM

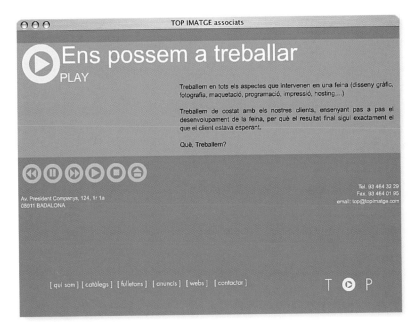

**WWW.TOPIMATGE.COM**
**D:** RAMON LLIBRE, **C:** LAMPROSSMEDIA
**A:** TOP IMATGE, **M:** TOP@TOPIMATGE.COM

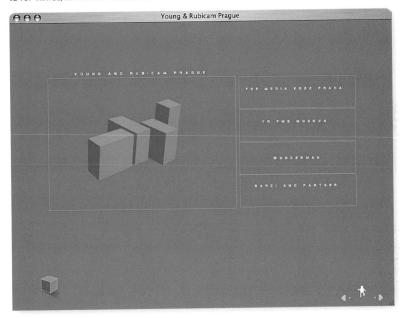

**WWW.YOUNG-RUBICAM.CZ**
**D:** MICHAEL CERVENKA, **C:** VACLAV KARGER
**A:** NE, **M:** VACLAV.KARGER@NE.CZ

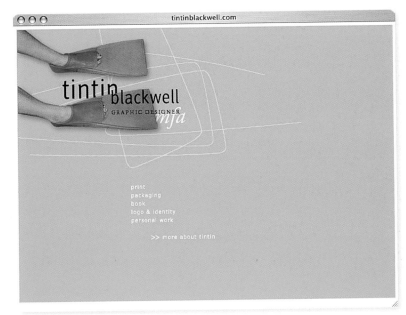

**WWW.TINTINBLACKWELL.COM**
**D:** TINTIN BLACKWELL, **C:** MARTIN LIDGARD
**A:** BLACKWELL'S STUDIO, **M:** TINTIN@TINTINBLACKWELL.COM

**PURETOUCH.NL**
**D:** JORIS MARJA
**A:** ID-LAB, **M:** JORIS@ID-LAB.N

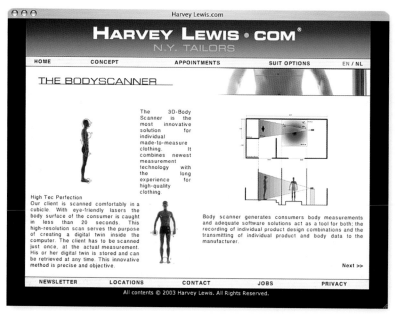

**WWW.POSSEN.COM**
**D:** BRET VLAZNY, **C:** TOMA CORCOTI
**A:** POSSEN.COM, **M:** BRET.VLAZNY@POSSEN.COM

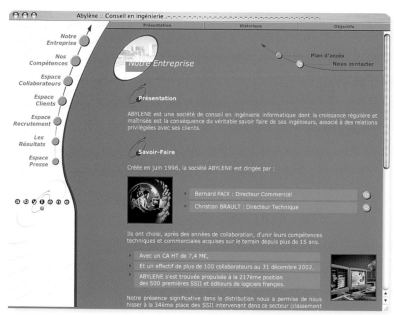

**WWW.ABYLENE.FR**
**D:** JEAN-LUC CHEVALLIER
**A:** MDB INFORMATIQUE, **M:** JEANLUC.CHEVALLIER@MDBINFORMATIQUE.NET

**WWW.MERC-BARCELONA.COM**
**D:** JORDI ORDÓÑEZ
**A:** BOSS-SOUNDS.ORG, **M:** GIORGIO@BOSS-SOUNDS.ORG

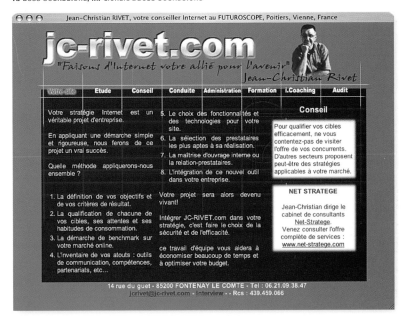

**WWW.JC-RIVET.COM**
**D:** JEAN-CHRISTIAN RIVET
**A:** NET-STRATEGE, **M:** JCRIVET@JC-RIVET.COM

**WWW.CELLA.IT**
**D:** ILARIA BOZ
**A:** VILLAGE S.R.L., **M:** IBOZ@VILLAGE.IT

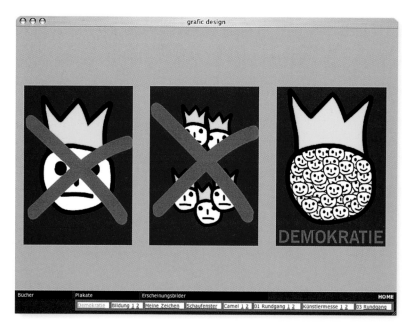

**WWW.BIRGIT-SCHMIDT.DE**
**D:** BIRGIT SCHMIDT
**M:** BSCHMIDT@TECO.EDU

**WWW.TEKISMSTUDIOS.COM**
**D:** BRIAN PULLIESE
**A:** TEKISM STUDIOS, **M:** BRIANP@TEKISMSTUDIOS.COM

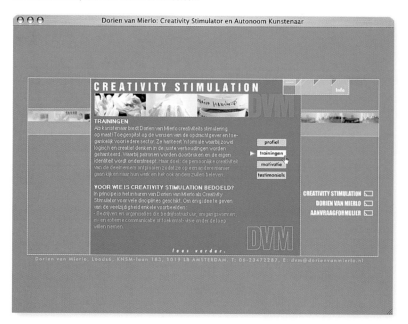

**WWW.DORIENVANMIERLO.NL**
**D:** ERWIN VD KRAAN, **P:** BIE KHO
**A:** SITE DIVISION, **M:** BIE@SITE-DIVISION.COM

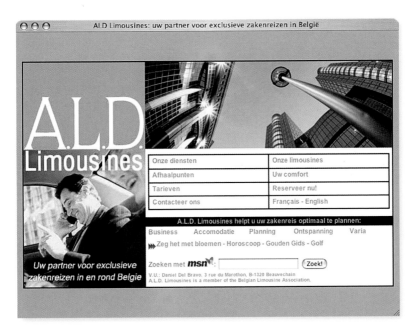

**WWW.ALDLIMOUSINES.COM**
**D:** GERDA VAN DAMME, **C:** GUIDO JANSSENS
**A:** DREAMMACHINE, **M:** INFO@DREAMMACHINE.BE

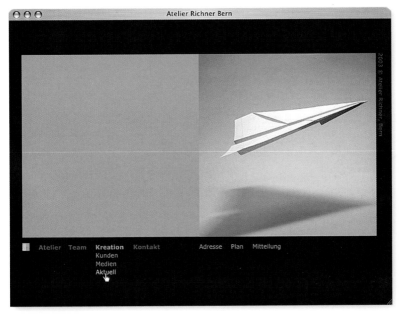

**WWW.ATELIERRICHNER.CH**
**D:** THOMAS RICHNER, **C:** MICHAEL BÄHNI, **P:** ATELIER RICHNER
**A:** APPROX. MEDIA, **M:** BAEHNI@APPROX.CH

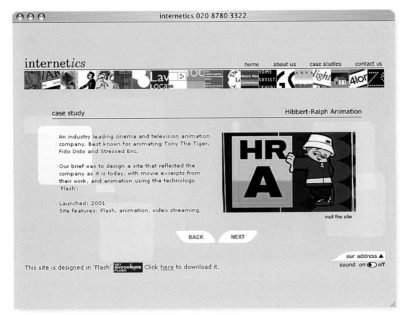

**WWW.INTERNETICS.CO.UK**
**D:** RUSS RASHID, **P:** CLIVE FRANCE
**A:** INTERNETICS, **M:** CHRIS@INTERNETICS.CO.UK

**WWW.CULTURA-CANTABRIA.ORG**
**D:** JORIS ORTUNO, **C:** JUAN MANUEL MOROTE, **P:** GLORIA GARCIA
**A:** IFIGENIA PLUS, **M:** JORTUNO@IFIGENIA.ES

**WWW.GRIZOO.NET**
**D:** MIRKO GRISENDI
**A:** GRIZOO.DESIGN, **M:** INFO@GRIZOO.NET

**WWW.ADVENSA.COM**
**D:** ALEX LEONOVA, **C:** VITALIY LEONOV
**A:** ADVENSA, **M:** INFO@ADVENSA.COM

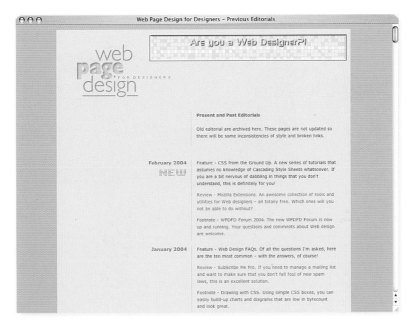

**WWW.WPDFD.COM**
**D:** JOE GILLESPIE
**A:** PIXEL PRODUCTIONS, **M:** JOE@PIXELP.CO.UK

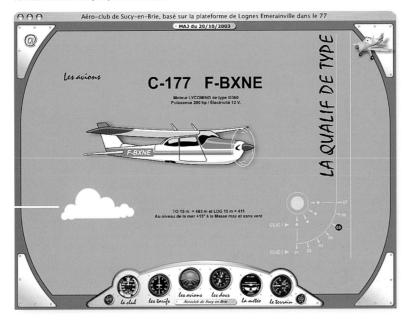

**WWW.AEROSUCY.ORG**
**D:** JEAN-LUC CHEVALLIER
**A:** MDB INFORMATIQUE, **M:** JEANLUC.CHEVALLIER@MDBINFORMATIQUE.NET

**WWW.XENEME.COM**
**D:** DESOÑOS
**A:** DESOÑOS, **M:** MULTIMEDIA@DESONHOS.NET

**WWW.BIWIS.COM**
**D:** ALEX CRECENDA, **P:** ADALBERTO FLORES MEDELLIN
**A:** CRECENDA FOUNDATION, **M:** AFMGF@BIWIS.COM

**WWW.EURO2000.NET**
**D:** MORELLI LUCA
**A:** IPERBOREO, **M:** HANGINGARDEN@INWIND.IT

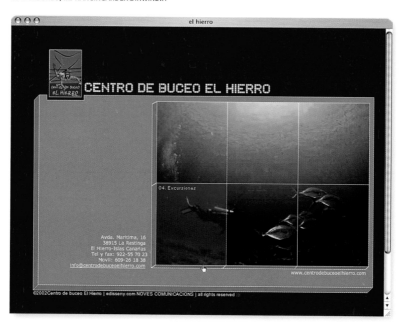

**WWW.CENTRODEBUCEOELHIERRO.COM**
**D:** EMILIO GARCIA VAZ
**A:** EDISSENY.COM*NOVESCOMUNICACIONS, **M:** INFO@EDISSENY.COM

**WWW.ATOMABOOKSHOP.BE/INDEX.HTML**
**D:** GERDA VAN DAMME, **C:** GUIDO JANSSENS
**A:** DREAMMACHINE, **M:** INFO@DREAMMACHINE.BE

**WWW.CERESBEER.COM**
**D:** DANILO ROLLE, **C:** PAOLO CASTELLI
**A:** DARTWAY, **M:** DROLLE@DARTWAY.COM

**WWW.GIVEMETHE5.COM**
**D:** FERNANDO MOSTACERO SERRA
**M:** MAKA_INA@HOTMAIL.COM

**WWW.THEA-WEIRES.DE**
**D:** RENÉ MARTIN, **C:** PETER GIERTZ, **P:** THEA WEIRES
**A:** VS.42, **M:** RECEPTION@VS42.COM

**WWW.STRATEGA.NL**
**D:** LEO HAMERS
**A:** YAIKZ!, **M:** INFO@YAIKZ.NL

**WWW.TYPE-O-GRAPHICS.DE**
**D:** ALEX SCHWARZ
**A:** TYPE-O-GRAPHICS, **M:** TYPE-O-GRAPHICS@T-ONLINE.DE

266

**Design**

**W**at is design? Tijdloze klasse; dat is design. Maar wat dan tijdloze klasse is, daarover kun je natuurlijk weer van mening verschillen. Over de klasse is iedereen het wel zo'n beetje eens. De chaise-longue van Le Corbusier: dat is design. Geen twijfel mogelijk. De Rietveld-stoel: idem dito met een sterretje. Maar ook recenter werk, van bijv. Minotti, Montis en Giorgetti, heeft de 'eeuwigheidswaarde' die je van design mag verwachten. En oh ja, niet te vergeten: de nieuw verpakte jaren 60 en 70 modellen van Moroso, Fritz Hansen en Artifort. Zo kun je nog wel even doorgaan, op de design afdeling van Sijben...

<< Terug

**WWW.SIJBEN.NL**
**D:** COBWEB WEBDESIGN
**A:** COBWEB WEBDESIGN, **M:** WEBDESIGN@COBWEB.NL

**WWW.KIFI.BE**
**D:** NOVIO
**M:** HANS_VANDEVELDE@YAHOO.COM

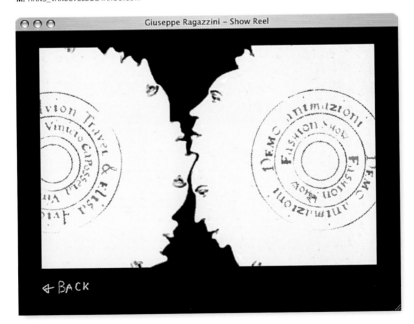

**WWW.GIUSEPPERAGAZZINI.IT/SHOW.HTM**
**D:** GIUSEPPE RAGAZZINI, **C:** PAOLO MANCINI
**A:** STUDIO RAGAZZINI, **M:** GIUSEPPERAGAZZINI@VIRGILIO.IT

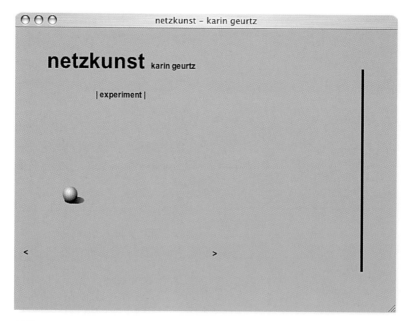

**WWW.KARINGEURTZ.DE**
**D:** TOBIAS HERRMANN
**A:** HTMWEB.DE, **M:** TOBIAS@ARTOBI.DE

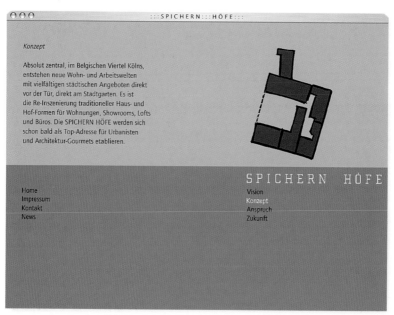

**WWW.SPICHERN-HOEFE.DE**
**D:** MÖSSLER
**A:** TOUCHEE, **M:** INFO@TOUCHEE.DE

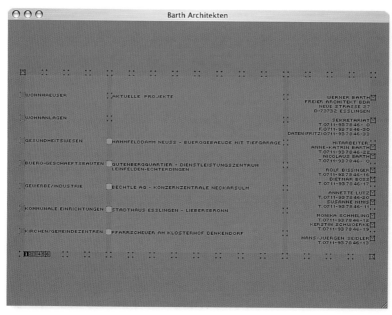

**WWW.BARTH-ARCHITEKTEN.COM**
**D:** HEINZ WITTHOEFT, **C:** [D-MIND] FUCHS/WEISS GBR, **P:** BARTH ARCHITEKTEN
**A:** ARCHITEKTURTAILE, **M:** HEINZ.WITTHOEFT@STATIONIST.COM

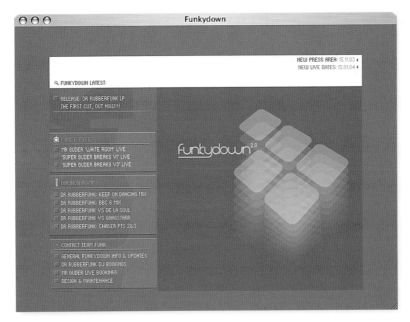

**WWW.FUNKYDOWN.CO.UK**
**D:** JIM MORGAN, **C:** NICK LAND, **P:** SIMON WARD
**A:** ACROYEAR DESIGN PROJECTS, **M:** INFO@FUNKYDOWN.CO.UK

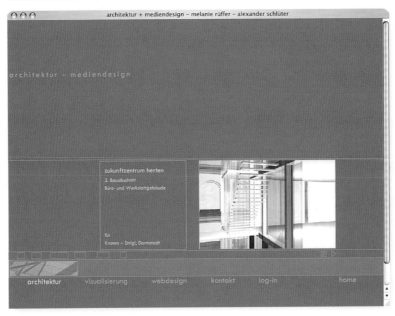

**WWW.ARCHITEKTUR-MEDIENDESIGN.DE**
**A:** WESTWERK-ARCHITEKTEN
**M:** INFO@ARCHITEKTUR-MEDIENDESIGN.DE

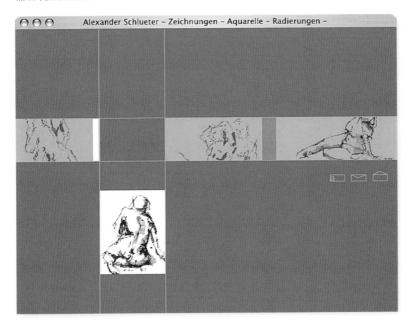

**WWW.ALEXANDERSCHLUETER.DE**
**D:** WESTWERK-ARCHITEKTEN
**A:** WESTWERK-ARCHITEKTEN, **M:** MAIL@ALEXANDERSCHLUETER.DE

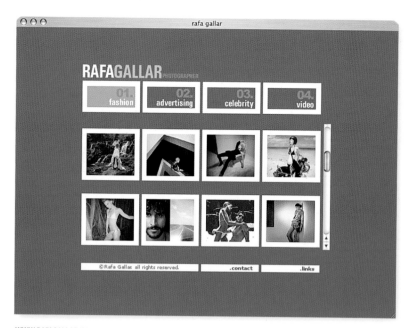

**WWW.RAFAGALLAR.COM**
**D:** SUSANA PÉREZ BERMEJO, **C:** EMILIANO BENÍTEZ
**M:** SPBERMEJO@YA.COM

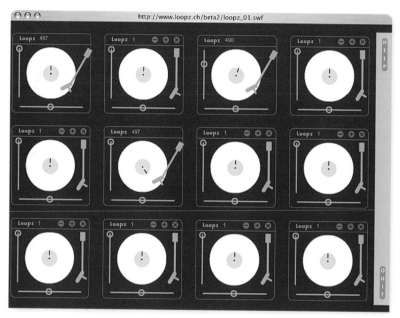

**WWW.LOOPZ.CH**
**D:** BATCHAS
**A:** SP-MULTIMEDIA, **M:** INFO@SP-MULTIMEDIA.CH

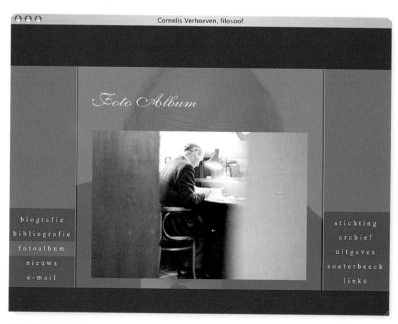

**WWW.CORNELISVERHOEVEN.NL**
**D:** LEO HAMERS
**A:** YAIKZ!, **M:** INFO@YAIKZ.NL

**WWW.CEROUNO.COM.AR**
**D:** BRUNO COPPOLA, **C:** SERGIO CIARAVINBO, **P:** PABLO CAROU
**A:** CEROUNO, **M:** PABLO@CEROUNO.COPM.AR

**WWW.RUSTBOY.COM**

**WWW.JANKNOFF.DE**
**D:** WOLFGANG KOHLERT, JAN KNOFF, **C:** WOLFGANG KOHLERT
**M:** SUSANNE.THIEMANN@KOELN.DE

**WWW.PAGONGSKI.COM**
**D:** MIGUEL VAZ
**A:** PÉS NEGROS, **M:** ME@PAGONGSKI.COM

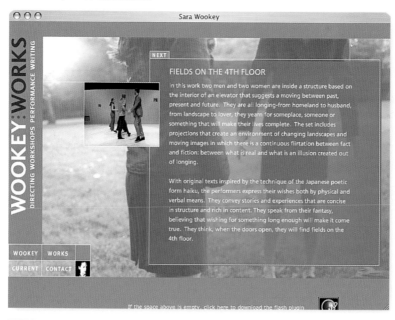

**WWW.SARAWOOKEY.COM**
**D:** ELLE LEPOUTRE

**WWW.MRP-STUDIO.DE**
**D:** MICHAEL RENNER
**A:** MRP-STUDIO, **M:** INFO@MRP-STUDO.DE

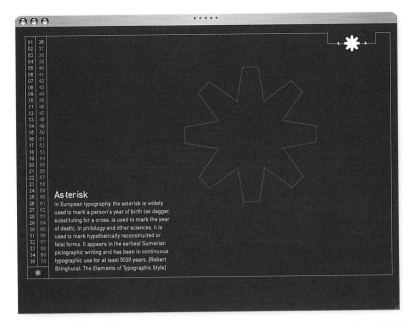

**WWW.JHWD.COM/ASTERISK/**
**D:** WILLIAM DRENTTEL / JEFFERY TYSON, **P:** COOPER-HEWITT NATIONAL DESIGN MUSEUM
**A:** HELFANDDRENTTEL STUDIO, **M:** WILLIAM@JHWD.COM

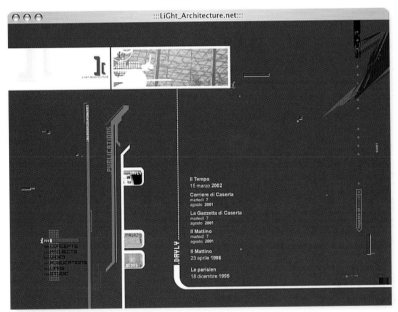

**WWW.RANAULO.COM**
**D:** STEFANO PEDRETTI
**A:** PULP, **M:** INFO@PULPIT.IT

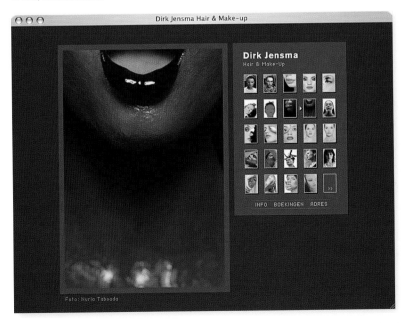

**WWW.JENSMA.NET**
**D:** YACCO VIJN
**A:** SKIPINTRO, **M:** INFO@SKIPINTRO.NL

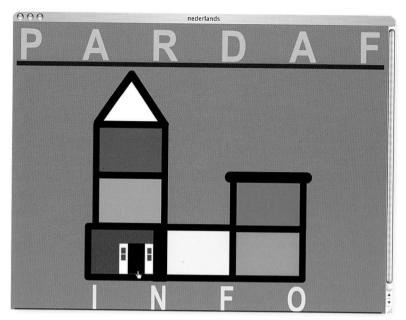

**WWW.PARDAF.BE**
**D:** NES
**A:** PINKER, **M:** INFO@PINKER.BE

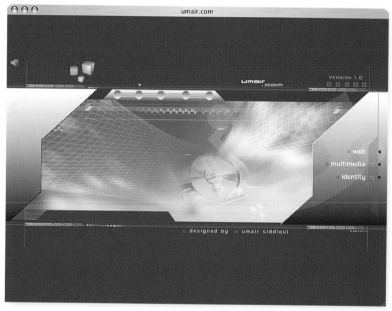

**WWW.UMAIR.COM**
**D:** UMAIR
**A:** UMAIR.COM, **M:** UMAIR@UMAIR.COM

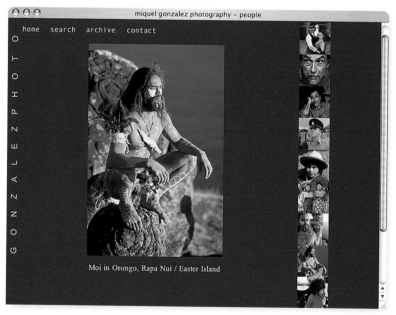

**WWW.GONZALEZPHOTO.COM**
**D:** MIQUEL GONZALEZ
**A:** GONZALEZPHOTO, **M:** MAIL@GONZALEZPHOTO.COM

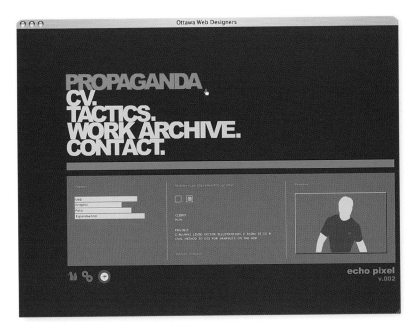

**WWW.ECHOPIXEL.NET**
**D:** DEREK MOROZ
**A:** ECHO PIXEL, **M:** RECOGNITION@ECHOPIXEL.NET

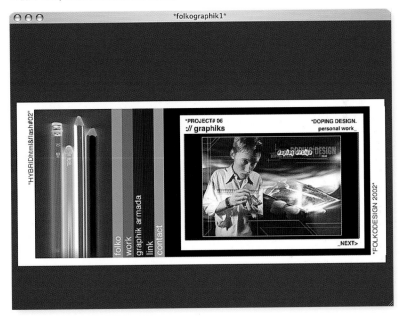

**WWW.FOLKODESIGN.COM**
**D:** FOLKO
**A:** *FOLKODESIGN*, **M:** FOLKO@LIBERO.IT

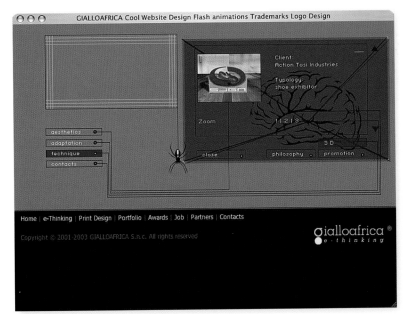

**WWW.GIALLOAFRICA.COM**
**D:** RICCI LORENZO
**A:** GIALLOAFRICA, **M:** INFO@GIALLOAFRICA.COM

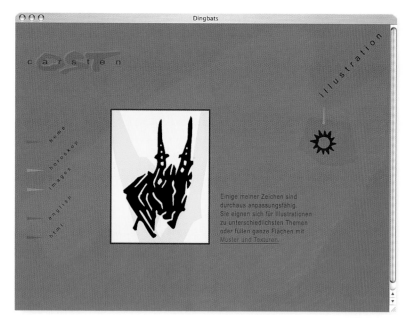

WWW.OSTSIGNS.DE
**D:** KARIN GEURTZ
**A:** CARSTEN OST, **M:** KARIN.GEURTZ@T-ONLINE.DE

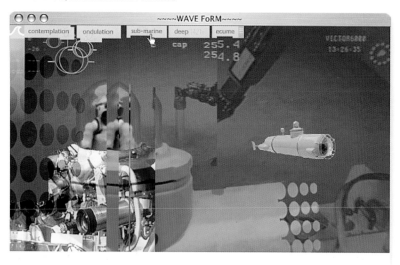

WAVEFORM001.FREE.FR
**D:** FRÉDÉRIC BONTEMPS
**M:** FRED_BONTEMPS@HOTMAIL.COM

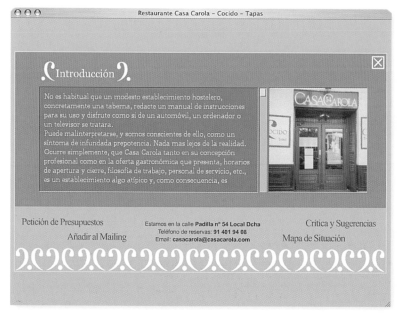

WWW.CASACAROLA.COM
**D:** CHILO RIVERO, **C:** JAIME RIVERO, **P:** CASA CAROLA
**A:** MAÑANAMAS, **M:** PROGRAMACION@M-MAS.COM

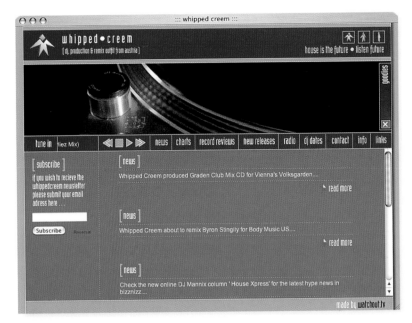

**WWW.WHIPPEDCREEM.COM**
**D:** ROBERT ONDROVICS
**A:** WATCHOUT, **M:** R.ONDROVICS@VIENNA.AT

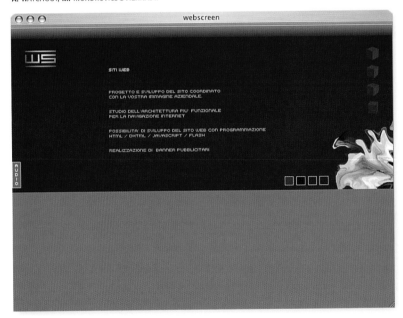

**WWW.WEBSCREEN.IT**
**D:** LEONARDO MARÈ, **C:** LEONARDO MARÈ
**M:** INFO@WEBSCREEN.IT

**WWW.DRESSFORSUCCESS.NL**
**D:** BIRGIT VAN DEN BEEMT, **C:** DUTCHWEB, **P:** BLAASJE
**A:** BLAASJEDOTCOM, **M:** PETER@DRESSFORSUCCESS.NL

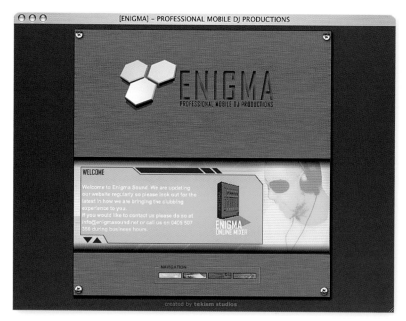

**WWW.ENIGMASOUND.NET**
**D:** BRIAN PULLIESE
**A:** TEKISM STUDIOS, **M:** BRIANP@TEKISMSTUDIOS.COM

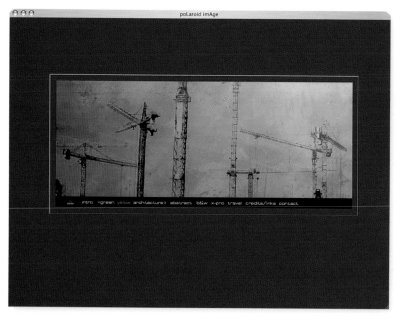

**POLAROIDIMAGE.COM**
**D:** LILLI N, **C:** YOSHI
**A:** LAMBIANCE-DESIGN, **M:** DANIEL_SHP@HOTMAIL.COM

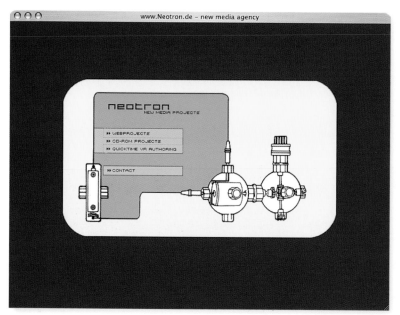

**WWW.NEOTRON.DE**
**D:** MICHAEL ZALEWSKI, **P:** NEOTRON
**A:** NEOTRON, **M:** INFO@NEOTRON.DE

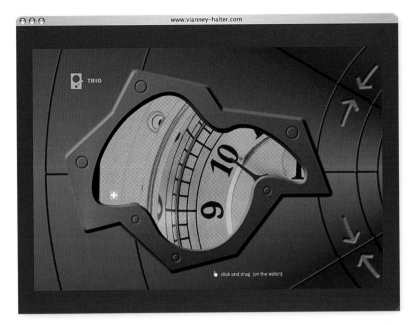

**WWW.VIANNEY-HALTER.COM**
**D:** RICHARD BIREN, **P:** VIANNEY HALTER
**M:** BIREN@ONLINE.FR

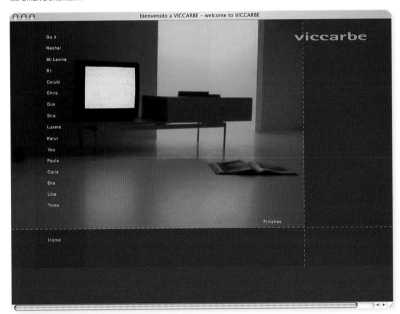

**WWW.VICCARBE.COM**
**D:** HÉCTOR DIEGO, **P:** VICCARBE HABITAT
**A:** HÉCTOR DIEGO PROJECTS, **M:** VICCARBE@VICCARBE.COM

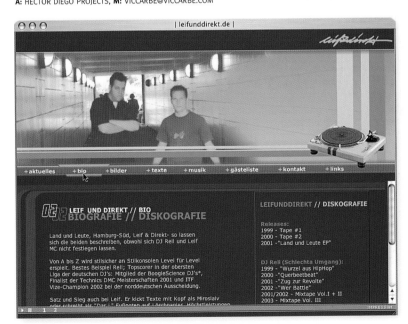

**WWW.LEIFUNDDIREKT.DE**
**D:** BENJAMIN WEISS
**A:** WEITIROOM, **M:** BENJAMIN@OST-KOMBINAT.DE

**JULIEN.MOULIN.FREE.FR**
**D:** JULIEN MOULIN
**M:** JULIEN.MOULIN@NOOS.FR

**WWW.LATINDOT.COM**
**D:** ENRIQUE BUSTIOS, **C:** PABLO SALCEDO, **P:** LATIN DOTCOM
**A:** LATIN DOTCOM, **M:** ASANMARTIN@LATINDOT.COM

**WWW.DARKELEPHANT.COM**
**D:** MELVIN DE LOS SANTOS
**A:** DARKELEPHANT, **M:** BABAR@DARKELEPHANT.COM

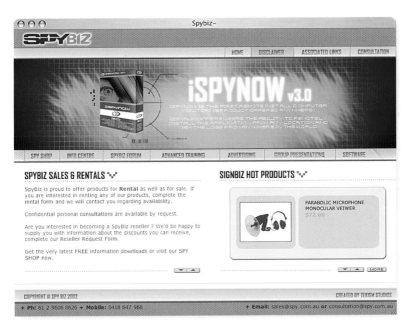

**WWW.SPY.COM.AU**
**D:** BRIAN PULLIESE
**A:** TEKISM STUDIOS, **M:** BRIANP@TEKISMSTUDIOS.COM

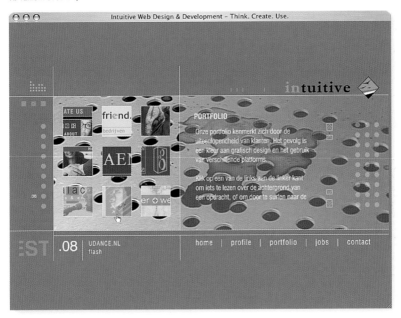

**WWW.INTUITIVE.NL**
**D:** D. ZUIJDERLAND, **P:** B. VAN DE VOORT
**A:** ::INTUITIVE, **M:** DAAN@INTUITIVE.NL

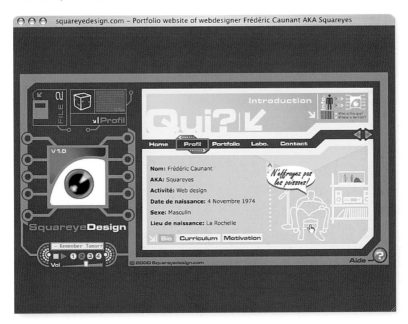

**WWW.SQUAREYEDESIGN.COM**
**D:** FRÉDÉRIC CAUNANT
**M:** CONTACT@SQUAREYEDESIGN.COM

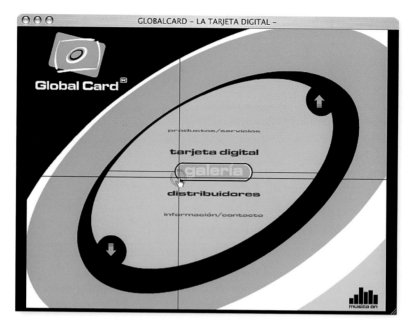

**WWW.GLOBALCARD.NET**
**D:** MIKEL BENITO
**A:** XARELAN, **M:** MIKEL.BENITO@TELELINE.ES

**WWW.E-SIENA.NET**
**D:** CAVAGNA ALESSIA, **C:** BECATTI FABRIZIO
**A:** MULTYMEDIA

**WWW.SERVAL.ES**
**D:** RICHARD TALUT
**A:** ESTUDIO ANA MORENO, **M:** RICHARD@ESTUDIOAM.NET

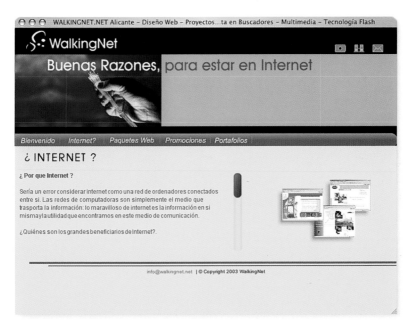

**WWW.WALKINGNET.COM**
**D:** ESLAVA VEZA
**A:** WALKINGNET, **M:** JUANC.ESLAVA@WALKINGNET.NET

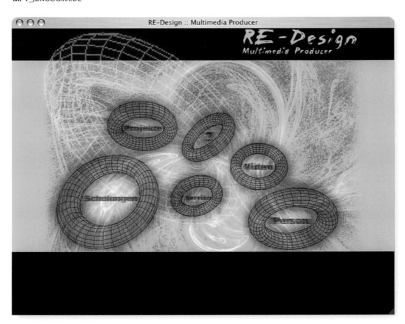

**WWW.BRITZONE.DE**
**D:** VERENA JUNG
**M:** V_JUNG@GMX.DE

**WWW.RE-DESIGN.DE**
**D:** ENRICO REINSDORF
**A:** RE-DESIGN, **M:** ENRICO@RE-DESIGN.DE

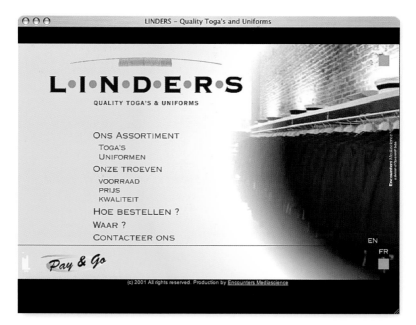

**WWW.LINDERSBRUSSELS.BE**
**D:** SVEN GODIJN, **C:** JAN BOLS
**A:** ENCOUNTERS MEDIASCIENCE, **M:** INFO@ENCOUNTERS.BE

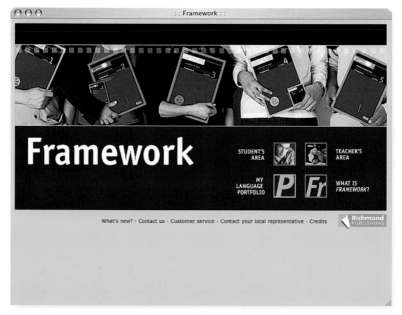

**WWW.OVO3.COM**
**D:** ANDREA MODENESE
**A:** OVO3 - VISU, **M:** ANDREAMOD@BOX.SEVEN.IT

**WWW.WEBFRAMEWORK.NET**
**D:** PATRICIA FUENTES
**A:** BLUE PLANET, **M:** INFO@BLPLANET.COM

**WWW.H-HOMMA.COM**
**D:** TAKAAKI YAGI
**A:** FORM::PROCESS, **M:** INFO@FORM-PROCESS.COM

**WWW.ANTHONY-THIBAULT.COM**
**D:** ANTHONY THIBAULT,
**M:** ANTHONY@GRAPHISMEDIA.COM

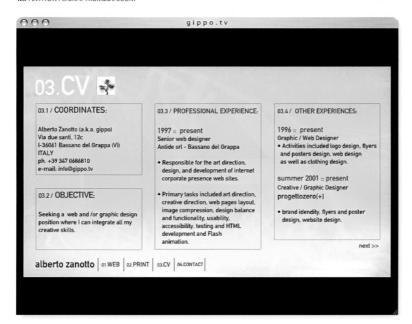

**WWW.GIPPO.TV/**
**D:** GIPPO
**A:** GIPPO, **M:** INFO@GIPPO.TV

**WWW.B-MEDIADESIGN.COM**
**D:** NÚRIA BLAY
**A:** B-MEDIADESIGN.COM, **M:** BLAY@B-MEDIADESIGN.COM

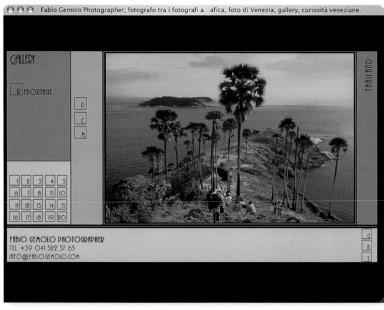

**WWW.FABIOGEMOLO.COM**
**D:** BEATRICE SUSA
**A:** ARTE LAGUNA, **M:** INFO@ARTELAGUNA.IT

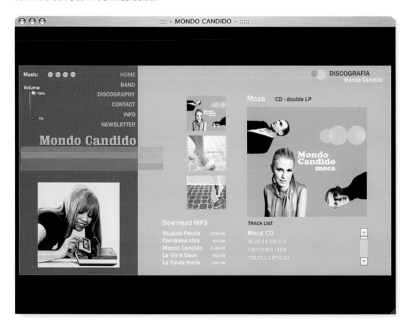

**WWW.MONDOCANDIDO.IT**
**D:** GCMEDIA/CACIALLI/SIGNORINI, **C:** GUIDO CACIALLI, **P:** MONDOCANDIDO
**A:** GCMEDIA, **M:** SIGMAo@SUPEREVA.IT

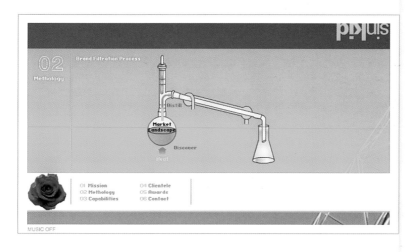

**WWW.SINKID.COM**
**D:** AGNES TAN
**A:** JUNKFLEA

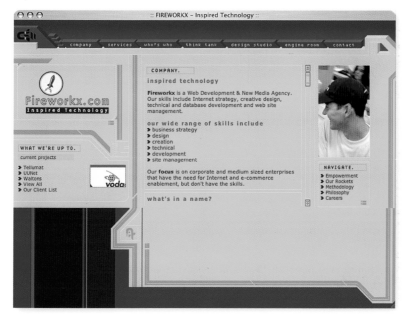

**WWW.FIREWORKX.COM**
**D:** FRANCOIS VAN DER MERWE, **P:** MICHELE MACKLIN
**A:** FIREWORKX, **M:** MICHELE@FIREWORKX.COM

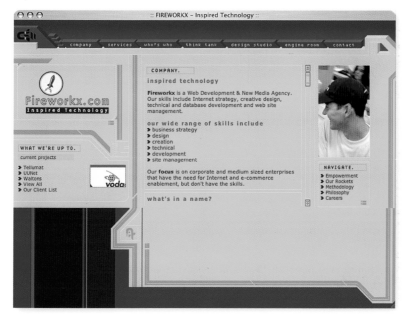

**WWW.VATE.COM.MX/AOM**
**D:** ANDRES ORTIZ MASSO
**A:** VATE, **M:** VATE@VATE.COM.MX

**WWW.NIEMANN-H.DE**
**D:** ANTJE WEBER, **C:** HANNO DENKER
**A:** DIE QUERDENKER, **M:** ANTJEWEBER2000@GMX.DE

**INKO.CJB.NET**
**D:** DAN NANAS
**A:** INKO GROUP, **M:** DAN@INKO.CJB.NET

**WWW.MORJAC.DK**
**D:** THOMAS BRIXEN
**A:** VISUELT DESIGNBUREAU, **M:** BRIXEN@ONCABLE.DK

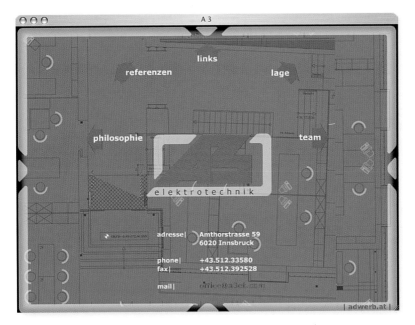

**WWW.A3ET.COM**
**D:** RAPHAEL LEPUSCHITZ, **P:** FLORIAN KOCH
**A:** ADWERB.AT, **M:** F.KOCH@ADWERB.AT

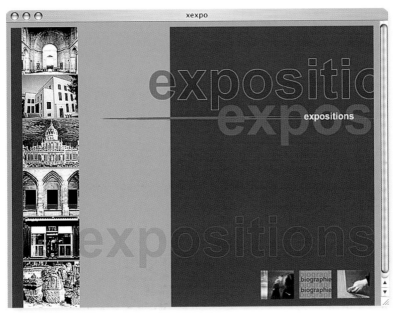

**WWW.KRGHETTOJUICE.COM**
**D:** GIOVANNI PALETTA
**M:** ME@KRGHETTOJUICE.COM

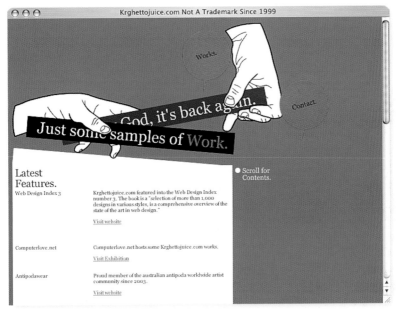

**DIDIER.GRAMMARE.FREE.FR**
**D:** JEANNE DIDIER
**M:** JEANNE.DIDIER@LIBERTYSURF.FR

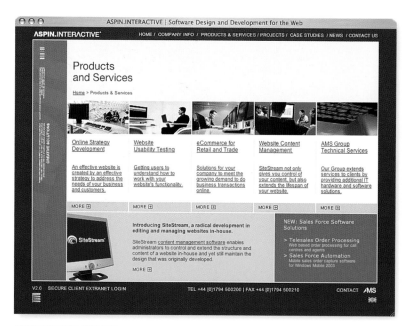

**WWW.ASPININTERACTIVE.COM**
**D:** NATHAN KINGSTONE **C:** MARCUS PULLEN **P:** MARCUS PULLEN
**A:** ASPIN INTERACTIVE **M:** MARCUSP@ASPIN.CO.UK

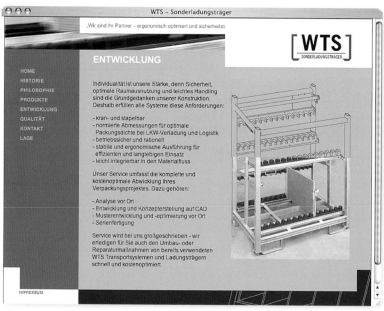

**WWW.WTS-TRANSPORTSYSTEME.DE**
**D:** ANJA URBAN, **C:** MATTHIAS MESSERER
**A:** QUERFORMAT - DIE WERBEAGENTUR, **M:** MESSERER@QUERFORMAT.INFO

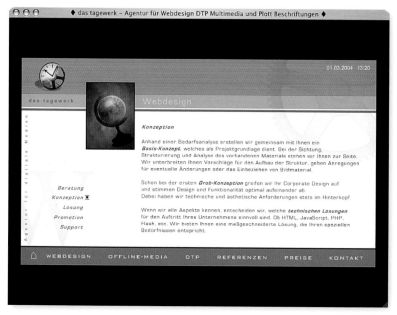

**WWW.DAS-TAGEWERK.DE**
**D:** SYLVIA TRAUTMANN
**A:** DAS TAGEWERK, **M:** TRAUTMANN@DAS-TAGEWERK.DE

WWW.AUTHENTIC-CAR.COM/INDEX8oo.HTML
**D:** LAURENT CHARTIER
**A:** DUC - DISTANCE ULTRA COURTE, **M:** INFOS@D-U-C.COM

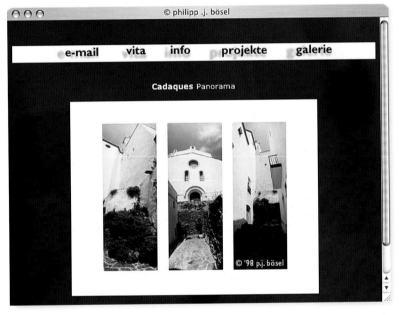

WWW.ENIGMART.DE
**D:** PHILIPP J. BOESE
**A:** AUGENBLICKE DIE BLEIBEN, **M:** PHILIPP.BOESEL@WEB.DE

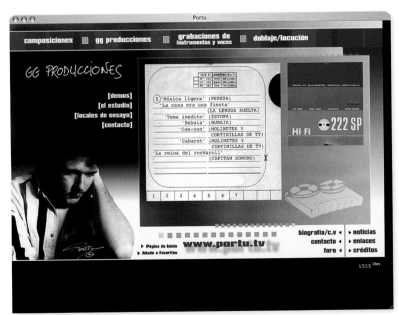

WWW.PORTU.TV
**D:** CUCO DARBONNENS / CHARLIE ARNAIZ, **C:** CUCO, **P:** JAVIER PORTUGUÉS
**A:** INDRAS, **M:** TOYMAN@TELEFONICA.NET

**WWW.REDOCTOBER.COM**
**D:** ANDI RUSU
**A:** REDOCTOBER INDUSTRIE, **M:** ANDI@REDOCTOBER.COM

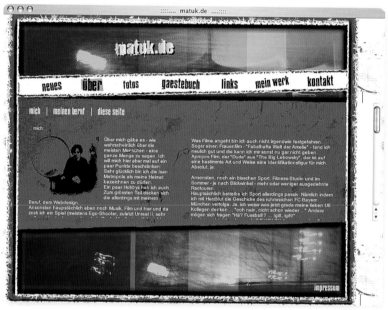

**WWW.MATUK.DE/**
**D:** MARCEL TUCHEK
**M:** ROTWEISSE_TRIKOT@FCBAYERN.DE

**WWW.ONISHENKO.COM/BOOK/**
**D:** MILAN NEDVED
**A:** PUPPETEERS, **M:** JP@PUPPETEERS.CZ

**WWW.BETANCOR.DE**
**D:** HERMANN KÖPF
**A:** NEOWELT MEDIA GMBH, **M:** HERMANN.KOEPF@NEOWELT.DE

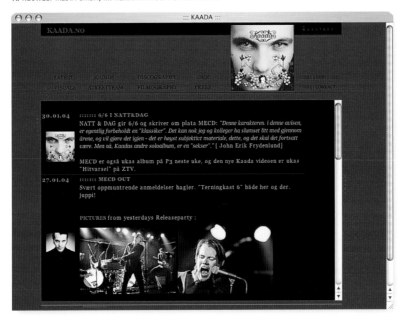

**WWW.KAADA.NO**
**D:** JOHN KAADA
**M:** CAPTAIN@KAADA.NO

**WWW.ARTDEVIVRE.COM.HK**
**D:** MARC SCOTT
**M:** MSCOTT@I-CABLE.COM

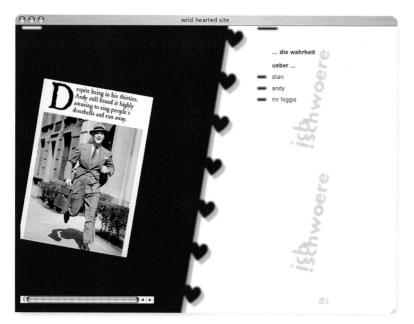

**WWW.FREISE.DE**
**D:** MARKUS FREISE
**M:** MARKUS@FREISE.DE

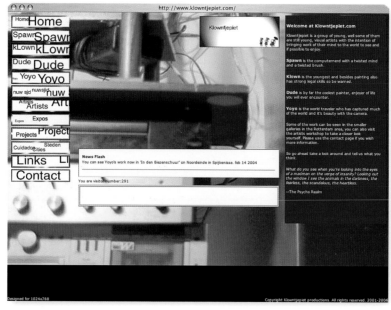

**WWW.KLOWNTJEPIET.COM**
**D:** JEROEN VESSEUR
**M:** JEROEN@KLOWNTJEPIET.COM

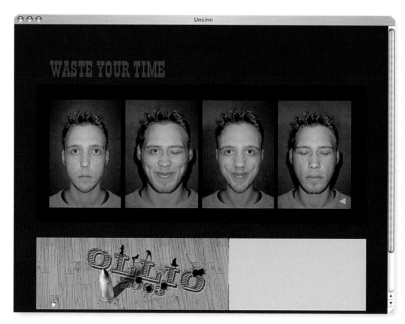

**WWW.OLLIO.DE**
**D:** OLIVER OERTEL, **C:** FRITZ KRAUSS
**A:** ANALOG MULTIMEDIA, **M:** ANALOG@ANALOG.DE

**WWW.INTERARCHDESIGN.COM.SG**
**D:** AGNES TAN
**A:** JUNKFLEA, **M:** INFO@JUNKFLEA.COM

**WWW.PRALLER.DE**
**D:** STEPHAN MERTEL, **C:** PETER WEISS
**A:** TOGETHER-MEDIA, **M:** MERTEL@TOGETHER-MEDIA.DE

**WWW.QUIRO-PRO.COM**
**D:** TAKEHIKO ICHIMURA
**A:** QUIRO PRO, **M:** INFO@QUIRO-PRO.COM

**WWW.MUNICHAFFAIRS.DE**
**D:** SEVERIN BRETTMEISTER
**A:** FA-RO MARKETING, **M:** SEVERIN@FA-RO.DE

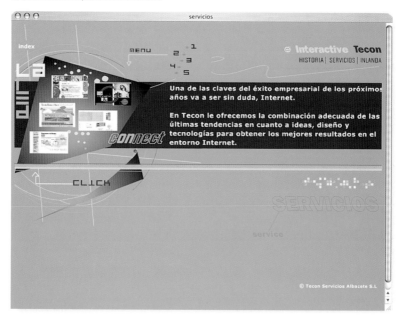

**WWW.TECON.ES**
**D:** ELENA JIMENEZ ARBOLEDA, **C:** MANUEL ALTAMIRANO, **P:** LUIS ZORNOZA
**A:** TECON, **M:** EJIMENEZ@TECON.ES

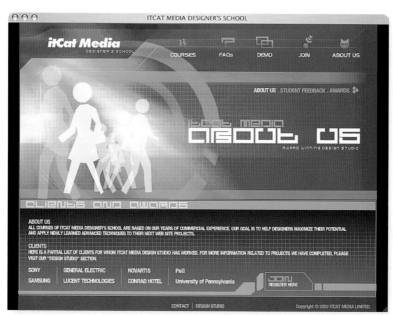

**WWW.ITCATMEDIA.COM/**
**D:** STEPHEN LO, **C:** PERIC SZE, **P:** NOVITA LEUNG
**A:** ITCAT MEDIA LIMITED, **M:** STEPHEN@ITCATMEDIA.COM

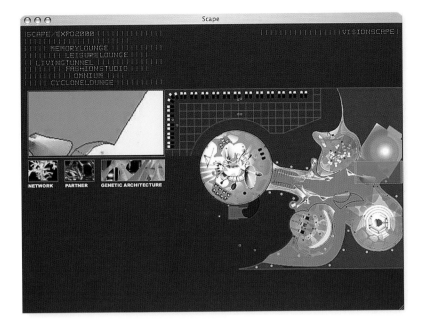

**VISIONSCAPE.DE**
**D:** NICOLETTA GERLACH / ETC, **C:** HOLGER HIRT, RALF DZISCHER
**A:** SCREENBOW, **M:** IDEFIX98@HOTMAIL.COM

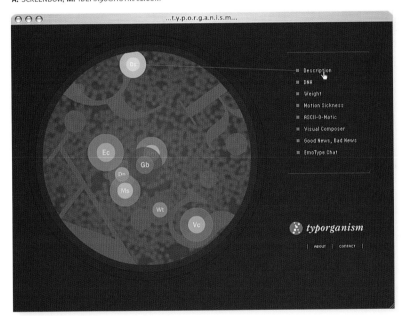

**WWW.TYPORGANISM.COM**
**D:** GICHEOL LEE
**A:** STUDIOTIMO, **M:** CAMEO@STUDIOTIMO.COM

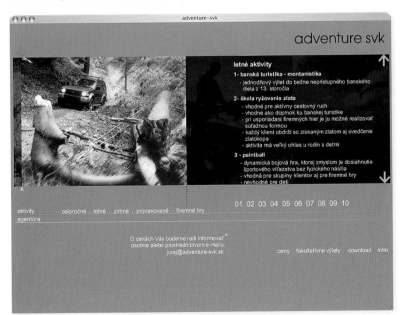

**ADVENTURE-SVK.SK**
**D:** MICHAL BARTKO, **P:** YURYA/ROS S.R.O.
**A:** BARTKO DESIGN, **M:** MODI@POBOX.SK

**WWW.WERBEBROCHER.DE**
**D:** STEFAN BROCHER
**A:** WERBETECHNIK STEFAN BROCHER, **M:** INFO@WERBEROCHER.DE

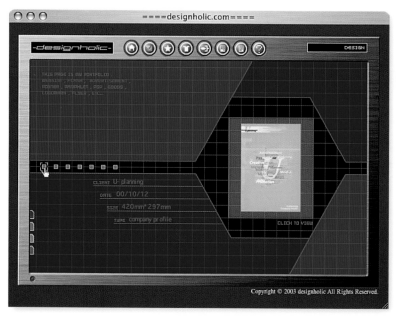

**WWW.PARASITE-MOI.COM**
**D:** CELINE VERHELST
**A:** DIPLOMATIC COVER, **M:** CELINE_VERHELST@HOTMAIL.COM

**WWW.DESIGNHOLIC.COM**
**D:** HIROYUKI KUROIWA
**M:** BLACK@DESIGNHOLIC.COM

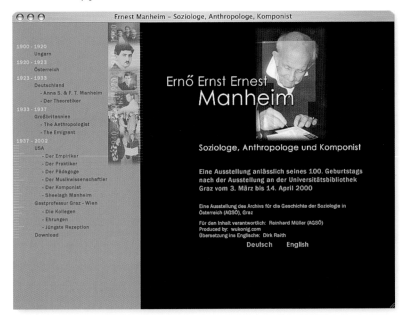

**WWW.YOLKS715.COM**
**D:** SENG KIT LOY
**M:** SENGKIT@YOLKS715.COM

**WWW.KFUNIGRAZ.AC.AT/SOZWWW/AGSOE/MANHEIM/**
**D:** JOERG WUKONIG
**A:** WUKONIG.COM, **M:** OFFICE@WUKONIG.COM

**WWW.IDEP.ES/JULIANSITE/BOMBARDEO**
**D:** ANGELES MORENO, **P:** JULIÁN ALVAREZ
**A:** ANAIMATION, **M:** NAIMA@ANAIMATION.COM

**WWW.ARHPA.COM/**
**D:** JOSE MANUEL FERNÁDEZ, **C:** JORGE LÓPEZ, **P:** JOSE LUIS MUÑIZ
**A:** RISQUELMEDIA, **M:** IMAGINA@TRISQUEL.COM

**WWW.JUSTPERSONAL.NL**
**D:** DUSTIN REMME, **C:** PETER HARNISCH, **P:** JARNO BONHOF / MARCEL RUTTE
**A:** SCRAPBOOK DESIGN®, **M:** INFO@SCRAPBOOKDESIGN.NL

**WWW.JOSHMURRAY.COM.AU**
**D:** JOSH MURRAY
**A:** JOSH MURRAY DESIGN, **M:** HELLO@JOSHMURRAY.COM.AU

300

**WWW.STINCHEN.DE**
**D:** CHRISTINA FREISE, **C:** THOMAS PEITZ
**M:** MARKUS@FREISE.DE

**WWW.LACENTRAL.ES**
**D:** TONI SANCHEZ, **C:** JORDI AMENGUAL
**A:** VIRTUALTEAM, **M:** TSANCHEZ@VIRTUALTEAM.WS

**WWW.PROJECTFIREWORKS.COM**
**D:** KLEANTHIS ECONOMOU
**M:** POLIVOTIS@YAHOO.COM

**WWW.INTERIOR-WEB.DE**
**D:** HELGA SALLERSTORFNER
**M:** HELGA.SAL@GMX.DE

**WWW.HDMDESIGNS.COM**
**D:** HERMAN MALDONADO
**A:** HDM DESIGN + PARTNERS, **M:** HDMALDONADO@HDMDESIGNS.COM

**WWW.HIGHLYGRAPHIC.COM**
**D:** JENS KARLSSON, **C:** SCOTT SNYDER
**A:** CHAPTER THREE, **M:** JENS@CHAPTER3.NET

**WWW.ART5AGENTUR.DE**
**D:** FSA
**A:** ART.5 TEXTKONTOR INTERNET SUPPORT, **M:** FSA@ART5AGENTUR.DE

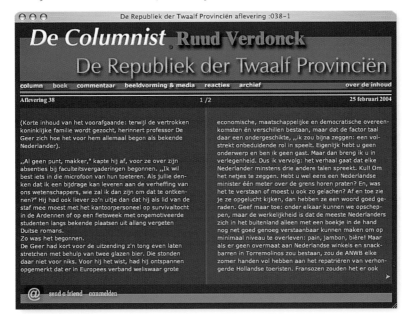

**WWW.RUUDVERDONCK.NL**
**D:** T VAN DER LAAN
**A:** BUREAUBROWSERBEEST, **M:** S.PEREIRA@WXS.NL

**WWW.MURRAYDUNLOPARCHITECTS.COM**
**D:** JIM GALL
**A:** THE PRESENTATION HOUSE

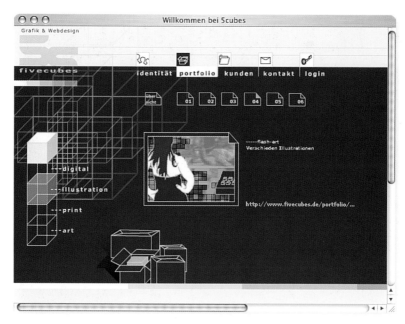

**WWW.FIVECUBES.DE**
**D:** ROLAND BILGER
**A:** FIVECUBES, **M:** INFO@FIVECUBES.DE

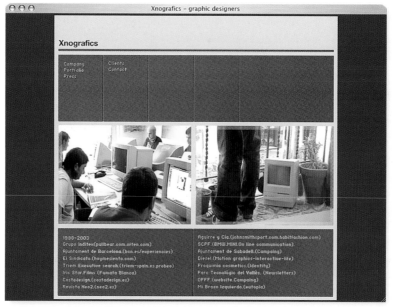

**WWW.XNOGRAFICS.COM**
**D:** XNOGRAFICS
**A:** XNOGRAFICS, **M:** LLUIS@XNOGRAFICS.COM

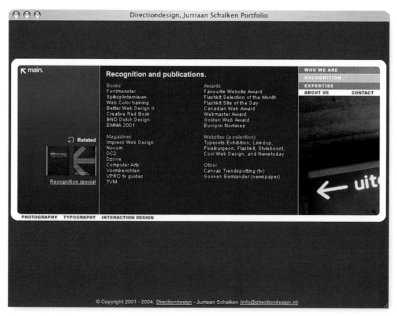

**WWW.DIRECTIONDESIGN.NL**
**D:** JURRIAAN SCHALKEN
**A:** DIRECTIONDESIGN.NL, **M:** JURRIAAN@DIRECTIONDESIGN.NL

WWW.FMLEAO.PT
**D:** CESAE-UCI
**A:** CESAE, **M:** UCI@MAIL.CESAE.PT

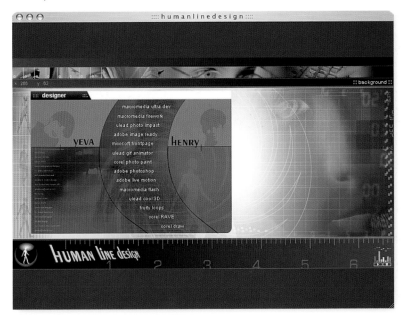

PLANET.TIME.NET.MY/CENTRALMARKET/HENRYYAP/
**D:** HENRY YAP SWEE CHENG
**A:** CARDOS MULTIMEDIA SDN. BHD., **M:** SC.YAP@CARDOS.COM.MY

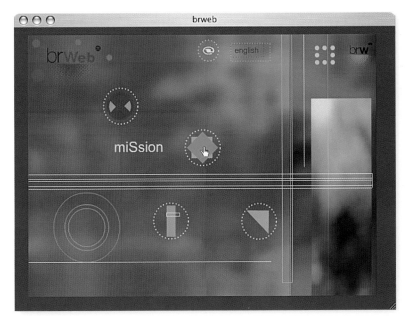

WWW.BRWEB.IT
**D:** CATERINA AGUECI
**A:** CATECF, **M:** CATE@MARKINO.NET

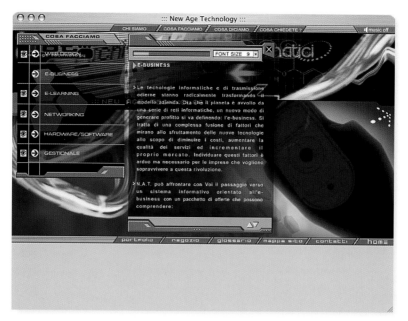

**WWW.NAT.IT**
**D:** OSCAR ANTINO, **P:** NEW AGE TECHNOLOGY
**M:** OSCAR@NAT.IT

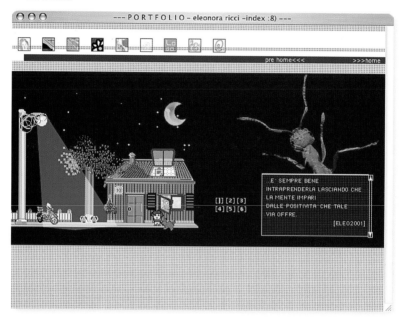

**WWW.ELEOLOLA.COM**
**D:** ELEONORA RICCI
**M:** ROLLE@TISCALINET.IT

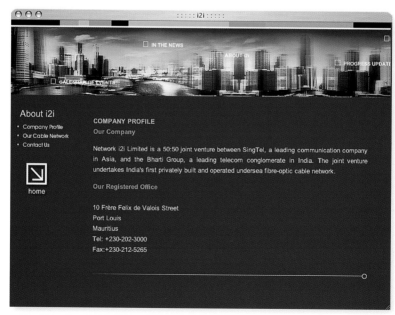

**WWW.I2ICN.COM**
**D:** VOXMEDIA, **C:** RAGHU, **P:** JOE CHUA
**A:** VOXMEDIA, **M:** GERALD@VOXMEDIA.COM.SG

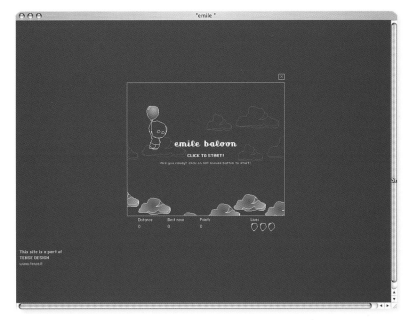

**WWW.EMILE.IT**
**D:** FRANCESCO BERTELLI
**A:** TENSE, **M:** INFO@TENSE.IT

**WWW.MODUSCREANDI.COM**
**D:** RICCARDO SCANDELLARI, **P:** PAOLO SCHIAVI
**A:** MODUSCREANDI MULTIMEDIA, **M:** INFO@MODUSCREANDI.COM

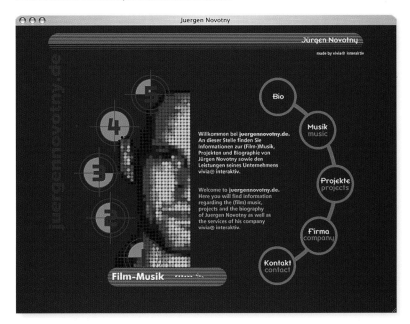

**WWW.FLYNNS.DE**
**D:** JÜRGEN NOVOTNY, **P:** FLYNN'S
**A:** VIVIA INTERAKTIV

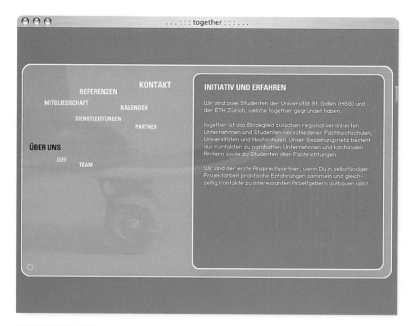

**WWW.TOGETHER-ONLINE.CH**
**D:** SANDRO FISCHER
**A:** VITAMIN2, **M:** FISCHER@VITAMIN2.CH

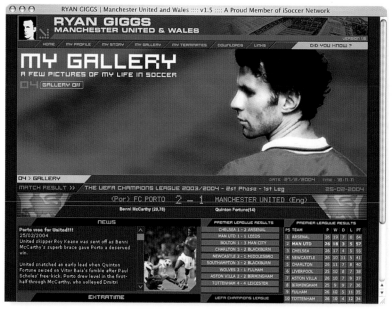

**WWW.RYANGIGGS.CC**
**D:** STEVEN TAN
**A:** MOTIONWORKS SDN.BHD., **M:** STEVEN11@PD.JARING.MY

**WWW.KLARKKENT.DE**
**D:** KRISZTIAN DEMETER

**WWW.2BDESIGN.IT**
**D:** DOMENICO FASANO
**A:** 2BDESIGN, **M:** INFO@2BDESIGN.IT

**WWW.VILLAMIMOSA.COM**
**D:** JOHNNIE MANEIRO
**A:** GRAFF.NET, **M:** JOHNNIEMANEIRO@MAC.COM

**INICIA.ES/DE/ESCUELAARTESEGOVIA/PRINCIPAL.HTM**
**D:** JOSÉ LUIS GILARRANZ LEONOR, **P:** ESCUELA DE ARTE DE SEGOVIA
**M:** ESARTESEGO@INICIA.ES

**WWW.SLOWBURN.IT**
**D:** STEFANO SCIACCA, **P:** SLOWBURN GOTHIC E-ZINE
**M:** NEFFYDJ@HOTMAIL.COM

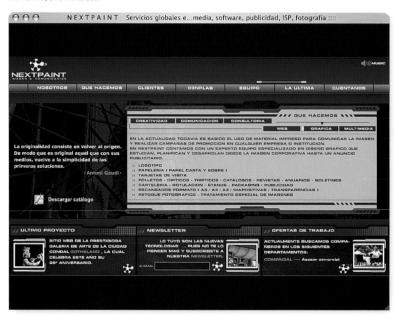

**WWW.NEXTPAINT.COM**
**D:** TONI AZNAR, **C:** KATHY TELLADO
**A:** NEXTPAINT, **M:** KTELLADO@NEXTPAINT.COM

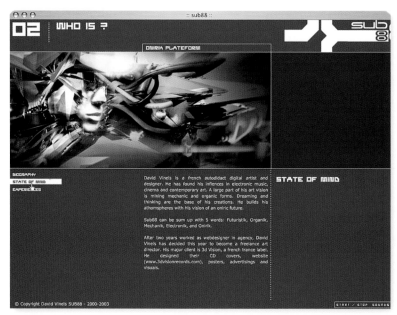

**WWW.SUB88.COM**
**D:** DAVID VINEIS
**A:** SUB88, **M:** DAVID@SUB88.COM

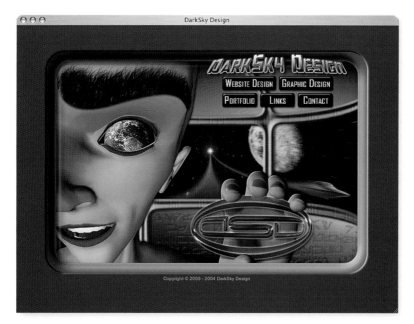

**WWW.DARKSKYDESIGN.COM**
**D:** ERIC DEMARAY
**A:** DARKSKY DESIGN, **M:** ERIC@DARKSKYDESIGN.COM

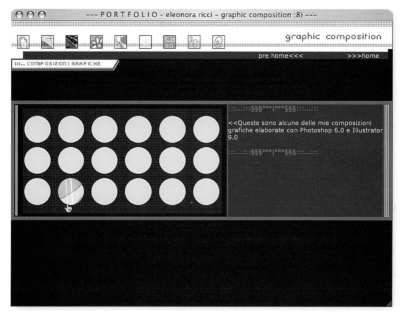

**WWW.ELEOLOLA.COM**
**D:** ELEONORA RICCI
**M:** E.RICCI@CALTANET.IT

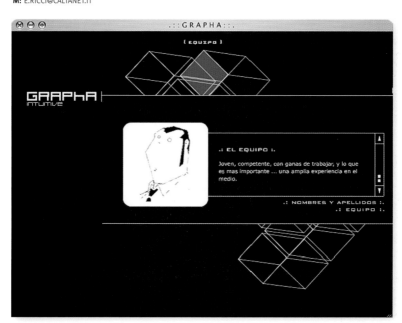

**WWW.GRAPHA.NET**
**D:** ANA BELÉN ALVAREZ, **C:** ENRIQUE VALENTIN
**A:** GRAPHA INTUITIVE, **M:** ALFONSO@GRAPHA.NET

**WWW.PRART.NET**
**D:** PAUL ROJANATHARA
**M:** PAUL@PRART.NET

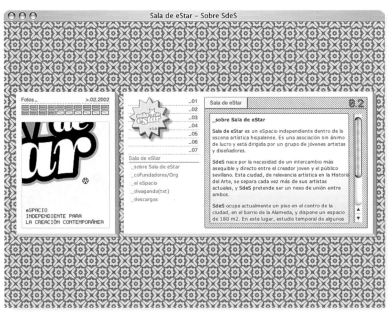

**WWW.SALADEESTAR.COM**
**D:** JOSE GIL GALIANO
**M:** JGGALIANO@HOTMAIL.COM

**WWW.SICKBASSIX.COM**
**D:** ALEXIS WRONA

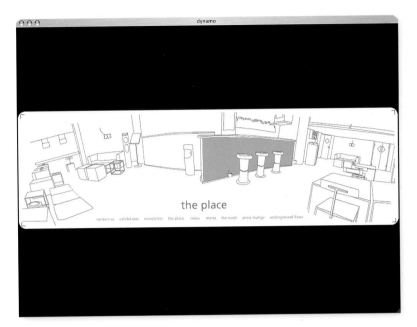

**WWW.DYNAMO.IT**
**D:** PAOLO SALA
**M:** INFO@PSDESIGN.IT

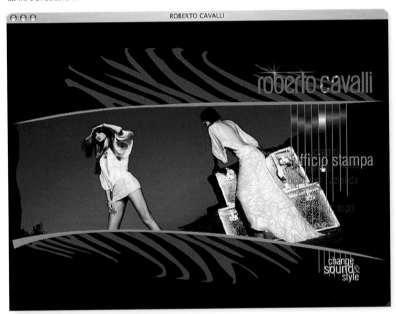

**WWW.ROBERTOCAVALLI.IT**
**D:** ALESSIO PAPI,
**A:** NEXTOPEN MULTIMEDIA, **M:** ALESSIO@NEXTOPEN.IT

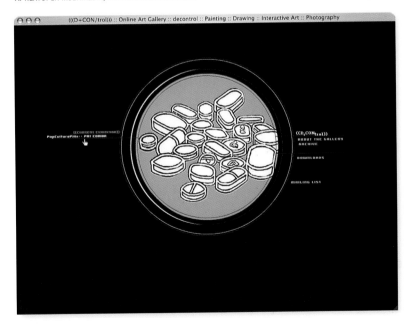

**WWW.DECONTROL.COM**
**D:** GEORGE SHAW
**A:** DECONTROL, **M:** GEORGE@DECONTROL.COM

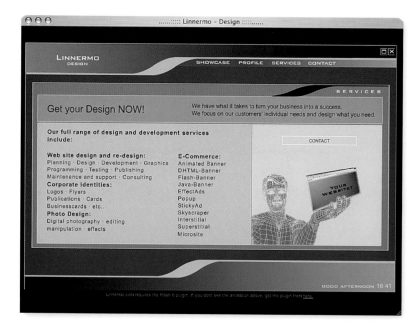

**WWW.UMTSMATRIX.DE**
**D:** JUUSO LINNERMO
**A:** J.A.LINNEMO DESIGN, **M:** J.A.LINNERMO@UMTSMATRIX.DE

**WWW.BUESA.NET/CURSOS/ALCORCON**
**D:** CARLOS BUSÓN BUESA, **P:** CURSO DE DISEÑO DE PÁGINAS WEB
**A:** BUESA.NET, **M:** CBUSON@BUESA.NET

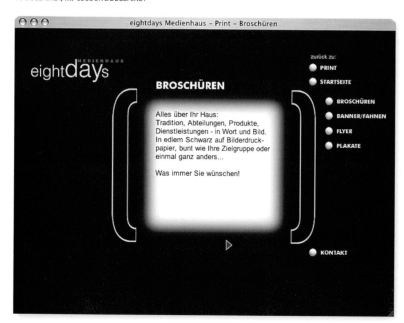

**WWW.EIGHTDAYS.DE**
**D:** PETRA J. SCHABERGER, **C:** GABRIELE HERBEL
**A:** EIGHTDAYS MEDIENHAUS, **M:** INFO@EIGHTDAYS.DE

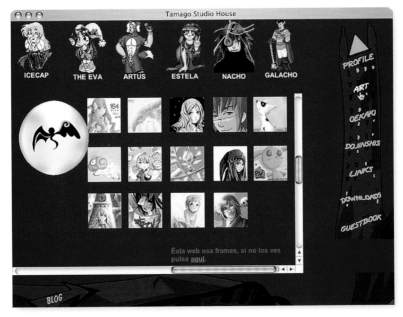

**WWW.TAMAGOSTUDIO.COM**
**D:** ARTURO SÁNCHEZ RODRÍGUEZ
**M:** ARTUS@TAMAGOSTUDIO.COM

**WWW.LITTLE-MOUSE.BE**
**D:** AYMERIC GUYOMARCH
**A:** LITTLE MOUSE, **M:** INFO@LITTLE-MOUSE.BE

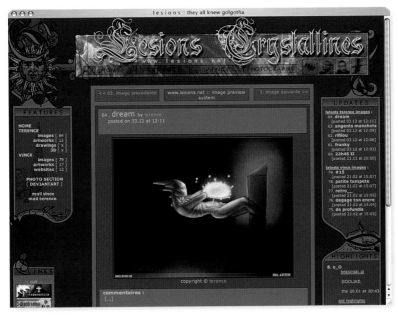

**WWW.LESIONS.NET**
**D:** VINCENT BIGUET
**M:** PASTOR@WANADOO.FR

**WWW.AUDIOTECH.CZ**
**D:** BARBORA KUKLÍKOVÁ, **C:** RADEK BALKOVSK
**A:** D-SIGN.CZ, **M:** KUKLIKOVA@D-SIGN.CZ

**WWW.DRAGONS-STUDIO.COM**
**D:** ANTONIO ARIAS EXPOSITO
**M:** AARIAS@DRAGONS-STUDIO.COM

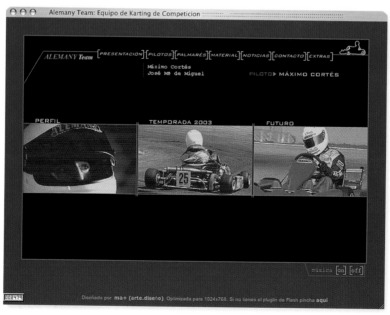

**WWW.ALEMANYTEAM.COM**
**D:** MAMAS
**A:** MAMAS, **M:** MAITEoo@OZU.ES

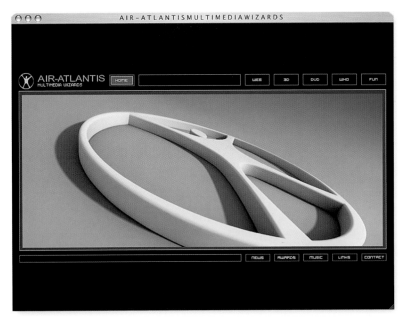

**WWW.AIR-ATLANTIS.COM**
**D:** STEFANO ARGENTI, **P:** AIR-ATLANTIS
**M:** S.ARGENTI@AIR-ATLANTIS.COM

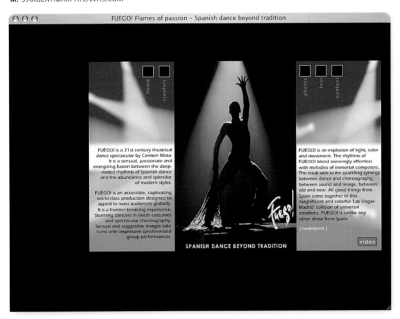

**WWW.FUEGOSHOW.COM**
**D:** VALERIA ZALAQUETT
**A:** VIZUALE MULTIMEDIA, **M:** V_ZALAQUETT@YAHOO.COM

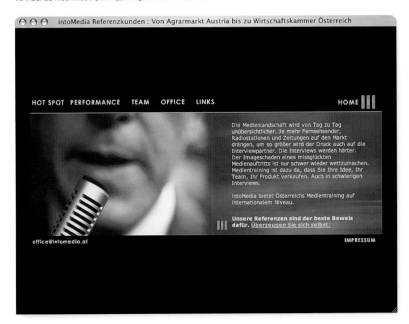

**WWW.INTOMEDIA.AT/**
**D:** JOERG WUKONIG
**A:** WUKONIG.COM, **M:** OFFICE@WUKONIG.COM

**WWW.SKYBLUECREATIONS.COM**
**D:** SIMON MCCABE
**A:** SKYBLUE CREATIONS, **M:** SIMON@SKYWALKER-RANCH.FREESERVE.CO.UK

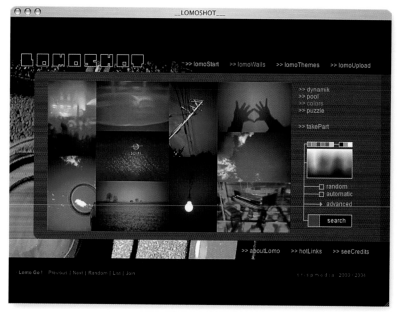

**WWW.LOMOSHOT.COM**
**D:** CHRIS HORSTMANN, **C:** HORSTMANN, RICHTER, GROTE
**M:** CHRIS@LOMOSHOT.COM

**WWW.C3MDESIGNS.COM**
**D:** CLAUDIA CARRANZA
**A:** C3M DESIGNS, **M:** CONTACT@C3MDESIGNS.COM

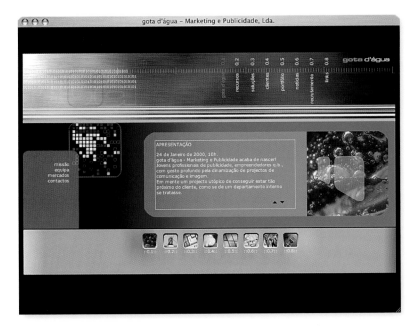

**WWW.GOTADAGUA.COM**
**D:** PEDRO MACHADO, **C:** PEDRO SANTOS, **P:** RUI GONÇALVES/ PRITESH
**A:** GOTA D'ÁGUA, **M:** PEDRO.MACHADO@GOTADAGUA.COM

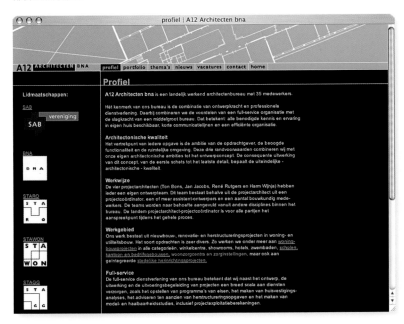

**WWW.BONANNIDESIGN.COM**
**D:** FABRIZIO BONANNI
**A:** BONANNI DESIGN

**WWW.A12ARCHITECTEN.NL/**
**D:** JOOST KUIJPERS
**A:** OIN / RDBMC, **M:** INFO@A12ARCHITECTEN.NL

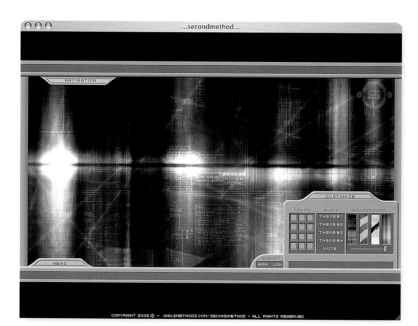

**WWW.2METHODS.COM/SECONDMETHOD**
**D:** VITALIY ONISHENKO
**A:** 2METHODS.COM, **M:** VITALIY@2METHODS.COM

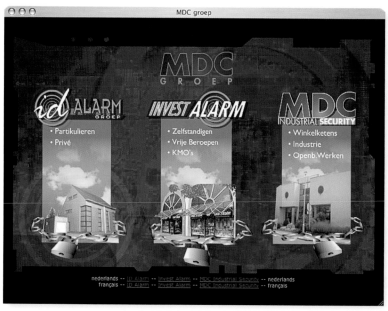

**WWW.MDCGROEP.BE**
**D:** SVEN GODIJN, **C:** JAN BOLS
**A:** ENCOUNTERS MEDIASCIENCE, **M:** INFO@ENCOUNTERS.BE

**GRAPIXEL.DR.AG**
**D:** VOLKAN PACACI
**A:** GRAPIXEL, **M:** VOLKANP@MSN.COM

**WWW.3D-ANIMATION.DK**
**D:** MARTIN NIELSEN, **C:** KEVIN SØRENSEN
**A:** 3D-ANIMATION.DK, **M:** KEVIN@3D-ANIMATION.DK

**WWW.YACHTFAITH.CO.NZ**
**D:** RONALD STALLMACH
**A:** TEXTUS DESIGN, **M:** INFO@TEXTUSDESIGN.CO.NZ

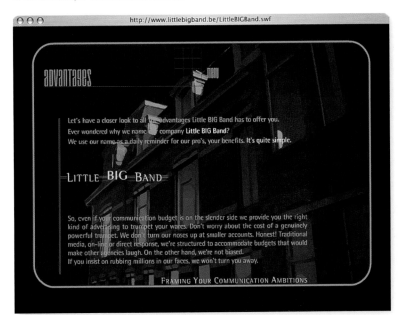

**WWW.LITTLEBIGBAND.BE**
**D:** KRISTOF VANDERBEKE
**A:** LITTLE BIG BAND, **M:** KRISTOF@LITTLEBIGBAND.BE

**PROJECT-EUH.COM**
**D:** SYLVAIN VRIENS
**A:** PROJECT-EUH, **M:** BSGLOUDE@CS.VU.NL

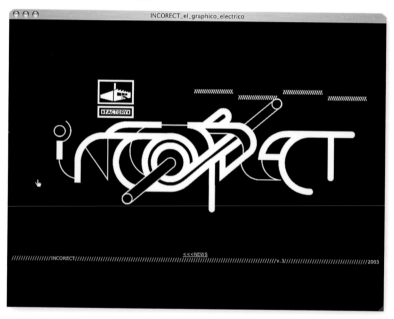

**WWW.INCORECT.COM**
**D:** OLIVIER BOGARTS
**M:** OLIVIER_BOGARTS@HOTMAIL.COM

**WWW.DANIELECASCONE.COM**
**D:** DANIELE CASCONE
**M:** KASKO@CIAOWEB.IT

**WWW.DUNASTUDIO.COM**
**D:** LUCA BARTOLINI
**A:** EQUILIBRISOSPESI, **M:** LUCA@EQUILIBRISOSPESI.COM

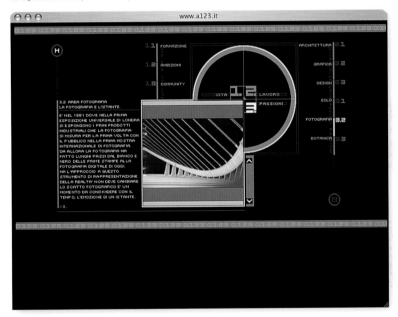

**WWW.A123.IT/**
**D:** ALESSANDRO DI LELIO
**A:** KORA S.R.L., **M:** ALESSANDRO.DILELIO@A123.IT

**WWW.EADESIGN.IT**
**D:** STEPHEN ALAN DAVIS
**A:** EADESIGN, **M:** STEPHEN@EADESIGN.IT

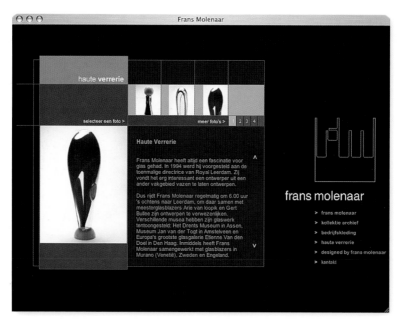

WWW.FRANSMOLENAAR.NL/
**D:** HALUK DEMIR, **P:** GLENN LEMING, NUMAN PEKGÖZ, TIJN TACKE
**A:** CLOCKWORK, **M:** DEMIRHALUK@HOTMAIL.COM

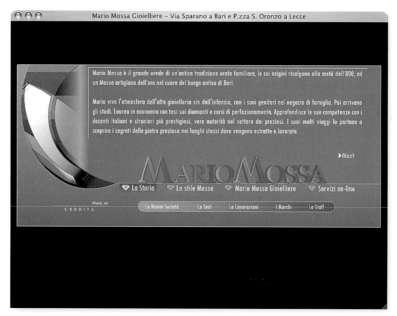

WWW.MARIOMOSSA.COM
**D:** FABRIZIO FIANDANESE, **P:** ALESSANDRO ANTONICELLI
**A:** THE WEB AGENCY, **M:** PROJECT@THEWEBAGENCY.IT

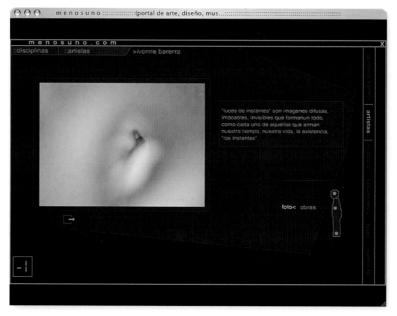

WWW.MENOSUNO.COM
**D:** MAITE CAMACHO PÉREZ, **C:** MARIO GUTIÉRREZ
**A:** ESTUDIO MAMÁS, **M:** MAITE@ESTUDIOMAMAS.COM

**WWW.MONIKAWOLTERING.COM**
**D:** MAIK WINKELMANN
**A:** AUCH, **M:** M.WINKELMANN@NETCOLOGNE.DE

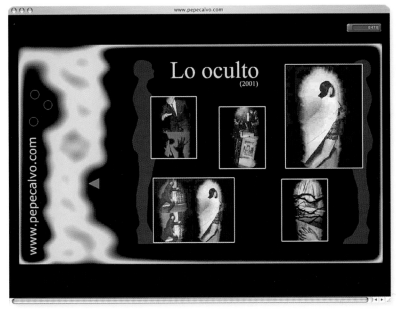

**WWW.PEPECALVO.COM**
**D:** CUCO DARBONNENS SAMPER, **P:** PEPE CALVO
**A:** INDRAS, **M:** TOYMAN@TELEFONICA.NET

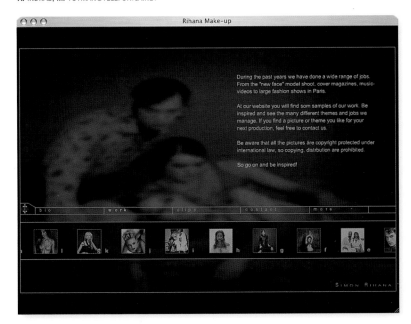

**WWW.RIHANA.DK**
**D:** MORTEN VILLADSEN/KIM VILE, **C:** KIM VILE, **P:** MORTEN VILLADSEN
**A:** ESTUPENDO INTERACTIVE I/S, **M:** MV@ESTUPENDO.DK

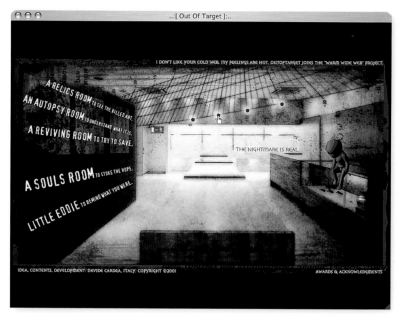

**WWW.OUTOFTARGET.COM**
**D:** DAVIDE CARDEA
**M:** ARTES@OUTOFTARGET.COM

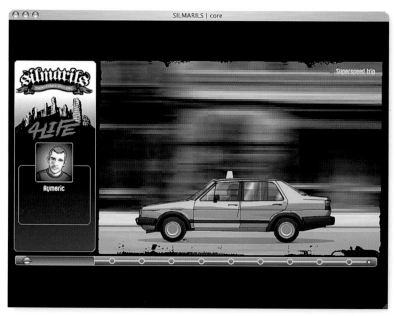

**WWW.SILMARILSNET.COM**
**D:** TINSEL FRÉDÉRIC, **C:** GALLEANO OLIVIER, **P:** SILMARILS
**A:** ADVISA, **M:** FTINSEL@ADVISA.FR

**WWW.URBANOMA.DE**
**D:** MIKE JOHN OTTO
**A:** MOD 73 - URBAN INFLUENCED MEDIA, **M:** INFO@MOD73.COM

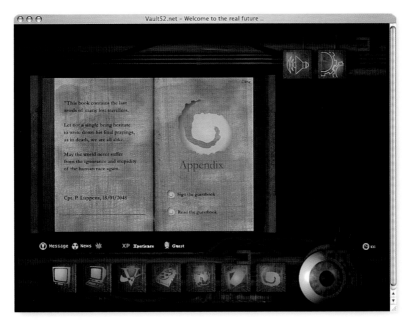

**WWW.VAULT52.NET**
**D:** PHILIP LUPPENS
**A:** VAULT52, **M:** WEBMASTER@VAULT52.NET

**WWW.OPENLAND.ES**
**D:** RICARDO RODRÍGUEZ DE LOS RÍOS
**A:** OPEN LAND, **M:** FALVA@OPENLAND.ES

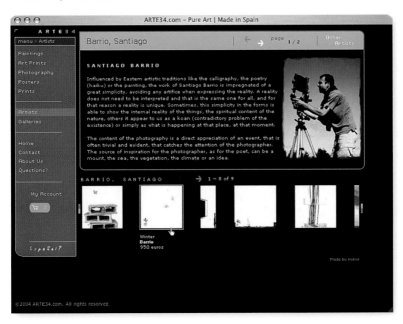

**WWW.ARTE34.COM**
**D:** LEE HSU
**A:** ARTE34.COM, **M:** NANO_TOPIA@HOTMAIL.COM

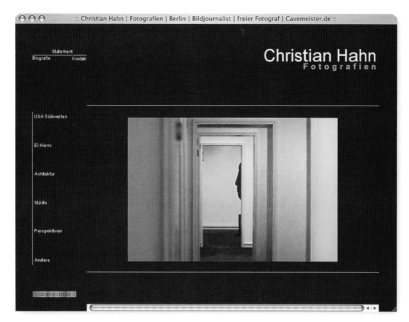

**WWW.CAVEMEISTER.DE**
**D:** CORDULA SEEL, **C:** RALF MITTERMUELLER
**A:** CAVEMEISTER.DE, **M:** CAVEMEISTER@T-ONLINE.DE

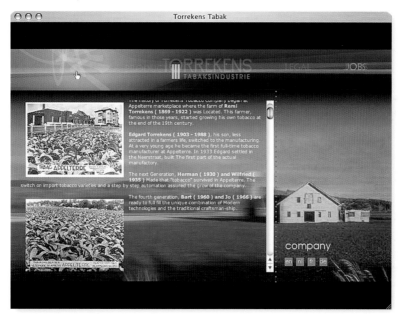

**WWW.TORREKENSTABAK.BE**
**D:** SVEN GODIJN, **C:** JAN BOLS
**A:** ENCOUNTERS MEDIASCIENCE, **M:** INFO@ENCOUNTERS.BE

**WWW.UMBRIAMBIENTE.IT**
**D:** ROSITA PAPARELLI
**A:** GRAFICHERÒ, **M:** INFO@GRAFICHERO.IT

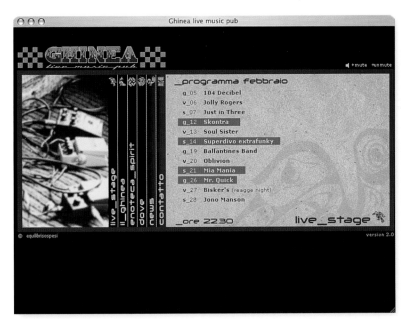

**WWW.GHINEAPUB.COM**
**D:** LUCA BARTOLINI
**A:** EQUILIBRISOSPESI, **M:** LUCA@EQUILIBRISOSPESI.COM

**WWW.MARGAUX-BERLIN.DE**
**D:** SASKIA VETTER
**A:** ICONNEWMEDIA, **M:** SASKIA.VETTER@ICONNEWMEDIA.DE

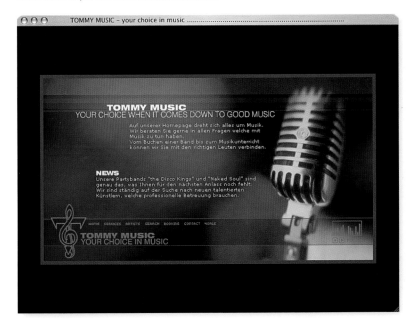

**WWW.TOMMYMUSIC.CH**
**D:** BEAT VON ROTZ
**A:** BEET.CH, **M:** BEAT@BEET.CH

**WWW.CGHUERTA.COM**
**D:** SUSANA PÉREZ BERMEJO, **C:** OSCAR DE AGUSTÍN
**M:** SPBERMEJO@YA.COM

**WWW.LEMERCIERS.COM**
**D:** JASON HENDRY
**A:** STORM, **M:** JASON@STORMCI.COM.AU

**WWW.POWERSOFT19.COM**
**D:** AIYAZ KIDWAI, **C:** ISRAR KHAN
**A:** POWERSOFT19, **M:** AIYAZ@HOTMAIL.COM

**WWW.THEANTSITE.COM**
**D:** ANTONIO CORNACCHIA
**M:** ANT@THEANTSITE.COM

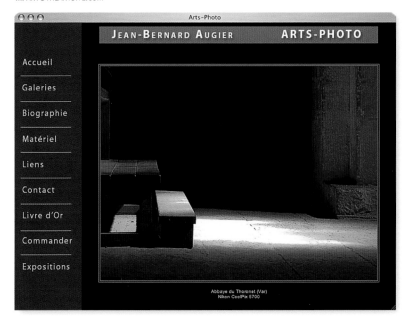

**WWW.ARTS-PHOTO.COM**
**D:** JEAN-BERNARD AUGIER, **C:** MYRIAM GRENIER
**M:** JB.AUGIER@TISCALI.FR

**WWW.PROGRIP.IT**
**D:** BEPPE DIENA, **C:** LOGICAL NET
**A:** BEPPE DIENA DESIGN, **M:** GIUSEPPE@LOGICAL.IT

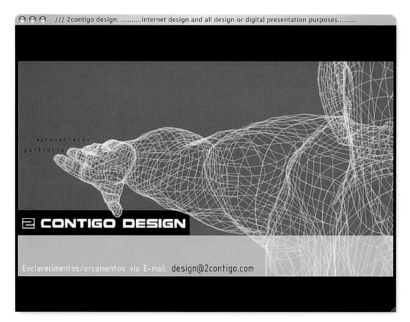

**2CONTIGO.COM**
**D:** GUSTAVO COUTO
**A:** 2CONTIGO DESIGN, **M:** DESIGN@2CONTIGO.COM

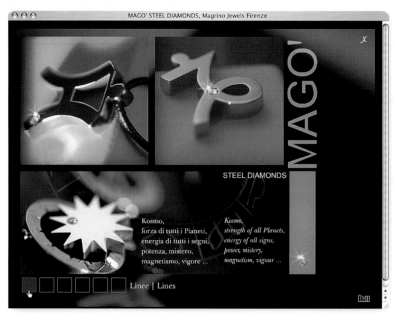

**WWW.MAGODIAMONDS.COM**
**D:** ALESSIO PAPI
**A:** NEXTOPEN MULTIMEDIA, **M:** ALESSIO@NEXTOPEN.IT

**WWW.FRANKOY.COM**
**D:** FRANCOIS MORIN
**A:** FRANKOY DESIGN, **M:** FRANKOY@SYMPATICO.CA

**WWW.ALLOALLO.NL**
**D:** PASCAL GOUW, **C:** MARNIX VAN WIJK, **P:** PASCAL GOUW
**A:** MEDIAXL, **M:** GOUW19@ZONNET.NL

**WWW.LUMINESSENCESTUDIOS.COM**
**D:** CYNTHIA JOHNSTON
**A:** LUMINESSENCE STUDIOS, **M:** CLJ@LUMINESSENCESTUDIOS.COM

**USERS.SKYNET.BE/GLYNN.SPEECKAERT**
**D:** INES VAN BELLE
**A:** PINKER, **M:** INFO@PINKER.BE

333

**WWW.LOCO-SHOP.COM**
**D:** NICOLAS BARNABÉ, **C:** STEPHANE LEVY, **P:** JOHN HASSAN
**A:** WS COM, **M:** ANJIE@NY.COM

**WWW.D5IVE.COM**
**D:** PAUL B. DROHAN
**A:** D5IVE.COM, **M:** PAULDROHAN@HOTMAIL.COM

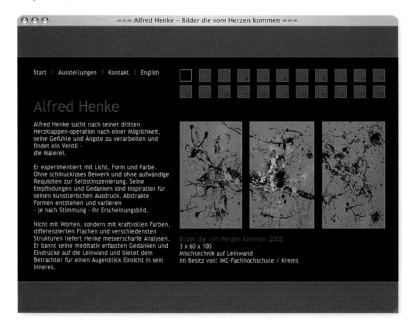

**ALFRED-HENKE.KH-MEDIENDESIGN.AT**
**D:** SUSANNE KROUPA
**A:** KH-MEDIENDESIGN.AT, **M:** KROUPA@KH-MEDIENDESIGN.AT

**WWW.LANDSCHAPSARCHITEKTEN.NL**
**D:** KOEN HAUSPY, **C:** PASCAL IMMERZEEL
**M:** KOEN@FLUIDO.AS

**WWW.TOATO.DE**
**D:** ALEXANDER TIECK, **P:** MAIER TYPO&LITHO
**A:** TO A TO MEDIENSERVICE, **M:** ATIECK@MAIER-TYPO-LITHO.DE

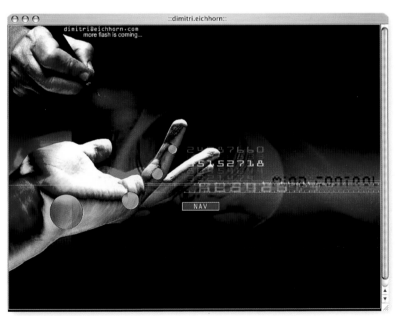

**WWW.DIMITRI.EICHHORN.COM**
**D:** DIMITRI EICHHORN
**M:** DIMITRI@EICHHORN.COM

**WWW.MONTAY.NL**
**D:** L. BULLENS, **C:** T. VAN ZANTVOORT, **P:** MONTAY AUTOMATISERING
**M:** INFO@MONTAY.NL

**WWW.KENVELO.COM**
**D:** MILAN NEDVED, **C:** JIRI PETVALDSKY
**A:** ISOLAB, **M:** E@ISOLAB.CZ

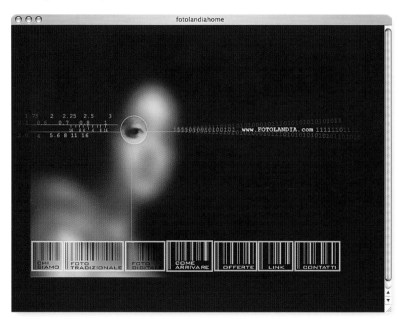

**WWW.FOTOLANDIA.COM**
**D:** GABRIELE CAVAZZANO
**A:** THE FORGE GROUP, **M:** CAVAZZANO@TISCALI.IT

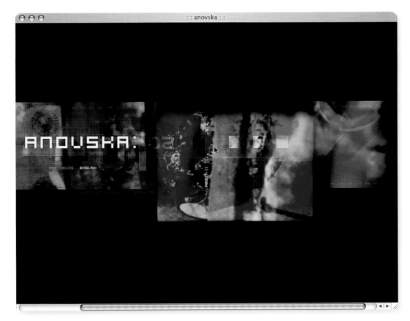

**WWW.ANOVSKA.COM**
**D:** ANA CARVALHO
**A:** : : ANOVSKA : :, **M:** ANOVSKA_@HOTMAIL.COM

**WWW.MORAVKOVA.COM**
**D:** BARBORA KUKLÍKOVÁ, **C:** RADEK BALKOVSK
**A:** D-SIGN.CZ, **M:** KUKLIKOVA@D-SIGN.CZ

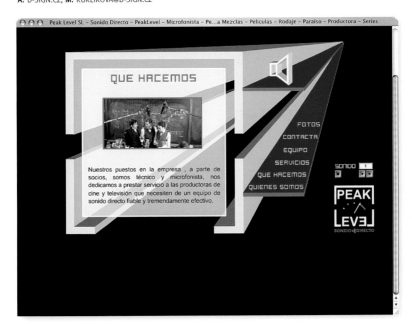

**WWW.PEAKLEVELSL.COM**
**D:** CHILO RIVERO, **C:** JAIME RIVERO, **P:** PEAK LEVEL
**A:** MAÑANAMAS, **M:** JAIMER10@HOTMAIL.COM

**WWW.TEAMWORKSPAIN.COM**
**D:** RICHARD TALUT
**A:** ESTUDIO ANA MORENO, **M:** RICHARD-STUDIO@MENTA.NET

**WWW.KIRAGLUSCHKOFF.COM/**
**D:** KIMMO KUUSISTO
**A:** AC-MAINOS, **M:** KIMMO@ACMAINOS.FI

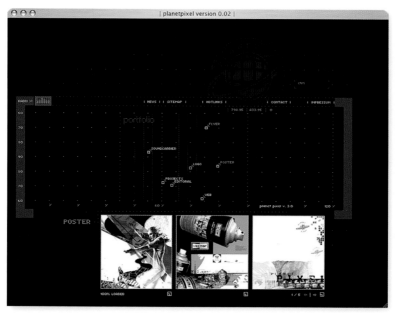

**WWW.PLANETPIXEL.DE**
**D:** PLANETPIXEL
**A:** PLANETPIXEL, **M:** TINASTOCKER@HOTMAIL.COM

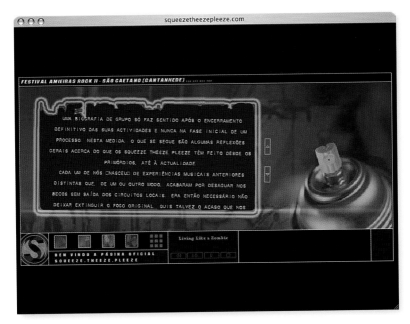

**WWW.SQUEEZETHEEZEPLEEZE.COM**
**D:** MIRO VAZ, NUNO FERREIRA, **C:** MIRO VAZ, **P:** SQUEEZETHEEZEPLEEZE
**A:** NUNOMFERREIRA.COM, **M:** NUNOMFERREIRA@NETVISAO.PT

**WWW.SOARTGROUP.COM**
**D:** NICOLA DESTEFANO
**M:** EMPUSA@SOARTGROUP.COM

**WWW.MARLOWESPACE.COM**
**D:** NICOLAS CÔTÉ
**A:** LEITMOTIV, **M:** NICOLASCOTE@YAHOO.COM

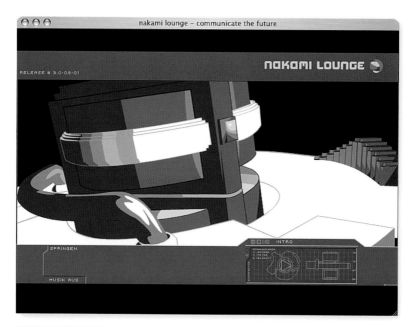

**WWW.NAKAMILOUNGE.DE**
**D:** M.KOENIG, B.RÜCKER, M. FANDRÉ
**A:** NAKAMILOUNGE GMBH, **M:** B.RUECKER@NAKAMILOUNGE.DE

**WWW.SUBFUSION.COM**
**D:** TOM MEARNS
**A:** SUBFUSION, **M:** TOM@SUBFUSION.COM

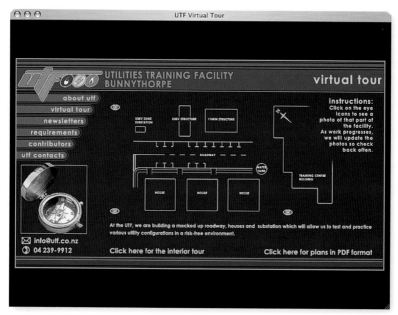

**WWW.UTF.CO.NZ/**
**D:** RONALD STALLMACH
**A:** TEXTUS DESIGN, **M:** INFO@TEXTUSDESIGN.CO.NZ

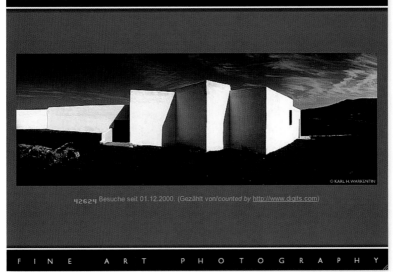

**WWW.WARKENTIN-FOTOGRAFIE.DE**
**D:** KARL H. WARKENTIN
**A:** DDS WARKENTIN, **M:** MAIL@DDS-WARKENTIN.DE

**WWW.KREISLICHT.DE**
**D:** SUSANNE STERNAGEL
**M:** SUSANNE.STERNAGEL@KREISLICHT.DE

**WWW.AGORAT.COM**
**D:** FREDERIC RIVOIRE
**M:** CONTACT@AGORAT.COM

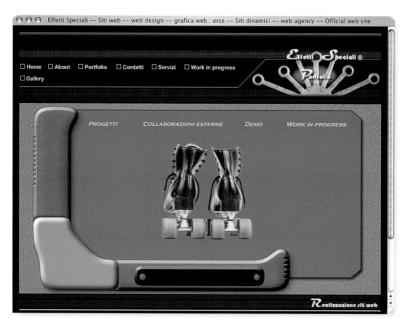

**WWW.EFFETTISPECIALI.NET**
**D:** FLAVIO CARBONI
**A:** EFFETTI SPECIALI, **M:** INFO@EFFETTISPECIALI.NET

**WWW.DANIEL-JANSEN.DE**
**D:** DANIEL JANSEN
**A:** JANSEN GRAFIK-WEBDESIGN, **M:** INFO@DANIEL-JANSEN.DE

**WWW.GIACOMOANDRICO.COM**
**D:** OTTAVIO BARBIERI
**A:** ICEDOME DESIGN, **M:** INFO@ICEDOMEDESIGN.COM

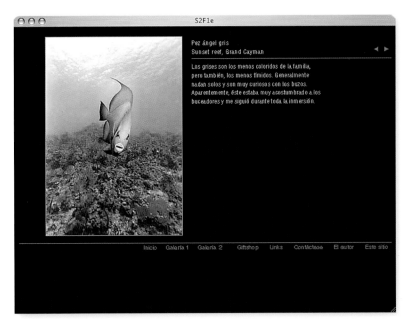

**WWW.LIGHT-UNDERWATER.COM**
**D:** MARCELO MAMMANA
**M:** MM@LIGHT-UNDERWATER.COM

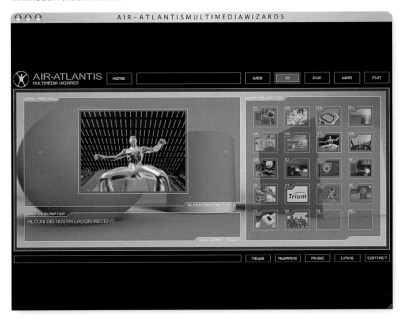

**WWW.AIR-ATLANTIS.COM**
**D:** STEFANO ARGENTI, **C:** LORENZO GIOVANNINI
**A:** AIR-ATLANTIS, **M:** M.BOTTI@AIR-ATLANTIS.COM

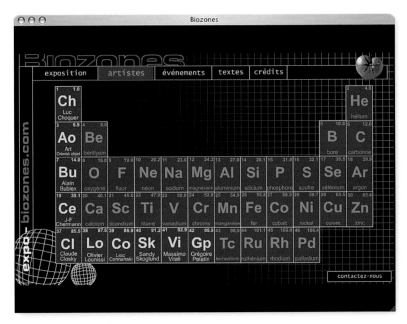

**WWW.EXPO-BIOZONES.COM/**
**D:** GUNTHER GROENEWEGE
**A:** G-DESIGN, **M:** GROENEWEGE@HOTMAIL.COM

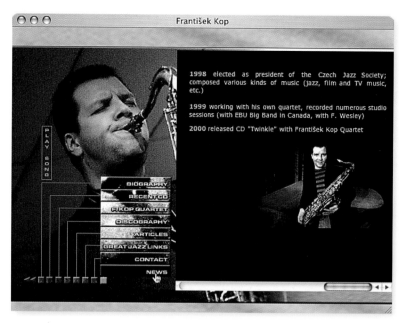

**WWW.KOPJAZZ.CZ**
**D:** BARBORA KUKLÍKOVÁ, **C:** RADEK BALKOVSK
**A:** D-SIGN.CZ, **M:** KUKLIKOVA@D-SIGN.CZ

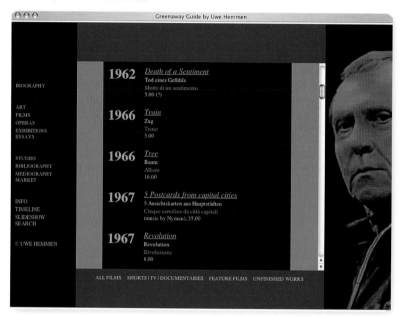

**WWW.GREENAWAY.DE**
**D:** UWE HEMMEN
**A:** WORLDS4, **M:** HEMMEN@WORLDS4.COM

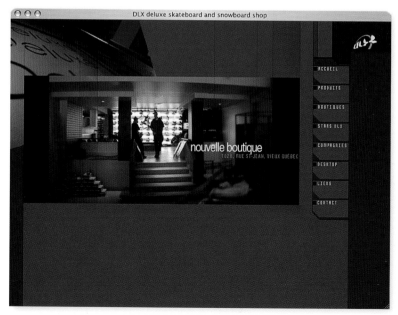

**WWW.DLXDELUXE.COM**
**D:** STEPHANE
**A:** BLASFEM INTERACTIF, **M:** SGROLEAU@BLASFEM.COM

**WWW.BATTILLOCCHI.COM**
**D:** MASSIMO RISCA
**A:** SINTETICA SRL, **M:** RISCA@SINTETICA.IT

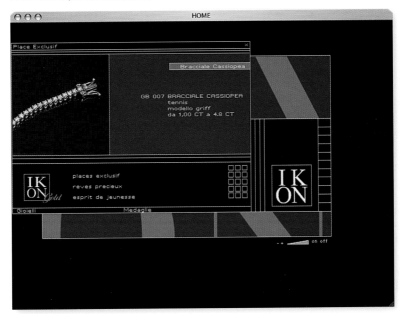

**WWW.IKONDIRECT.IT/**
**D:** GIANLUCA DALMASSO, **P:** IKON S.R.L.
**A:** SISTEMI UNO S.R.L., **M:** G.DALMASSO@SISTEMIUNO.IT

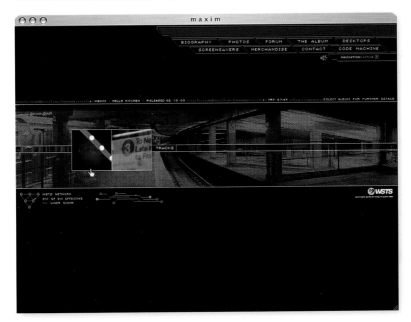

**WWW.MAXIM.UK.NET**
**D:** DAN SMITH, JIM MORGAN, **C:** NICK LAND
**A:** DEEPEND, **M:** JIM@DEEPEND.IT

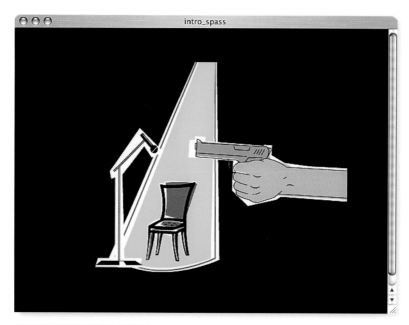

**WWW.SPASSGESELLSCHAFTSABENDE.DE**
**D:** JUAN PABLO PÁEZ
**A:** MEDIENPARK, **M:** PAEZ@MEDIENPARK.NET

**WWW.STUDIO-BASE.IT**
**D:** ALESSIO PAPI
**A:** NEXTOPEN MULTIMEDIA, **M:** ALESSIO@NEXTOPEN.IT

**BASE.MARCIALPONS.ES/ISROOT/MARCIALPONS/QUIENESSOMOS/FLASH.HTM**
**D:** MANUEL ESTRADA DISEÑO GRÁFICO
**A:** MANUEL ESTRADA DISEÑO GRÁFICO, **M:** DIGITAL@MANUELESTRADA.COM

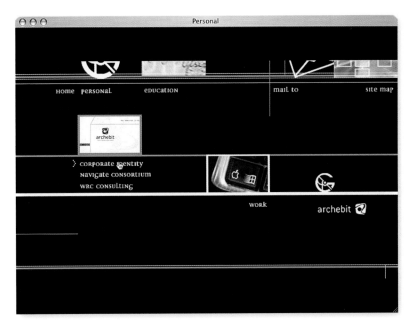

**WWW.GRAFICAROTA.IT**
**D:** GABRIELE ROTA
**A:** GRAFICA E COMUNICAZIONE, **M:** GABRIELE@GRAFICAROTA.IT

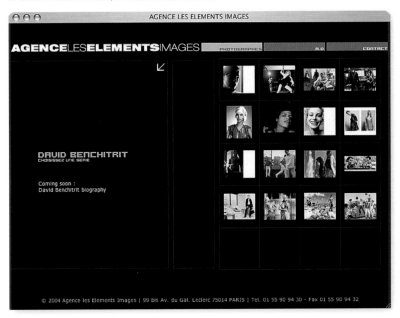

**WWW.AGENCE-ELEMENTS.COM/**
**D:** SAMUEL BERNARD
**A:** WEBIRIUM-TREMENS.COM

**WWW.HOLGERHEIX.DE**
**D:** HOLGER HEIX
**M:** HH@HOLGERHEIX.DE

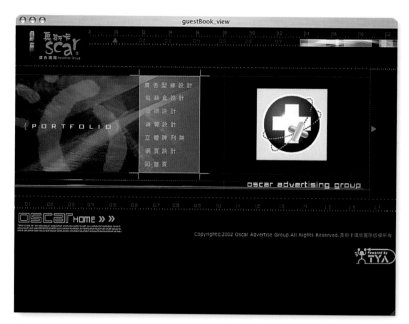

**WWW.OSCARAD.COM.TW**
**D:** JONATHAN HSU, **C:** JERRY LIN, **P:** SETTHA LEE
**A:** TYA STUDIO LTD., **M:** SETTHA@TYA.COM.TW

**WWW.NEXUS-DS.COM/**
**D:** FABRIZIO SILVETTI
**A:** NEXUS DIGITAL SOLUTIONS, **M:** INFO@NEXUS-DS.COM

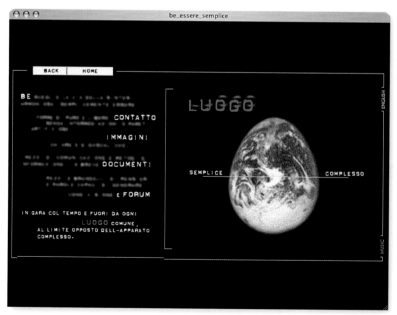

**WWW.BESIMPLE.IT**
**D:** FRANCESCO CANGIANO
**A:** SHENA, **M:** FCANGIANO@SHENA.IT

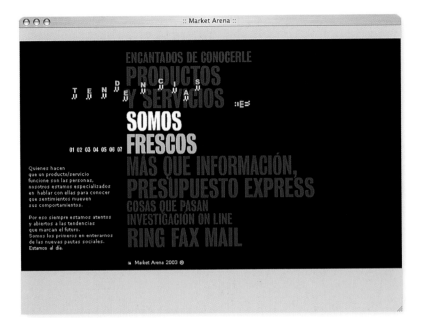

**WWW.MARKETARENA.ES/PROTO**
**D:** FERNANDO PALMEIRO / GABRIEL MARTINEZ, **C:** GALFANO CARBONI, **P:** GMI/ASPACI
**A:** LSD, **M:** GABRIEL@WEBGMI.COM

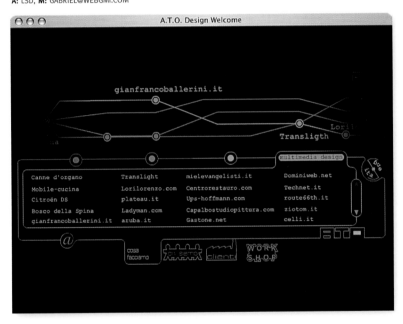

**WWW.ATODESIGN.IT**
**D:** ATO DESIGN SRL
**A:** ATO DESIGN SRL, **M:** TOMMASO@ATODESIGN.IT

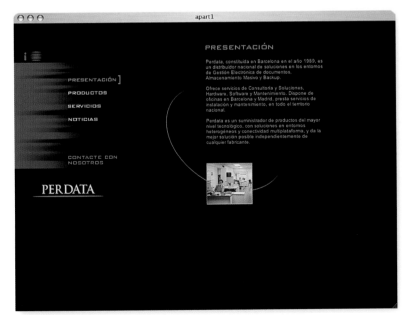

**WWW.PERDATA.ES**
**D:** SANTI SALLÉS
**A:** TUNDRABCN, **M:** INFO@TUNDRABCN.COM

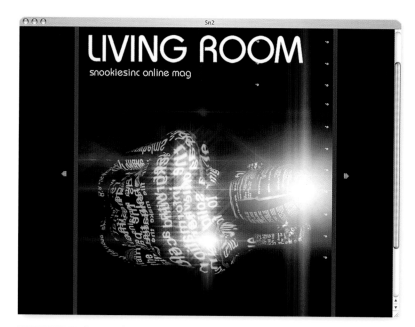

**MY.DREAMWIZ.COM/SNOOKIES/**
**D:** OHMIN, **P:** SNOOKIES

**WWW.DADOMAIN.COM**
**D:** ANUBANDH
**A:** DIGITAL ALCHEMY, **M:** ANUBANDH.KADAM@DADOMAIN.COM

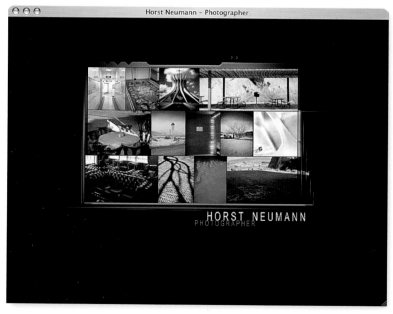

**WWW.HORSTNEUMANN.COM**
**D:** CHRISTIAN CHAMPAGNE
**A:** VISTAKUVA, **M:** CHRIS.CHAMPAGNE@VISTAKUVA.FI

**WWW.MEDIAVIEW.IT/**
**D:** DANIELA DANTI, **C:** DATATEC
**A:** NODOT, **M:** DANIELA@NODOT.IT

**WWW.SHARRAPAGANO.IT**
**D:** CATERINA ‹CATECF›
**A:** CATERINA ‹CATECF›, **M:** CATE@MARKINO.NET

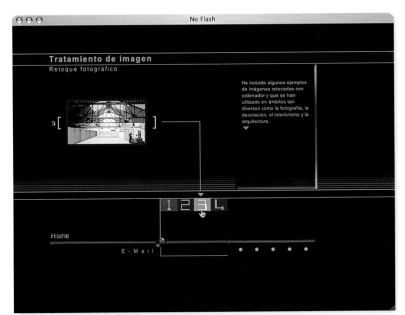

**WWW.LOCOPALIDO.COM**
**D:** JUAN CARLOS HERNÁNDEZ
**A:** JUAN CARLOS HERNÁNDEZ, **M:** JUANCARLOS@LOCOPALIDO.COM

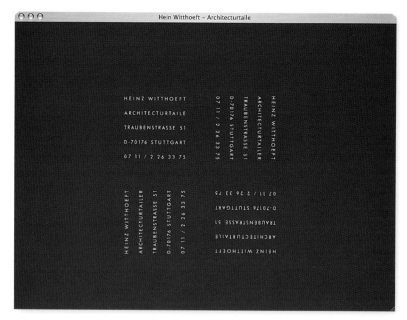

**WWW.STATIONIST.COM**
**D:** HEINZ WITTHOEFT, **C:** [D-MIND] FUCH/WEISS GBR, **P:** BARTH ARCHITEKTEN
**A:** ARCHITEKTURTAILER, **M:** HEINZ.WITTHOEFT@STATIONIST.COM

**WWW.LUISACOSTA.CL**
**D:** LUIS ACOSTA ABARZUA
**A:** FDX.CL, **M:** LUIS@FDX.CL

```
We are lucky.


We work as a web designers and we love this job.

But is sad to do always the same things:
        - same links.
        - same fashion colors.
        - same buttons.
        - same rollover images.
        - same designs...
The Net is becoming something boring.

We say STOP:
We are not users of web-design-software!!!
we are interface designers!!!.


A web page is just a web page but a new interface is a new experience:
an open window to a new world where something special can be possible.

Now, explore this interface, our first interface

            'labellalola.com in OLD STYLE' v1.05

Are you ready?
y/n
```

**WWW.LABELLALOLA.COM**
**D:** MIKEL SEIJAS ALONSO
**M:** DE_MIKEL@LABELLALOLA.COM

# INDEX

## GREECE

## HONG KONG